COLLEGE STUDY SKILLS

FIFTH EDITION

James F. Shepherd
Queensborough Community College, Emeritus
The City University of New York

HOUGHTON MIFFLIN COMPANY Boston Toronto

Dallas Geneva, Illinois
Palo Alto Princeton, New Jersey

Sponsoring Editor: Mary Jo Southern
Senior Development Editor: Barbara Roth
Associate Project Editor: Danielle Carbonneau
Associate Production/Design Coordinator: Jennifer Waddell
Senior Manufacturing Coordinator: Marie Barnes
Marketing Manager: George Kane

Cover Image: C.D. Geissler/XING Munich
Cover Design: Len Massiglia
Book Design: George McLean
Part-opening photographs: Part I, Part II, Part III: Copyright © Terry Wild Studio; Part IV: Copyright © Thom Duncan/Adventure Photo; Part V: Copyright © David Madison 1991

We would like to acknowledge and thank the following sources for permission to reprint material from their work:

Chapters 1–4, 10, and 11 are based in part on material in Shepherd, James F., *RSVP: The College Reading, Study, and Vocabulary Program,* 4th ed. Copyright © 1992 by Houghton Mifflin Company. Used with permission.

Page 69: From *How to Use the Reader's Guide to Periodical Literature,* rev. ed., © 1984, H. W. Wilson Company, p. 11. Reprinted with permission of The H. W. Wilson Company.

Page 116: From "Mass Media and American Politics." John H. Aldrich et al., *American Government.* Copyright © 1986 by Houghton Mifflin Company. Used by permission.

Page 129: "The SQ3R Study Method" from Shertzer, Bruce, *Career Planning,* 3rd ed. Copyright © 1985 by Houghton Mifflin Company. Used with permission.

Pages 134–142, 151, 190, and 192–194: from William Pride et al., *Business,* 3rd ed. Copyright © 1991 by Houghton Mifflin Company. Used with permission.

Page 148: Microbiology Cartoon FAR SIDE copyright 1987 FARWORKS, INC. Reprinted with permission of Universal Press Syndicate. All rights reserved.

Page 149: "The Hydrologic Cycle" from Joseph S. Weisberg, *Meteorology,* 2nd ed. p. 80. Copyright © 1981 by Houghton Mifflin Company. Used by permission.

(Credits continued on page 320.)

Printed in the U.S.A.

Library of Congress Catalog Card Number: 93-78677

ISBN: 0-395-67581-2

123456789-B-97 96 95 94 93

Contents

Preface

College Study Skills teaches the study and test-taking skills that are needed for success in college and it promotes the improvement of reading comprehension and analytical skills. Written in a supportive tone and in language that is easy for almost all college students to understand, it contains more than one hundred practical exercises that help students to acquire skills through practice. *College Study Skills* in its various editions has been used with great success by thousands of students, both in classes under the supervision of instructors and in other settings, including learning centers and skills laboratories.

Improvements in the Fifth Edition

This new Fifth Edition of *College Study Skills* includes updated exposition, improved exercises, and many other changes.

Organizational Changes. The book is now organized into five parts rather than four.

- Part 1, "Plan to Succeed," orients students to college life and study skills instruction.
- Part 2, "Use Time Wisely"—new to this edition—explains how to make better use of time by setting goals, scheduling time, and increasing ability to concentrate while studying.
- Part 3, "Learn Organizational Skills," develops analytical and organizational skills that are the foundation for underlining, making notes, and other study tasks. The exercises in this part have been redesigned so that they are now printed on fewer pages.
- Part 4, "Study for Tests," explains how to take good class notes, survey before reading, underline or highlight books, make notes of information in books, anticipate test questions, and recite and rehearse in preparation for tests.
- Part 5, "Do Well on Tests," explains methods for answering true-false, multiple-choice, matching, fill-in, and essay questions. Chapters have been combined so that this part now contains seven rather than nine chapters.

New Chapters. Four chapters are new to this edition.

- Chapter 5, "Improve Your Memory," provides background for study skills instruction by explaining the three stages of memory, the information-processing model of memory, and forgetting theory.
- Chapter 6, "Understand Your Learning Style," explains learning strategies and learning styles and offers students an opportunity to assess the study strategies they use.

- Chapter 7, "Deal with Stress," discusses sources of stress, symptoms of stress, and how to cope with stress.
- Chapter 9, "Work Toward Goals," shows how goals give direction to life and it suggests how to write and work toward them.

Expanded Instruction. Additions have been made to the instruction in most chapters, including the following:

- Chapter 2, "Do Your Best," now includes suggestions about selecting a curriculum, building a reference library, doing extra-credit work, participating in class, and establishing good relations with instructors.
- Chapter 8, "Use the Library," now includes an explanation of electronic data base searches.
- Chapter 10, "Manage Your Time," teaches how to analyze demands on one's time and it gives more suggestions for making better use of time.
- Chapter 11, "Increase Concentration," relates suggestions in Chapter 6, "Understand Your Learning Style," to strategies for increasing concentration.
- The formats for exercises in Chapter 12, "Learn to Label Outlines," and Chapter 13, "Make Well-Organized Outlines," have been redesigned to be printed on fewer pages.
- Chapter 14, "Use Effective Study Methods," provides a more comprehensive overview of the study process and a means for students to compare their study strategies to the ones prescribed by the SQ3R and SOAR study formulas.
- Chapter 16, "Survey Chapters," includes explanations about how photographs, cartoons, and circle graphs are used in textbooks.
- Chapter 20, "Remember and Recall Information," is revised to reflect the information about memory in Chapter 5; it relates rehearsal and retrieval cues to the learning process and discusses additional aids to recitation and rehearsal.
- Chapter 21, "Strategies for any Test," includes additional information about test anxiety and a checklist for students to analyze their anxiety.

Other Changes. Other prominent changes in this Fifth Edition of *College Study Skills* include the following:

- The textbook chapter in the appendix is used as the basis for improved exercises in surveying (Chapter 16), marking books (Chapter 18), making notes for books (Chapter 19), reciting and rehearsing (Chapter 20), and taking tests (Chapter 21). Both the Instructor's Resource Manual and Chapter 21 contain tests based on information in this chapter.
- Words in the textbook selections in Chapter 18 that may be unfamiliar to students are underscored in blue and they are defined in the Vocabulary List on pages 308–315. A test based on these underscored words is provided in the Instructor's Resource Manual.

The book concludes with an appendix which contains an entire textbook chapter, a vocabulary list, a glossary, an index, forms for keeping records of assignments, and forms for study schedules.

Teaching Suggestions

The chapters are arranged in a logical teaching sequence, but they are written so that students can study one of them without first having studied any others. Thus, skills may be taught in any sequence that a teacher prefers. I recommend, however, that students be taught the labeling system for outlines in Chapter 12 before they are asked to make well-organized outlines in Chapter 13. Also, it would be extremely helpful to students if they read about basic study procedures in Chapter 3, memory in Chapter 5, and effective study methods in Chapter 14 before they study Chapters 15–20, which explicate the steps in the study process.

Instructor's Resource Manual

College Study Skills is accompanied by a manual for instructors which contains teaching suggestions, quizzes, tests, and a complete answer key to exercises. The manual is printed on 8½-by-11-inch paper to facilitate duplicating materials in it for classroom use.

Acknowledgments

I am indebted to Mary Jo Southern for her guidance and support and to Barbara Roth and Danielle Carbonneau for their assistance and expertise; these colleagues made it a particular pleasure to prepare this revision of *College Study Skills.* I am also grateful to Jennifer Waddell, Marie Barnes, George Kane, George McLean, and Jennifer Schmidt for their many contributions and to the following reviewers for their comments and suggestions that helped me in revising this book.

John Adamski, II, *Indiana Vocational Technical College, Gary, Indiana*
Wanda S. Hartman, *Black Hawk College, Moline, Illinois*
Lois M. Hassan, *Henry Ford Community College, Dearborn, Michigan*
Cynthia A. Hilden, *Blue Mountain Community College, Pendleton, Oregon*
Carlotta Hill, *Oklahoma City Community College*
Dawn L. Leonard, *Charleston Southern University, South Carolina*
Susan L. Smith, *Black Hawk College, Moline, Illinois*
Michaeline Wideman, *University of Cincinnati, Ohio*

In writing this revision I was inspired by the continued interest in this book, which had its beginning in materials I created to teach students at Queensborough Community College—my academic home for more than twenty years.

I want *College Study Skills* to be as useful to you as I can make it. If you write to me to let me know what I should or should not change when I prepare the sixth edition, I will answer you. Address your letter to James F. Shepherd, c/o Marketing Services, College Division, Houghton Mifflin Company, 222 Berkeley Street, Boston, Masachusetts 02116.

J.F.S.

To the Student

The skills you will learn about in *College Study Skills* are the ones that thousands of college students told me helped them most to do well in their courses.

You may, at first, find it difficult to believe that you should modify your study procedures in the ways that are recommended in this book. If so, read Chapter 5 and Chapter 20 to understand what you must do to remember all the things you will be required to learn in college. Those chapters should help you understand that the study strategies I suggest can help you do your best in college and learn more in less time!

Also, I hope you will carefully work out the exercises that are provided in this book, even the ones that aren't collected by your instructor. Then, when you study or take tests, practice using the skills you have learned in this book. If you do these things, I believe that your chances for earning a degree will be greatly enhanced.

It is not possible to learn, all at once, everything in *College Study Skills.* When you have a study problem, consult the table of contents at the beginning of the book or the index at the end. For instance, if you know that you must answer multiple-choice questions for a test, consult the index to find where multiple-choice questions are discussed, and study those pages.

As soon as possible, read the chapters about how to do your best in each course (Chapter 2), how to use effective study methods (Chapter 14), and how to take good class notes (Chapter 17). These chapters explain information that is essential for you to know in order to succeed in each of your courses.

I would enjoy knowing your reactions to *College Study Skills.* If you take the time to write to me, I will take the time to answer you. Address your letter to James F. Shepherd, c/o Marketing Services, Houghton Mifflin Company, 222 Berkeley Street, Boston, Massachusetts 02116-3764.

I sincerely hope that you use what you learn in this book to do your best in school. I—and many others you have never met—want you to enjoy the benefits of a college education.

J.F.S.

PART 1

Prepare to Succeed

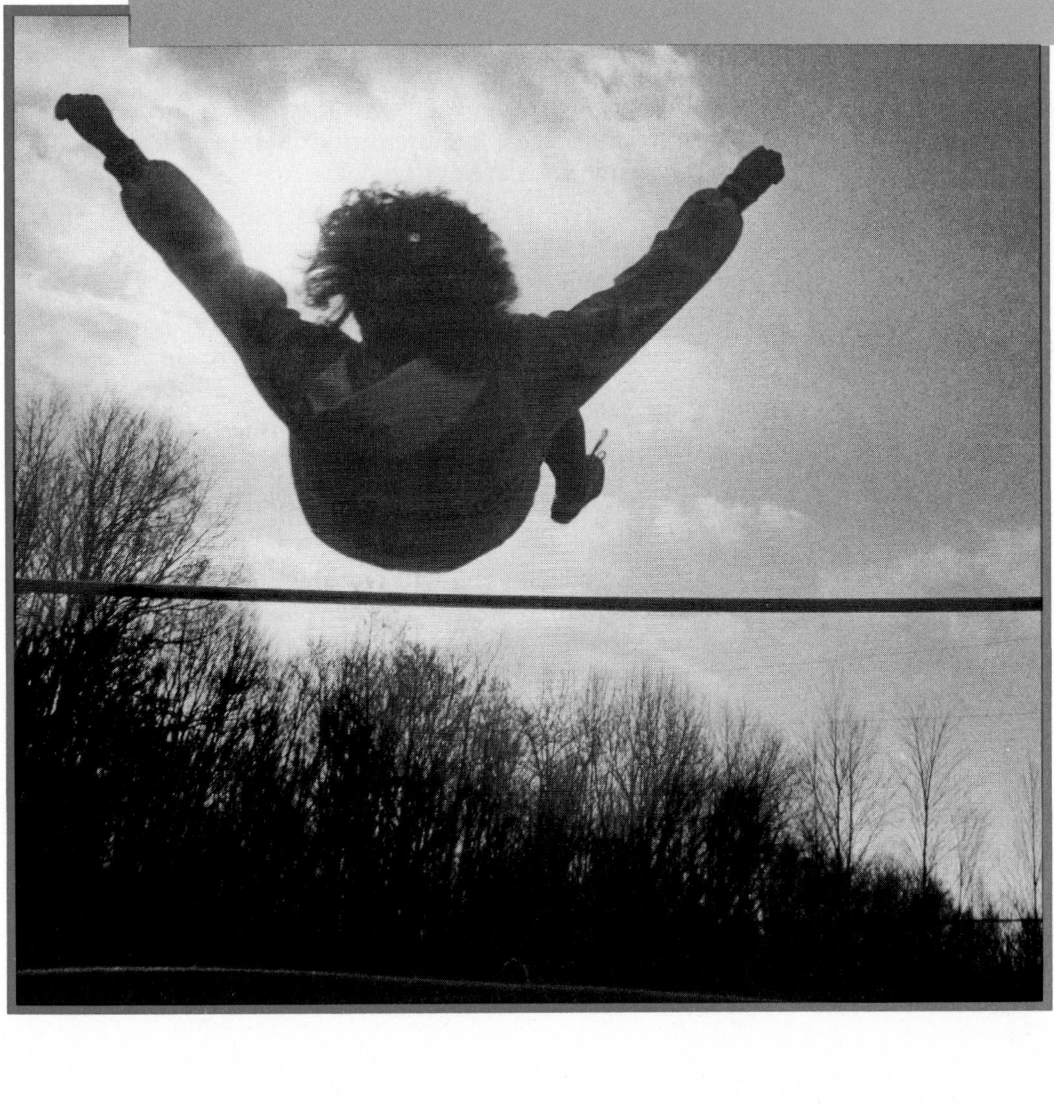

Preview of PART I

This first part of *College Study Skills* explains basic methods you may use to successfully pursue a college education.

- Chapter 1, "Adjust to College," suggests ways to make a smooth transition to college life.
- Chapter 2, "Do Your Best," summarizes procedures used by successful college students.
- Chapter 3, "Understand Degree Requirements," helps you learn about the academic standards at your school.
- Chapter 4, "Find Help If You Need It," discusses sources of help that are available to you in case you have academic difficulty.
- Chapter 5, "Improve Your Memory," explains how memory functions and how it can be improved.
- Chapter 6, "Understand Your Learning Style," gives you an opportunity to analyze your study procedures.
- Chapter 7, "Deal with Stress," includes suggestions for adapting to and coping with stress.
- Chapter 8, "Use the Library," is an introduction to library facilities and services.

If this is your first year in college, you will probably find a great many facts about college that are new to you as you study these eight chapters in Part I.

1

Adjust to College

The first weeks of college may be disturbing to you—they are for most students. You will need to make new friends, and you will have new teachers to get used to. You will need to learn where classrooms are located and to find the easiest way to travel from one place to another. You will want to buy your books, plan where you will study, and schedule when you will study. Also, you may feel uncomfortable because you don't know the difference between a *bursar* and a *registrar* or where to go for help if you have a problem.

This chapter suggests some basic ways to adjust to college life, and it explains the meanings of some important words you may not know.

Free Time

Some of the most noticeable differences between high school and college are that in college your report card is not sent home to your parents and you are not required to go to study hall or to carry a hall pass. In addition, you probably will not have classes scheduled every day, and you may sometimes have long breaks between classes. You will be responsible to decide what you will do during the time that you are not in classes.

This is why *College Study Skills* provides many ideas for making effective use of time. Chapter 10 explains basic strategies for managing time, Chapter 11 gives suggestions for making better use of time by increasing concentration, and Chapter 7 describes methods for coping with stress that interferes with your ability to use your study time well. In addition, Chapters 14–20 teach study techniques that you may use to learn material more thoroughly and quickly.

Textbooks

Another way that college differs from high school is that college students must buy their own **textbooks***.Some students encounter unnecessary difficulty because they wait too long to purchase required books or because they try to get by without buying the books they need.

*Boldface terms are defined in the glossary on pages 316–320.

Textbooks are expensive, but they are a small cost of attending college in comparison to tuition, housing, and other expenses. Do what experienced students do—purchase your required books immediately and get a head start in your classes by beginning to read them even before your teachers give reading assignments.

The Catalog or Bulletin

Your college publishes a book called a **catalog** or **bulletin** that contains important information, such as descriptions of courses, graduation requirements, names of instructors, and locations of buildings and offices. If you do not have a copy of your school's catalog, obtain one immediately. It is probably available at the admissions office of your school.

The School Calendar

Colleges prepare calendars that list holidays and other important days, such as the ones for **orientation,** registration, and final examinations. If you do not find a calendar printed in your catalog, ask a **counselor** or **adviser** for a copy. It is important for you to familiarize yourself with your school's calendar. For one thing, holidays at your school are not necessarily the same as the holidays at local public schools or at other colleges in your community.

Academic calendars are divided into **terms,** which are periods of study that usually end with final examinations. A term may be a semester, a quarter, or a trimester. When a school uses the **semester system,** the school year is divided into two parts, usually a fall and a spring term of about fifteen weeks each. When either the **quarter system** or the **trimester system** is used, the school year is usually divided into fall, winter, and spring terms of about ten weeks each.

Some colleges offer students opportunities to study during summer sessions or intersessions, which are not regarded as terms for the purposes of school business. A **summer session** is a period in the summer during which students may take courses; an **intersession** is a short session of study offered between two terms, such as a four-week session offered in January between a fall term and a spring term.

New Friends

You will enjoy school more if you have friends to talk with before and after classes. In addition, you need friends in your classes whom you can call to learn about assignments given when you are absent and from whom you can copy notes teachers give on days you are not in class. You may also find it is helpful to discuss assignments or to study for tests with students who are taking the same courses you are taking. Therefore, put a high priority on making friends in each class you take.

Social Activities

Your college experience will be more enjoyable if you make the effort to attend social functions, join clubs, and participate in sports.

Your student government sponsors social events, such as movies, concerts, athletic events, and dances. These and other activities are available to you at little or no cost. Read student newspapers and notices on bulletin boards for announcements of these events.

In addition, the students at your school have organized clubs for interests that may range from bowling to creative writing and from photography to karate. There are probably organizations for students who want to learn more about various religions, countries, or hobbies and opportunities for students to swim or to play basketball, baseball, volleyball, or other team sports. Information about clubs may be printed in a brochure or pamphlet that was distributed during orientation. Clubs not only provide you with opportunities to participate in activities you enjoy; they are also a way for you to meet people and to make new friends.

If you have difficulty learning about social events and clubs, visit the student government office, student activities office, or the student affairs office. Somebody there can give you the information that you need to involve yourself in campus life.

Counseling Services

Most colleges have **counselors** who provide students with guidance in achieving their educational and occupational goals and in resolving their personal problems. In addition, counselors are usually experts in helping students with such matters as changing curriculums and dropping courses.

If any of the statements in the "Checklist for Counseling Services" on page 6 describe you, a counselor at your school can either help you or tell you where you can find help. You may be advised to visit another office on campus. For instance, if you have difficulty in paying tuition, a counselor may refer you to a financial aid office. Or, if you have a problem for which your school provides no services, you may be advised to visit an agency in the community that can give you the assistance you need.

Health Services

Most colleges have an office that provides health services for students who become ill or injured while they are on campus. Call this office if you have an illness or injury that prevents you from attending classes for an extended period. Someone in the office may notify your teachers so they can make special arrangements for you to keep up to date with course work during the time you are unable to attend classes.

Checklist for Counseling Services

Check any statement in this list that describes you.

- ☐ I need a part-time job.
- ☐ I need a place to live.
- ☐ I need financial assistance.
- ☐ I need somebody to care for my children.
- ☐ I want to improve my grades.
- ☐ I am very anxious when I take tests.
- ☐ I want an explanation of my placement test scores.
- ☐ I want help in deciding what occupation to pursue.
- ☐ I want help in deciding what I should study in college.
- ☐ I want to know about job opportunities after I graduate.
- ☐ I want to transfer to another college.
- ☐ I am extremely displeased with one of my teachers.
- ☐ I have a serious physical disability or chronic illness.
- ☐ I have been out of school for years, and I feel lost.
- ☐ I feel very lonely.
- ☐ I have a serious problem with my parents (or spouse).
- ☐ I have poor relations with members of the opposite sex.
- ☐ I want help to overcome my drug (or alcohol) problem.

A counselor at your school can help you with your problems or tell you where you can find help.

Departments, Divisions, and Schools

The courses you are taking are probably offered by several departments. A **department** is an organizational unit that offers courses in a specific subject or a specific group of subjects. For example, a history department may offer courses only in history, but a social science department may offer courses in psychology, sociology, anthropology, and other subjects.

At some colleges, departments are organized in groups called **divisions.** For example, the social science division of a college may include a psychology department, a sociology department, an anthropology department, and other departments. Some universities refer to divisions as **schools.** For instance, schools of business, schools of law, and schools of medicine are usually divisions of universities.

The President and Deans

The senior administrative officer at most colleges and universities is the **president,** who has ultimate responsibility for all aspects of the functioning of a school. **Deans** are members of the administration who are in charge of specified areas of the school's activities, such as a dean of students or a dean of instruction. Sometimes there are also deans of divisions or schools within a college or university. At most schools, students come in contact with deans only when they are given awards or are in serious trouble.

At some schools, the senior administrative officer is called a **chancellor,** and deans are sometimes called **vice chancellors** or **vice presidents.** At a few colleges and universities, a chancellor or **ombudsman** serves as a special assistant to the president.

The Registrar and the Bursar

The administration includes a **registrar,** who oversees registering students for courses and keeps records of the courses students take and the grades they receive. Shortly after you complete each term, the registrar will send you a **transcript,** which is a report of your grades for the courses you took.

The registrar may be located in the registrar's office, the admissions office, or the student records office. Visit the registrar when you have questions about your transcript or your registration in courses, and when you want a transcript mailed to an employer or another school.

The **bursar,** or **cashier,** is the person who is responsible for money transactions; he or she may be located in the bursar's office, the cashier's office, the business office, or the office of the treasurer. Visit the bursar when you have questions about tuition or fees and when you need to pay a bill.

Teachers, Professors, and Doctors

Teachers in colleges and universities may be called "professor" or "doctor." "Professor" is sometimes an honorary or courtesy title, but more often it is a title for faculty members who hold the rank of **professor, associate professor,** or **assistant professor. Doctor** designates a person who has earned the highest degree awarded by a college or university. For instance, when professors of music are called "doctor," this is usually because they have earned the Doctor of Music degree.

In *College Study Skills,* I use "teacher," "instructor," and "professor" interchangeably when I refer to a person who teaches in a college or a university.

Adjunct and *tenure* are words sometimes used in discussions about college faculty members. An **adjunct** is a person hired to teach part-time or for a specified period, such as one term or one school year. **Tenure** is a status in which faculty members, having fulfilled certain requirements, hold their positions permanently.

EXERCISE 1.1 Your Required Textbooks

List the titles of the textbooks that you must purchase for the courses you are taking this term.

1. ______________________________
2. ______________________________
3. ______________________________
4. ______________________________
5. ______________________________

EXERCISE 1.2 Your School's Calendar

The following questions are about your school's calendar, which may be printed in the front of your catalog.

1. What is the last day this term you can add a course to your program?

   ____

2. What is the last day this term you can drop a course from your program and get a full tuition refund?

   ____

3. What is the next day when there will be no classes because your school is observing a holiday?

   ____

4. What is the next week when there will be no classes because your school is observing a recess of one week or longer?

   ____

5. What is the last day of classes for the current term at your school?

   ____

6. On what days will final examinations be given for the current term at your school?

   ____

EXERCISE 1.3 Office Locations

The answers to these questions are probably in your catalog and in materials that you got during orientation.

1. Where are the counselors' offices located?

   ____

2. Where is the registrar's office located? (It may be called the admissions office or the student records office.)

   ____

3. Where is the bursar's office located? (It may be called the cashier's office, the business office, or the office of the treasurer.)

   ____

4. Where is the financial aid office located?

   ____

5. Where is the office of testing located?

   ____

6. Where is the student activities office located?

   ____

7. Where is the health services office located?

   ____

   What is the telephone number of this office (in case you must report that you are unable to attend classes for an extended period because of illness)?

   ____

8. List the names and locations of the offices of the departments that offer the courses you are taking now.

   a. ______________________________

   b. ______________________________

   c. ______________________________

   d. ______________________________

   e. ______________________________

EXERCISE 1.4 Social Activities

List three clubs on your campus that you may want to join.

1. ______________________________

2. ______________________________

3. ______________________________

EXERCISE 1.5 Other Services

1. Where on campus can you go to use a computer?

____

2. Where is the bookstore located?

____

3. Where is the lost-and-found office located?

____

4. If lockers are available on your campus, where do you go to rent one?

____

5. If your school makes medical insurance available to you at special rates, where do you purchase it?

____

6. If students need parking stickers for their cars, where are the stickers purchased and how much do they cost?

____

7. If your school has a child care center, where is it located and what children does it serve?

____

8. What exercise, swimming, or sports facilities are available for your use during your free time and what hours are they open?

____

2

Do Your Best

Many of today's famous entertainers had to work at everyday jobs in restaurants, construction, offices, and factories before they became successful in show business. At one time, Tom Hanks was a hotel bellboy, Elayne Boosler was a waitress, and Harrison Ford was a carpenter. However, we don't think of these celebrities as a bellboy, waitress, and carpenter; we think of them as the famous performers they have become by doing the things that are necessary to succeed in the entertainment industry.

The same is true of you in your pursuit of a college degree. Today others may think of you as a recent high school graduate, working person, or homemaker, but you can become known as a successful college student by doing the things that successful college students do:

- Take the right courses.
- Be serious about each course you take.
- Do the things teachers expect of you.
- Participate in your classes.

This chapter explains these and other methods you may want to use to help ensure that you will have a successful experience in college.

Know Why You Are Attending College

It may seem obvious that the reason people go to college is to acquire an education, but the reasons for attending a college or university are actually extremely varied. Young people who have completed high school recently may go to college because they cannot find work; older people may go to college because the opportunity has been made available to them by their employers. The "Checklist of Reasons for Attending College" on page 12 lists the reasons students most often give for being in college. Read the list and check the boxes in front of the three reasons that best describe why you are in school.

Did you check boxes in front of the reasons that are ways of saying "I want to improve myself"? If so, you believe in the possibility of a better life for yourself, and you believe that if you attend college, your life will be better for it. On the other hand, if you are attending school *only* to please your parents, *only* because you cannot find work, *only* for some reason other than self-improvement, you may not have sufficient motivation to do well in school.

Checklist of Reasons for Attending College

Check the boxes in front of the three reasons that best describe why you are in school.

- ☐ I want to earn a college degree.
- ☐ I need a better education to get a good job.
- ☐ I want to prepare myself for a specific occupation.
- ☐ I want to be a well-educated person.
- ☐ I want to increase my appreciation for the arts.
- ☐ I want to learn to think more clearly.
- ☐ I want to be more responsible for my own life.
- ☐ I want a better job than the one I have now.
- ☐ I want to be promoted at the place where I work.
- ☐ I want to decide what I will do with my life.
- ☐ I want to use the money that is available for my tuition.
- ☐ I cannot find a job right now.
- ☐ I do not want to go to work right now.
- ☐ My parents want me to go to college.
- ☐ I like the social life at college.
- ☐ I like the feeling it gives me to be on campus.
- ☐ I want to find a boyfriend or girlfriend.
- ☐ I want to find a husband or wife.

Most students check three boxes in front of the first ten reasons, which are all ways of saying "I want to improve myself."

Enroll in the Right Curriculum

You will be awarded a **degree** when you satisfactorily complete all the course work and other requirements in your **curriculum,** or program of study. Following is an example of a program for first-semester accounting students:

		Credits
BU-101	Principles of Accounting I	4
BU-210	Business Organization	3
BU-205	Business Management	3
EN-101	English Composition I	3
HE-202	Health Education	1
PE-	Physical Education	1
		15

If you do not have a copy of your curriculum, ask your counselor or adviser where you can get a copy of it. It is extremely important for you to know exactly what courses you must take to earn a degree.

When you obtain a copy of your curriculum, refer to your college catalog to read the descriptions of your required courses to decide if they are the types of things that you want to study. You will benefit from college more if your required courses are ones that you want to take.

If you are not pleased with your curriculum, examine the courses that are required for *other* curriculums at your school; you may find a program of study that is more appealing to you and change to that curriculum. For most people, college is a time to explore possibilities and to learn about themselves; as a result, more than half of all college students change their curriculum at least once during their college careers.

Take the Right Courses

In addition to enrolling in the right curriculum, it is important that you take the right courses. Use the following suggestions to guide you during course **registration** each term:

Suggestions for Selecting Courses

- Enroll in courses as early during the registration period as you can; if you wait until the last minute, the courses you want to take may be closed because they are filled with other students.
- Enroll in prerequisite courses. A **prerequisite** is a course for which you must receive a satisfactory grade before you can enroll in some other course. For instance, the prerequisite for Accounting II may be a grade of C or better in Accounting I. It is essential for you to enroll in prerequisites so that you will take courses in the correct sequence and not be delayed in graduating from college.
- Enroll in learning skills courses. Colleges usually test students' reading, writing, and mathematics skills when they apply for admission. After testing, many students are required or advised to improve learning skills. Take full advantage of any learning skills instruction that you are offered. The faculty of your school believes that this instruction will help you do your best and earn a degree.
- Schedule difficult classes at the times you are most alert and concentrate best. If you like to get up early, schedule difficult classes as early in the day as you can. On the other hand, if you're not fully awake until noon, schedule your most challenging courses after lunch, late in the afternoon, or even in the evening.
- If you believe you might eventually change your curriculum, study your catalog to find courses that apply to any curriculum to which you may someday transfer, and take those courses as electives.

If you use these suggestions, you will be more likely to enroll in courses in which you will do your best.

Choose Your Instructors Carefully

Some students who take great care in selecting who will cut their hair or repair their automobile give no thought to choosing who will teach their courses. However, a good teacher can make any subject more enjoyable and satisfying to study. When two or more instructors teach a course, you have a chance to pick the teacher you prefer.

You probably already have a good idea about the characteristics you like in a teacher. Most students prefer instructors who are well organized and easy to understand, enthusiastic about their subject matter, available to answer questions, fair in testing, and reasonable in grading. On the other hand, students often report that they try to avoid teachers who come to class unprepared, conduct aimless class discussions, read aloud from the textbook, talk in an expressionless voice, ramble from topic to topic, show a preference for certain students, have unnecessarily difficult course requirements, or who are disrespectful or condescending to students.

Other students are your best source of information about the teachers at your school; therefore, if at all possible, enroll in courses taught by instructors who have been recommended to you by students whose judgment you trust. If you are unable to get recommendations from other students, investigate whether students' evaluations of the teachers at your school are published by your student government.

Know Your Teachers' Requirements

Students who don't know what their instructors require usually don't do all the things that are expected of them. As a result, they usually do not earn very good course grades.

During the first class meeting, instructors usually give an overview of the course, explain course requirements, and distribute a syllabus or other handout. A **syllabus** is a printed outline of the main topics of a course. When course requirements are listed in a syllabus or on other printed pages, keep them in a safe place; when they are presented orally, maintain accurate and complete notes about them. In either case, understand them completely and follow them exactly.

Use the "Checklist for Course Requirements" on page 15 to make certain that you know exactly what your teachers expect of you. Some teachers require only that students take **midterm** and final examinations, but other instructors require most of the things that are mentioned in the checklist.

Attend Classes Faithfully

At some colleges there are teachers who do not take attendance, thus giving students the impression that it is not important for them to go to class. However, even teachers who don't take attendance are not likely to be sympathetic toward students who cut class. Students who are frequently absent should not expect their teachers to do favors for them if they have a problem, and chances are that they will have a problem.

Checklist for Course Requirements

Use this checklist for each course you are taking.

- ☐ I know what books or other materials I must purchase.
- ☐ I know what books or materials I must take to class.
- ☐ I must take notes during class.
- ☐ I must participate in class discussions.
- ☐ I must do homework assignments.
- ☐ I must read materials that are on reserve in the library.
- ☐ I must attend a laboratory (and I know where it is located and when I must attend it).
- ☐ I must have conferences with the teacher (and I know when and where I must go for the conferences).
- ☐ I must write a paper (and I know the format for the paper and when it is due).
- ☐ I must go on field trips or to concerts or museums.
- ☐ I know the class policy on missed and late assignments.
- ☐ I know the class policy on lateness and absence.
- ☐ I know how many tests I must take and when they will be given.
- ☐ I know how my final grade will be determined.

If you are uncertain about requirements for a course, ask the instructor to explain them.

Faithful class attendance is essential because you are responsible for everything that happens in each of your classes, even if you are absent. For instance, you are expected to know about all assignments and tests even if they are announced on a day you are not in class! In addition, it is only by attending class that you can know what material your instructors emphasized by writing it on the board, by repeating it, or by other means; you cannot get this information from another student's notes. If you don't know what material your teachers consider to be most important, you will not know what to emphasize when you study for tests.

What to Do If You Miss a Class

- Contact a classmate to learn about assignments or tests announced in your absence.
- Hand-copy or photocopy notes taken by a classmate while you were absent.
- Deliver due assignments to the instructor as soon as possible
- When you return to a class, check with your teacher to make certain that your classmate gave you correct information about assignments and tests, and ask the instructor for suggestions about how you can catch up with work you missed.

Following an absence, do not ask an instructor, "Did I miss anything?" The answer is yes. Also, do not tell a teacher that an absence is "excused" because of illness or some similar reason. Excused absences are noted in high schools but not in most colleges and universities. When a serious student is absent from a college class, the teacher assumes that the absence is unavoidable.

If an injury or illness makes it impossible for you to attend class for an extended period, contact the health services office of your school. Someone in that office may notify your instructors why you are not attending classes. If so, your teachers may make special arrangements for you to catch up with course work; however, if your teachers do not make special arrangements, you may need to withdraw from your courses (see page 37).

In addition to attending all classes, arrive on time. Students who are frequently late to class communicate the message to their teachers and classmates that they are disorganized, inconsiderate, or immature. Do not create an unfavorable impression of yourself; arrive at class on time.

Use the Right Study Equipment

Professional chefs don't try to cook gourmet meals without the right cooking utensils, and qualified carpenters don't try to build houses without the tools of their trade, but many students try to pursue a college career with not much more than a ballpoint pen and a spiral notebook.

You will find that it is easier to be a student if you have the equipment that you need to do the work of a student efficiently. The "Study Equipment Checklist" on page 17 may include some items that you need to purchase.

When you purchase study equipment, take special care in selecting a notebook; the notebook you choose can help or hinder you in maintaining the well-organized records of class notes you need to do well in your college courses. Though most students choose spiral notebooks, a ring binder is probably a better choice.

Reasons for Using a Ring Binder

- A ring binder can hold all the notes for all of your classes.
- Since you will have only one ring binder, you will always take the right notebook to class.
- Using a hole punch, you can insert papers teachers distribute exactly where they belong in your notebook.
- You can add paper to a ring binder. As a result, you can always have enough paper in your notebook for courses in which teachers give long lectures.
- If you are absent, you can insert notes you copy from a classmate exactly where they belong.
- You can have an assignment section in a ring binder, so you don't have to have a separate assignment book.
- It is less expensive to buy paper for a ring binder than to buy spiral notebooks.

When a desk is too small to accommodate a ring binder comfortably, remove some paper from the binder for note taking. Or leave your ring binder at home, take notes on loose-leaf paper that you carry in a folder with double pockets, and insert the notes where they belong in your ring binder when you return home.

Study Equipment Checklist

Put checks in front of the items you own.

- ☐ Desk or table
- ☐ Desk chair
- ☐ Reading lamp
- ☐ Typewriter or computer
- ☐ Bulletin board
- ☐ Bookshelves
- ☐ File
- ☐ Required textbooks
- ☐ Calculator
- ☐ Pencil sharpener
- ☐ Paper clips
- ☐ Transparent tape
- ☐ Household glue
- ☐ Stapler and staples
- ☐ Staple remover
- ☐ Ruler
- ☐ Hole punch
- ☐ Notebook
- ☐ Notebook paper
- ☐ Typing paper
- ☐ Index cards
- ☐ File folders
- ☐ Pencils and pens
- ☐ Pencil bag
- ☐ Highlight pens
- ☐ Eraser
- ☐ Rubber bands
- ☐ Scissors
- ☐ Clock or watch
- ☐ Backpack, bag, or briefcase

Figure out how you can acquire any of this equipment that you need but don't have.

If you decide to use spiral notebooks, it is a good idea to purchase a separate notebook for each class. Buy notebooks with pockets on the inside covers so you will have a place to keep papers your teachers distribute, or use transparent tape to attach these papers to inside covers. Write the names of your courses in large print on the outside front covers of your notebooks to ensure that you take the right notebooks to your classes.

Organize Your Notebook

Organize your notebook so that notes for each class are completely separate from the notes for your other classes. For example, notes for a biology, a math, and an English course should be kept in three separate sections of a notebook. If you mix your notes for one class with your notes for another class, your notes will not be properly organized when you study them to prepare for tests. In addition, be sure you set aside in your notebook a place to keep records about assignments, tests, instructors, and classmates.

Important Records for Your Notebook

- Information about assignments should explain exactly what they are, how they are to be done, and when they are due.
- Information about tests should include exactly what materials and topics will be covered on each test and the dates, times, and places that the tests will be given.
- Information about instructors should include their names, office locations, office telephone numbers, and office hours.
- Information about classmates should include the names, addresses, and telephone numbers of at least two people in each class whom you can contact for assignments and notes you miss when you are absent.

On page 90 there is an explanation of a method you may want to use to keep accurate records of your assignments, and a form for keeping assignments is found in the back of the book.

Build a Reference Library

In addition to textbooks, you need reference books to help you in doing your college assignments. Your basic reference library should include a standard desk dictionary, a thesaurus, and an English handbook.

A Basic Reference Library

- In addition to a paperback dictionary to take to classes, you need a standard desk dictionary to use where you study. When you shop for a desk dictionary, pay special attention to the clear definitions, usage notes, word histories, and illustrations in *The American Heritage Dictionary of the English Language,* Third Edition, Boston: Houghton Mifflin, 1992.
- Your library should include a **thesaurus,** which is a book that lists synonyms; it will provide you help in finding the best words to express your ideas. I recommend *The Random House Thesaurus* because it is complete and easy to use.
- A good English handbook is an essential reference book because it contains a great deal of information, including answers to your questions about grammar, usage, and the correct format for term papers. *The Riverside Handbook,* published by Houghton Mifflin Company, is an excellent English handbook.

Eventually you should add an almanac, atlas, and other books to your reference library. An **almanac,** such as *The World Almanac,* is an annual publication that contains a wealth of information on many topics, including facts and statistics about famous people, history, the countries of the world, and various sports. An **atlas,** such as *The Rand McNally World Atlas,* is a collection of maps of all the countries of the world followed by a detailed index that assists in locating the thousands of places indicated on the maps.

Keep Up-to-Date with Course Work

College terms start out slowly. They gradually get busier and busier, reaching a peak of activity at final examination time. If you fall behind in the work for a course, you may find yourself trying to catch up just when you are very busy with all of your other courses. Don't fall behind—keep up-to-date with work in all your courses.

This is doubly important when you must master information or **skills** taught early in a course in order to learn information or skills that are taught later in the course. Mathematics, science, technology, and foreign language courses are some of the courses that fit this description. When you study, ask yourself this question: "Do I need to learn this information or skill in order to learn other information or skills later in the course?" If the answer to this question is yes, learn the information or skill immediately and review it often.

Do Assignments on Time

Instructors give assignments to provide practice for skills and for other purposes. They expect students to have assignments ready on time; many teachers do not accept late work, and other instructors give lower grades for assignments that are turned in late.

Some teachers give assignments that they review in class but do not collect and grade. Do these assignments faithfully; their purpose is to help you acquire a skill or to learn other things that you need to know.

Teachers sometimes require students to write papers that are five, ten, or more pages long. The grades for papers such as these usually account for substantial proportions of course grades. Therefore, before you start work on any paper for which you will receive college credit, make certain that you know the answers to the following questions:

- How many pages long must the paper be?
- What topics are acceptable for the paper?
- In what format must the paper be presented?
- When is the paper due?

When you are uncertain about the requirements for a paper, schedule a conference with the teacher to receive the clarification you need.

English handbooks, such as *The Riverside Handbook,* mentioned on page 18, explain the steps in writing papers and reports of various kinds. It is wise to begin work on long papers as soon as they are announced. If you put off writing a paper, you may need to devote many hours to it just when you want to prepare for midterm tests or final examinations. If you are unable to complete a paper on time, you may need to request your instructor to give you an incomplete grade (see page 38).

Keep a photocopy of each paper you write so you will not need to rewrite it if a teacher misplaces or loses it and so you will have a record of references and other information in the paper to which you may want to refer in the future.

Submit Neat Assignments

Before you submit any written work, keep in mind that college instructors usually give higher grades to papers that are neat in appearance and free of errors than to ones that are sloppy looking and full of mistakes. Therefore, ask a friend or relative to proofread your written work before you give it to an instructor, and submit only papers that are as neat as you can make them.

If you do not know how to use a word processor, it would be a good idea for you to learn. Computers are probably available for you to use in an instructional resource center or some other facility on your campus. Studies have found that teachers tend to give higher grades to papers that are prepared on word processors than to those that are typed or handwritten. It is very time consuming to retype or rewrite an entire page to make a minor change; however, slight changes can be made very easily and quickly on a word processor, and a corrected page can be retyped by simply pushing a button. Papers written using a word processor tend to receive higher grades because they usually have fewer errors than typed or handwritten papers.

Always Do Extra-Credit Work

When instructors offer special assignments or projects for extra credit, be certain that you do them. By giving extra credit for special work, teachers have a convenient way to find out which students are most eager to earn high course grades. Thus, the good work you do for extra credit might raise your final course grade from C to B or from B to A. However, doing *only* extra-credit assignments is not enough; students who do failing work all term are not likely to raise their grades much by doing extra-credit assignments at the last minute.

Participate in Class

It is your responsibility as a student to contribute to your classes, and one of the easiest ways to do this is to ask questions. Write down the questions that occur to you while you are reading assigned material or while you are listening to the teacher explain course content; they may be about things you don't understand or statements with which you disagree.

Guidelines for Asking Questions

- Ask questions at the times instructors indicate they want to answer them. Some teachers prefer to answer questions at the beginning or end of class, whereas others stop from time to time and ask, "Are there any questions?"
- Be polite and specific. "Will you please give more examples of palindromes?" is polite and specific. On the other hand, "Did you expect me to understand what you said?" is neither polite nor specific.
- Ask only questions that may benefit other students. Requesting an explanation of palindromes may benefit other students who are also interested in the answer. However, "May I have another copy of the syllabus to replace the one I lost?" benefits only you; ask this sort of question before or after class.

Another basic way to participate in any class is to answer teachers' questions about homework, class notes, or the lecture topic.

- Answer questions about homework by referring to your completed homework.
- Prepare to answer questions about your class notes by looking them over before class to refresh your memory about the information in them.
- Anticipate questions your teacher might ask about the lecture topic when you read the assignment before class.

Think out your answers silently in your mind before you give them, and try to answer questions in a manner that will communicate to your teachers that you are serious about learning the content of their courses. However, if you are not prepared to answer questions, it is best to say nothing. It is obvious to teachers when students are unprepared and bluff answers to questions.

In addition to asking and answering questions, you may sometimes be required to contribute to class discussions. If an instructor announces there will be a class discussion, prepare for it by reading assigned material about the discussion topic before you go to class. As you read, list your questions about information you don't understand and statements with which you disagree; use these questions to make contributions to the discussion.

Most students are not comfortable when they have to talk in front of a group. If speaking in a group embarrasses you, keep the following thoughts in mind:

GOOD TEACHERS CREATE A CLIMATE THAT IS SAFE FOR DISCUSSION + QUESTIONS

Dealing with Fear of Class Participation

- Remember that it is normal for you to be nervous when you speak in a group. Most of your classmates are nervous, too, and most of them are more concerned with how they appear to others than the impression you make.
- When you speak in class, concentrate on what you want to say and not on how you appear to others. If you concentrate on what you want to say, you will speak more intelligently and look better to others.
- Remind yourself that by speaking in class now, you will gain experience that will help you be more comfortable during future discussions in school and at work.

You do not need to do a great deal of talking during a discussion. It is usually better to say too little than to say too much. Make statements and ask questions that are directly related to the points under discussion and that keep the discussion moving toward the goal that has been established. Try using some of the following strategies:

How to Participate in Discussions

- If somebody says something that you do not fully understand, ask for a more complete explanation.
- If somebody gives information on a topic and you have additional information about the same topic, offer the information.
- If somebody asks a question that you can answer, give the answer.
- When it is appropriate, ask one of the questions in the list that you prepared while you were reading about the discussion topic.

You may grow weary of some students who try to dominate discussions by talking too much and by always trying to put in the last word on every point that is made. This is inappropriate behavior during a discussion. Teachers may ask students who talk too much to give others a chance to speak, and they may also correct students who engage in other inappropriate behaviors, such as those in the following list:

Inappropriate Behaviors During Discussions

- Being unprepared by failing to read required material about the topic
- Not paying attention while other students speak
- Stating opinions and experiences without referring to information in required reading material about the topic
- Interrupting others while they are speaking
- Doing anything that is distracting while others are speaking
- Engaging in arguments with others
- Making unkind statements to others

Polite disagreement is appropriate during a discussion, but unkindness is not. When people discussing a topic disagree, they are more likely to make a statement such as "I understand your point, but I don't fully agree because . . ." rather than "That's the dumbest idea I've ever heard."

Be Prepared for Tests

Some first-year students make the mistake of not preparing properly for the first test their teachers give. Being poorly prepared, they do not go to class on test days, or they take tests and receive low grades. Either way, they start the term at a great disadvantage.

If you are absent the day a test is given, you may be required to take a make-up test that is more difficult than the test the other students took. Or if a teacher does not offer make-up tests, you may be given a failing grade for the test you missed.

If you receive a low grade for the first test in a course, you might become discouraged because you realize that it will be extremely difficult for you to earn a good grade in the course. Do not create an unnecessary source of discouragement for yourself. Be prepared to do your best on all tests.

Chapters 14 through 20 explain how to prepare for examinations, and Chapters 21 through 27 describe methods for answering test questions.

Build Good Relationships

It is to your benefit to have good relations with your instructors. If you have a problem, teachers will be more interested in helping you find a solution if you have made a favorable impression on them. Also, when they can't decide which of two grades to give you, they are more likely to give you the higher grade if they have positive feelings about you.

THE ONE VARIABLE YOU CAN CONTROL IS YOU.

One way to make favorable impressions on your teachers is to pronounce and spell their names correctly and to address them using the titles they prefer. Notice the titles they place before their names on materials they distribute to you. If your instructors show their names as "Prof. Joseph Hosey," "Dr. Elaine Morton," "Mr. John Snyder," and "Ms. Kitty Bateman," they probably would like you to use these titles when you say their names.

Students also create a good impression on instructors when they show that they are willing and ready to learn by attending class faithfully, arriving on time, sitting in an attentive position, and contributing to the class by asking and answering questions. Most of your teachers will also appreciate it if you smile and say hello when you see them on campus.

Following is a list of student behaviors that are a source of annoyance to many college teachers:

Annoying Behaviors

- Cutting, arriving late, and leaving early
- Being unprepared for class
- Not having a notebook or pen
- Holding a conversation
- Not paying attention
- Acting bored or going to sleep
- Reading or writing something for another class
- Criticizing the course or subject matter
- Making comments about the teacher's private life
- Eating, drinking, or chewing gum noisily
- Passing notes or making wisecracks

Work at creating a good impression of yourself; there are few assets more valuable than the good opinion others have of you.

EXERCISE 2.1 Checklist for Course Requirements

Use the "Checklist for Course Requirements" on page 15 to analyze what your teachers require. Use your analyses to write a summary of the requirements for each of your courses.

EXERCISE 2.2 Attendance Requirements

Find the answer to question 1 by looking in your college catalog.

1. What are the official attendance requirements at your college?

____

____

____

2. If any of your teachers have attendance requirements that are more or less strict than those stated in your college catalog, write their requirements on the following lines.

____

____

____

____

____

EXERCISE 2.3 Your Study Equipment

Which items that you didn't check on the "Study Equipment Checklist" (page 17) do you intend to purchase?

1. ____________________ 4. ____________________

2. ____________________ 5. ____________________

3. ____________________ 6. ____________________

EXERCISE 2.4 Your Teachers' Names

List the names of all your teachers and the titles by which they prefer to be addressed.

1. ____
2. ____
3. ____
4. ____
5. ____

EXERCISE 2.5 Course Information Chart

List information about your courses, instructors, classmates, and tests on the "Course Information Chart" on the inside front cover of this book.

3

Know Degree Requirements

To graduate from your college or university, you must satisfy requirements that are stated in your school's catalog or bulletin. The information and exercises in this chapter will help you to learn what you must do to earn a degree at the school you are attending.

Degrees

When students graduate from colleges and universities, they are awarded **degrees,** which are ranks for those who successfully complete specified courses and other requirements.

If this is your first year in college, you are probably studying for an associate degree or a bachelor's degree. **Associate degrees** are usually offered by two-year and community colleges. They are most commonly the A.A. (Associate of Arts), the A.S. (Associate of Science), and the A.A.S. (Associate of Applied Science). **Bachelor's degrees** are offered by four-year colleges and universities. They are usually the B.A. (Bachelor of Arts) and the B.S. (Bachelor of Science). Some colleges and universities offer **master's degrees** and **doctoral degrees.**

You will be awarded a degree when you satisfactorily complete all the course work and other requirements that are listed in your **curriculum,** or program of study.

Credits and Hours

Credits and hours are assigned to most college courses. **Credits** are units given for the satisfactory completion of study that applies toward a degree. **Hours** are units that designate time spent in classrooms, laboratories, or conferences—they may be shorter or longer than sixty minutes. For example, at many colleges students earn three credits when they satisfactorily complete a three-credit English composition course. However, the students devote *four* hours each week to the course—*three* hours in class and *one* hour in conference with their composition teachers.

FIGURE 3.1

The Usual Correspondences Between Letter Grades, Number Grades, and GPA Values

Letter grades	**Meaning**	**Number grades**	**GPA values**	
			System 1	***System 2***
A	Excellent	96–100	4.00	4.00
A−		90–95	4.00	3.70
B+		87–89	3.00	3.30
B	Good	84–86	3.00	3.00
B−		80–83	3.00	2.70
C+		77–79	2.00	2.30
C	Satisfactory	74–76	2.00	2.00
C−		70–73	2.00	1.70
D+		67–69	1.00	1.30
D	Passing	64–66	1.00	1.00
D−		60–63	1.00	0.70
F	Failing	0–59	0.00	0.00

Letter and Number Grades

Instructors evaluate papers, tests, and other student work using letter or number grades. Figure 3.1 above shows the correspondences between letter grades and number grades used at most schools. Notice, for example, in Figure 3.1 that the **letter grade** of B+ corresponds to the **number grades** 87, 88, and 89. Study your catalog to learn the correspondences between letter grades and number grades that are used at your school. Sometimes there are important differences between colleges. For instance, some schools offer the letter grade of A+ and do not offer the grade of D−.

The Grade Point Average (GPA)

Most colleges compute students' average grades using the **grade point average** or **GPA,** which is a number that ranges from 0.00 to 4.00. Following final examinations, instructors submit letter grades to the registrar, who enters the grades on students' transcripts and assigns numerical values to them for the purpose of computing GPAs.

Figure 3.1 above shows two widely used methods for assigning **GPA values** to letter grades. Notice in Figure 3.1 that when system 1 is used, letter grades have the same value whether they are accompanied by a plus or a minus (for example, B+, B, and B− all have a value of 3.00). But when system 2 is used, letter grades have larger values when they are accompanied by a plus and smaller values when they are accompanied by a minus (for example, B has a value of 3.00, but B+ has a value of 3.30 and B− has a value of 2.70). "How to Compute the GPA" on page 27 explains methods you may use to compute your grade point average.

How to Compute the GPA

Letter grades	Credits		GPA values		Grade points
A	3	×	4.00	=	12.00
B −	6	×	2.70	=	16.20
C −	6	×	1.70	=	10.20
	15				38.40

$$\frac{38.40}{15} = 2.56 \text{ GPA}$$

The grade point average is computed using the following procedures.

- Assign GPA values to letter grades.
- Multiply GPA values by credits.
- Add credits and add grade points to find totals.
- Divide total grade points by total credits.

In the example above, the GPA of 2.56 was found by dividing total grade points (38.40) by total credits (15).

Final Course Grades

It may surprise you to learn that most instructors find grading to be their most painful responsibility. A few teachers avoid the discomfort of grading by giving all students high grades. But most accept the obligation to compare students and to award the highest grades to students who do the best work and the lowest grades to students who do the poorest work.

Instructors use a variety of methods for computing final grades; it is impossible to list them all. Following are descriptions of three commonly used methods:

1. *An instructor may determine final course grades by finding the averages for students' number grades.* For example, if a student has test grades of 77, 82, 86, and 75, an instructor will add the scores (320) and divide by the total number of scores (4) to find the average, which is 80. Figure 3.1 shows that a number grade of 80 is equivalent to a letter grade of B −; this is the final course grade the instructor will submit for the student.

2. *An instructor may determine final course grades by finding the average for letter grades students have received.* For example, if a student has the three letter grades of C +, B −, and B +, the instructor may convert these letter grades to the GPA values shown in Figure 3.1 (2.70, 3.00, and 3.30), add the values

(9.00) and divide by the total number of grades (3) to find the average, which is 3.00. Figure 3.1 shows that 3.00 is equivalent to a letter grade of B. The instructor will enter a final course grade of B.

3. *An instructor may give extra value to one score in a set of scores.* For example, one psychology professor computes final grades from scores on a term paper, a midterm examination, and a final examination, giving double value to the final examination score. Following is an example of how the teacher computed a student's final grade:

Term paper	B+	= 3.30 × 1	=	3.30
Midterm exam	B	= 3.00 × 1	=	3.00
Final exam	A	= 4.00 × 2	=	8.00
		4		14.30

The professor divided 14.30 by 4 to find the average, which is 3.575. Figure 3.1 shows that 3.575 is equivalent to B+ (3.70 is needed for an A−). The student's final course grade is B+.

These are only three examples of the many different methods instructors may use to determine final course grades. If an instructor does not tell you how he or she will determine your final grade, ask, so you will know what you must do to earn the grade you want for the course.

The Importance of Your GPA

In high school, students pass from one grade to the next if they pass all of their courses. However, college students can fail out of school even if they pass all of their courses, because most colleges require students to maintain a minimum GPA of 2.00. Students who have passing grades of D, D+, or C− often have GPAs lower than 2.00.

Strive to maintain a good grade point average. An unsatisfactory GPA will have a devastating effect on your college career, and it may cause you to have a poor opinion of yourself. You must have a satisfactory GPA

- to graduate.
- to avoid probation and dismissal.
- to transfer credits to another school.
- to participate in athletics.
- to join certain clubs.
- to be eligible for scholarships and grants.
- to run for class or student government offices.

When a student's GPA drops below 2.00, it is usually difficult or impossible to raise it to a satisfactory level. For example, students who complete fifteen credits in their first term with a GPA of 1.65 must have a GPA of at least 2.35 for fifteen credits in their second term to bring their GPA up to 2.00. Unfortunately, students who have a D+ average in their first term seldom have a C+ average in their second term. On the other hand, the GPA works to the advantage of students who earn good grades. If you have a GPA in the 2.50 to 3.50 range for many courses, you can receive a D, D+, or C− in one or two courses and still have a good average.

EXERCISE 3.1 Credits and Hours

The answers to questions 3, 4, and 5 are probably printed in your catalog.

1. For how many credits are you registered this term?________________
2. For how many hours are you registered this term?________________
3. How many credits are required in your curriculum?________________
4. What is the minimum number of credits for which you must register to be classified as a full-time student?

   ____

5. What is the maximum number of credits for which you can register without receiving special permission?

   ____

EXERCISE 3.2 Letter Grades and Number Grades

Study your catalog to learn the correspondences between letter grades and number grades at your school. Then write the letter grades that correspond to the following number grades.

1. 85 ______	7. 84 ______	13. 89 ______
2. 70 ______	8. 90 ______	14. 76 ______
3. 77 ______	9. 79 ______	15. 73 ______
4. 63 ______	10. 83 ______	16. 69 ______
5. 74 ______	11. 64 ______	17. 60 ______
6. 59 ______	12. 67 ______	18. 87 ______

EXERCISE 3.3 Letter Grades and GPA Values

Study your catalog to learn the correspondences between letter grades and GPA values at your school. Then write the GPA values that correspond to the following letter grades.

1. C ______	5. D ______	9. C− ______
2. B+ ______	6. B ______	10. F ______
3. A− ______	7. D+ ______	11. A ______
4. C+ ______	8. D− ______	12. B− ______

EXERCISE 3.4 Minimum Grade Requirements

1. What is the minimum GPA required for graduation?____________________

2. Most schools have lower minimum GPA requirements for the first term or two of study and higher requirements for subsequent terms. If your school has such a policy, describe it below.

____

____

3. A college may require students to have minimum grades in specified courses (such as grades of at least C for courses in major subjects). If your school has minimum grade requirements for specified courses, state them below.

____

____

4. List the grades that have a value of 0.00 for computing the Grade Point Average at your school.

____

5. When students are put on probation because of low grades, how much time are they given to raise their grades?

____

6. What action is taken against students who fail to raise their grades sufficiently during the time they are on probation?

____

EXERCISE 3.5 Your Teachers' Grading Practices

Find the answers to the following questions:

1. What grading policies do your teachers have for assignments that are turned in late?
2. What grading policies do your teachers have for students who are frequently late to class?
3. What arrangements do your teachers make for students who are absent on the days when tests are given?
4. How will your final grades be determined for the courses you are taking this term?

EXERCISE 3.6 Computation of the GPA

Compute GPAs for the following problems, using the method that is used at your school. If you own a calculator, use it to help you make the computations.

1.

Letter grades	Credits		GPA values		Grade points
A	12	×		=	
B	8	×		=	
C	15	×		=	______

GPA = ______

2.

Letter grades	Credits		GPA values		Grade points
B	10	×		=	
C	6	×		=	
D	2	×		=	______

GPA = ______

3.

Letter grades	Credits		GPA values		Grade points
B	6	×		=	
C	6	×		=	
D	6	×		=	
F	3	×		=	______

GPA = ______

4.

Letter grades	Credits		GPA values		Grade points
B	6	×		=	
C	7	×		=	
D	4	×		=	______

GPA = ______

5.

Letter grades	Credits		GPA values		Grade points
B+	5	×		=	
C	4	×		=	
C−	6	×		=	______

GPA = ______

4

Find Help if You Need It

Most students have difficulty with a course at some time during their college careers. Academic difficulty often begins when a student falls behind in doing assignments, misses a quiz or test, or is absent from classes.

The first step in solving a problem is to acknowledge that it exists. Don't make the mistake of thinking that the problem will go away—it probably won't. If you have trouble in a course during the third week of a term, you are likely to be in worse trouble later on. Therefore, begin immediately to explore possible solutions to your problem. Don't be hasty; take time to investigate all possible remedies to your situation and weigh the advantages and disadvantages of each alternative before you set a course of action. "Strategies for Solving Academic Problems" on page 34 summarizes what you can do if you have trouble with a course.

Use This and Other Books

Your first source of answers to study problems is books you may own, purchase, or borrow from a library.

College Study Skills provides help for taking class notes, studying for tests, answering test questions, and many other study problems. You may also own other books that contain answers to problems you encounter in college courses. For example, your English handbook should explain the format to use for a research paper you must write for a psychology course, and a math book you own may provide the review of mathematics you need for a chemistry course.

When you have extreme difficulty understanding the textbook for a course, visit the library and bookstore to locate an easier-to-understand book on the same subject. If you are unable to find an understandable book on the topic, use one of the other strategies explained in this chapter.

Strategies for Solving Academic Problems

There are six basic strategies you may use to help yourself resolve an academic problem:

- **Study a book.** Investigate whether the answer to the problem is printed in a book you own, borrow from a library, or purchase in a bookstore.
- **Talk with helpful people.** Confer with a teacher, counselor, adviser, experienced student, or other person who may suggest a solution to your problem.
- **Improve your learning skills.** If your learning skills are deficient, take advantage of instruction your school provides in writing, math, reading, or studying.
- **Balance your responsibilities.** If work, family, or some other activity or interest is interfering with your college studies, you may need to reduce the number of courses you take or spend less time with the conflicting activity.
- **Drop a course.** You may find it necessary to drop a course and take it again later; the withdrawal grade is provided for this purpose.
- **Request more time.** If you request, a teacher may give you additional time to complete a term project or to study for a final examination; special grades are provided for this purpose.

Talk with Helpful People

Advisers, counselors, teachers, and other students are sources of help when academic difficulties arise. **Advisers** are teachers who are assigned to help students select the college courses in which they register; the services counselors provide are explained on page 5.

Teachers can sometimes offers solutions that do not occur to students. A young man told his chemistry teacher that he was having trouble because his laboratory sessions were taught by an inexperienced laboratory assistant. His teacher arranged for him to sit in on laboratory sessions taught by another assistant. Instead of attending one laboratory each week, he attended two, but he did well in his chemistry course.

If you have established a good relationship with a teacher, you may be able to make a special arrangement with him or her. For instance, if you didn't do well on an important test, you might schedule a conference with your professor to explain why you didn't do your best and to ask whether there is anything you can do to offset the low test grade. Some teachers take an interest in students who show that they are concerned about doing good work.

Teachers, counselors, and advisers also usually know if there are study groups, laboratories, **tutors,** or other sources of help available. If they do not know, they may advise visiting the office of the department that offers the problem course. Or they may suggest visiting an office of academic skills, a learning center, a tutorial service, or some other department or service on your campus.

Also, students who have already taken a course that gives you trouble may sometimes be your best source of help—they have already solved problems you are having. Make friends with second-, third-, and fourth-year students who are enrolled in your curriculum and who will give you suggestions on how to study for courses they have already taken.

Improve Your Learning Skills

Colleges usually test students' reading, writing, and mathematics skills when they apply for admission. After testing, many students are required or advised to improve learning skills. Take full advantage of any learning skills instruction that you are offered. The faculty of your school believes that this instruction will help you do your best and earn a degree.

Some students who do poorly in college are the ones who do not take reading, writing, and mathematics instruction when they are supposed to because they aren't aware of how important these skills are to their success in college. Other students believe that their skills are better than they actually are. For instance, it is fairly common for students to complain about being required to take a special writing course even though they did well in high school English classes. The misunderstanding arises because sometimes high school and college teachers use different criteria for evaluating student writing. For instance, a high school teacher might read students' work looking especially for original thinking, whereas a college professor might give as much attention to whether written work is free of grammatical errors and misspellings as to the ideas presented in it.

When learning skills instruction is offered for no credit or for partial credit, students sometimes believe that they will learn nothing or that the courses are extremely easy. However, learning skills courses usually are not easy, because they require students to master skills that they did not master earlier in their schooling. You may need to work as hard in these courses as you do in courses that you take for full academic credit.

Balance Your Responsibilities

The simplest solution to an academic problem is to spend more time studying. Unfortunately, some students don't study enough because they devote much of their time to a job, family responsibilities, a sport or hobby, or some other activity. If you are so busy with another activity that it interferes with your ability to do well in college, you may need to reduce the number of courses you take or you may need to spend less time engaging in the conflicting activity.

Place checks in the boxes in front of any of the statements in the following multiple-choice questions that describe you:

1. I have been absent from classes because of
   - ☐ a. my job.
   - ☐ b. family responsibilities or friends.
   - ☐ c. a sport or hobby.
   - ☐ d. something else I do.

2. I have been late to classes because of
   - ☐ a. my job.
   - ☐ b. family responsibilities or friends.
   - ☐ c. a sport or hobby.
   - ☐ d. something else I do.

3. I am sometimes tired in classes because of
   - ☐ a. my job.
   - ☐ b. family responsibilities or friends.
   - ☐ c. a sport or hobby.
   - ☐ d. something else I do.

4. I have done poor work on assignments because of
   - ☐ a. my job.
   - ☐ b. family responsibilities or friends.
   - ☐ c. a sport or hobby.
   - ☐ d. something else I do.

5. I have failed to turn in assignments because of
   - ☐ a. my job.
   - ☐ b. family responsibilities or friends.
   - ☐ c. a sport or hobby.
   - ☐ d. something else I do.

6. I have been poorly prepared for a test or quiz because of
   - ☐ a. my job.
   - ☐ b. family responsibilities or friends.
   - ☐ c. a sport or hobby.
   - ☐ d. something else I do.

7. I have been absent from a test or quiz because of
   - ☐ a. my job.
   - ☐ b. family responsibilities or friends.
   - ☐ c. a sport or hobby.
   - ☐ d. something else I do.

If you checked any box, your job or some other responsibility or interest is interfering with your ability to do your best in college. You need to figure out how you can balance your desire to do well in college with your other responsibilities or interests. For instance, if you are a full-time student having academic difficulty because of your job, following are some alternatives you might consider:

How to Balance Work and School

- Work a great deal during the summer and very little, or not at all, during the school year.
- If you spend much time traveling to and from work, find a job on campus, near campus, or near where you live (even if it pays less money).
- If the hours that you must work are the problem, find a job with more suitable hours (even if it pays less money).
- If you are working only because you want to enjoy a luxury, such as an expensive automobile, consider doing without the luxury.
- If you are working mainly because you receive more approval from your parents for working than you do for being a student, consider explaining the demands of college study to your parents.

If none of these alternatives are solutions for you, or if you are a part-time student working full-time to support yourself or your family, you may need to enroll in fewer courses next term or to use one of the other suggestions in this chapter.

Drop a Course

When an academic problem cannot be solved in any other way, you may find that it is necessary to drop a course and take it again later. It is always advisable to drop a course when a final course grade is likely to be an F, and it is usually better to drop a course than to end up with a low grade, such as a D. The grade of D is acceptable only for an extremely difficult course that is not in your area of specialization. For example, students who specialize in computer technology may be satisfied with a grade of D in a very difficult history course, but not in a computer course.

It is essential to drop courses officially, by making the proper arrangements with the admissions office or the registrar's office. If you just stop going to a class without officially dropping it, you will receive a grade of F or some other grade that has the same value as F in computing your grade point average.

For the first few days of a term, dropped courses are usually not recorded on students' transcripts. After this period, it is necessary to request a **withdrawal grade,** or **W.** The W grade is not usually used to compute grade point averages; thus, it usually does not lower (or raise) GPAs. However, there are strict limitations on the time period during which this grade may be requested.

Before you request a W grade, keep in mind that when you drop a course, the total number of credits in your program may be reduced to fewer than you need for full-time student status. If you lose full-time status, you may lose important benefits, such as financial aid or the privilege of playing varsity athletics. Therefore, before you withdraw from a course, you may want to discuss your intentions with a financial aid counselor or other adviser.

Also, it is not a good idea to develop the habit of withdrawing from courses frequently. A transcript with several W grades creates the impression that it belongs to a person who had difficulty following through on commitments—an impression you do not want to convey to prospective schools or employers who examine your transcript.

Request More Time

If your problem in a course is that you need more time to finish a term paper or other project or to study for a final examination, your professor may give you additional time if you request it.

The **incomplete grade,** or **INC,** is provided for students who did satisfactory work in a course but who did not complete a term paper or other important project. For instance, when students do satisfactorily on all tests for a course but do not submit a required written report, a teacher may give them INC grades rather than grades such as B or C. When the report is completed, the INC grade is changed to A, B, C, or some other letter grade.

However, there are deadlines after which past-due work is not accepted. At most schools, INC grades are automatically changed to Fs when work is not turned in by deadlines. It is much better to keep up-to-date with course work than to request an INC grade and to run the risk of having it changed to an F.

Some schools also give students a chance to take make-up final examinations if they are absent from the final for a course in which all of their other work is satisfactory. They are given a course grade that is similar to the INC grade; when a make-up test is not taken by a specified deadline, the grade is automatically changed to an F. Investigate whether your school makes provisions for students who are absent from final exams.

EXERCISE 4.1 Using This Book

Consult the table of contents of this book to answer the following questions.

1. What chapter of this book can you read to learn how to take good lecture notes?

   ____

2. What chapter of this book can you read to learn how to remember and recall information?

   ____

3. What chapter of this book can you read to learn methods for selecting correct answers to multiple-choice questions?

   ____

4. What chapter of this book can you read to learn how to write good answers to essay questions?

   ____

EXERCISE 4.2 Finding Helpful People

Seek the help of others if you have academic problems.

1. List the names of all your current teachers with whom you would feel comfortable in discussing any difficulty you might have in fulfilling the requirements for their courses.

____

____

____

____

2. List the names of two counselors or advisers with whom you would talk if you were having difficulty with a course.

____

____

3. List the names of at least three second-, third-, or fourth-year students enrolled in your curriculum from whom you would seek help if you were having difficulty with a course.

____

____

____

EXERCISE 4.3 Learning Skills

If you have taken a writing, math, reading, or study skills course in college, write an explanation of whether you believe the course helped you improve learning skills.

EXERCISE 4.4 Balancing Responsibilities

If a job, family responsibilities, a sport or hobby, or some other activity or interest is preventing you from doing your best work in college, write an explanation of what adjustments you will make to accommodate the conflict.

EXERCISE 4.5 Dropping a Course

The answers to the following questions are probably printed in your catalog.

1. What is the last day this term you can drop a course and not have the course recorded on your transcript?

____

2. What is the last day this term to request a W grade (or drop a course without academic penalty)?

____

EXERCISE 4.6 Requesting More Time

The answers to the following questions are probably printed in your catalog.

1. What is the deadline for completing past-due work for INC grades students receive at the end of this term?

____

2. What happens to INC grades when past-due work is not completed by the deadline?

____

____

3. If your school has a grade for students doing satisfactory work who are absent from the final exam, write the grade on the line.

____

What happens to this grade when a final exam is not made up by the deadline?

____

____

5

Improve Your Memory

Have you ever wondered why you sometimes forget people's names a few seconds after you are introduced to them or why you are unable to recall the answers to test questions that you have studied thoroughly? This chapter gives the answers to questions such as these, and it also provides general background for your study of Chapters 12–20 of *College Study Skills,* which are devoted to helping you improve your ability to analyze, organize, remember, and recall information. Chapter 20, "Remember and Recall Information," provides practical suggestions for applying the information you will read about memory in this chapter.

The Three Stages of Memory

The most generally accepted theory about human memory is that it consists of three stages: sensory memory, short-term memory, and long-term memory. The characteristics of these three stages are summarized in Figure 5.1 on page 42.

Sensory memory registers all information that enters through the five senses—sight, hearing, taste, touch, and smell. Each bit of incoming information stays in sensory memory for a fraction of a second so that we experience consecutive bits of information in a smooth, uninterrupted flow. For example, when you listen to a speaker, your sensory memory holds each speech sound for a fraction of a second so that you experience a smooth flow of words and sentences rather than a series of unconnected sounds. Sensory memory is essential for interpreting experiences, but it is not useful for remembering information or events. For something to be remembered, it must first be transferred from sensory memory to short-term memory.

Short-term memory holds between five and nine pieces of information for about twenty seconds. The information stored in short-term memory is usually meaningful groupings of letters or numbers, such as "The Boer War was fought 1899–1902." After information has been in your short-term memory about twenty seconds, you will forget it unless it is transferred to long-term memory.

FIGURE 5.1

The Three Stages of Memory

Sensory Memory		Short-Term Memory		Long-Term Memory
Registers incoming information for a fraction of a second.	→	Holds up to nine pieces of information for about twenty seconds.	→	Stores a vast amount of information for as long as a lifetime.

When people use the word *memory,* they usually mean **long-term memory,** which is the stage of memory that holds an enormous amount of information for long periods, even a lifetime. The following discussions in this chapter are about long-term memory, because it is in long-term memory that you keep information to recall for answering test questions. *In the following discussions, the word* memory *refers to long-term memory.*

The Information-processing Model

The **information-processing model** applies to human memory the processes that pertain to computer memory: encoding, storage, and retrieval. The characteristics of these basic memory processes are summarized in Figure 5.2 on page 43.

MOTIVATION FOR REMEMBERING

MAKING INFO. MEANINGFUL

OVERHEAD

Encoding

Encoding is the process by which information enters memory. Many kinds of information are encoded, including memories about how to ride a bicycle and memories of events that took place on birthdays and vacations. However, the focus of this discussion is on college subject matter, which is usually encoded into memory through the use of semantic codes or visual codes.

Semantic Codes

The word *semantic* means "pertaining to meaning in language," and a **semantic code** is a representation of information by its general meaning. For instance, a student wanted to learn the following definition for a business course:

A Definition

Selective advertising promotes the sale of brand name products, such as Bayer aspirin.

She encoded this definition in the following way, using the general meaning of the statement rather than the exact words:

Semantic Coding of a Definition

Selective advertising is used to sell specific brand name products, such as Cannon towels and Skippy peanut butter.

FIGURE 5.2
The Three Basic Memory Processes

Encoding		**Storage**		**Retrieval**
Information is put into memory.	→	Information is held in memory over time.	→	Information is recalled from memory.

Compare the definition of *selective advertising* and the semantic coding of the term to notice that they are identical in meaning though they are worded differently. The comparison illustrates the basic characteristic of a semantic code—it is a general representation of a meaning rather than a rote, word-for-word memorization of it.

Visual Codes

FORMER STUDENT VISUAL-SPATIAL PH. #

A **visual code** is a mental image of information or an event. My memory of meeting my newborn sister was encoded as an image. When I want, I can visualize the moment I first met my sister many years ago. Visual coding can be used to remember many kinds of information. For example, an effective way to learn the locations of the countries of South America is to visualize a map of the continent with the names and boundaries of countries clearly marked on it. Or, the function of *selective advertising* could be remembered by visualizing the images of brand name products, such as Bayer aspirin, Cannon towels, Skippy peanut butter, and Reebok shoes.

Storage

In the information-processing model, the act of holding information in memory over time is called **storage.** Any facts you can recall, any events of the past that you can recollect, and any information you can use to answer test questions is stored in your memory.

Automatic Processing

Information is stored in memory in a variety of ways. Some is stored by **automatic processing,** which is an effortless transfer of information. My memory of my baby sister was no doubt stored in my memory through automatic processing. Your recollection of the places you were yesterday were also stored in your memory by this means unless you made a conscious effort to remember those places.

Recitation

— REPEATING INFO.

Most information is stored in memory through recitation and rehearsal. **Recitation** is the act of repeating information over and over. For instance, when you are introduced to somebody and repeat his name several times to remember it, you use recitation.

Rehearsal

Recitation is most effective when it is used together with **elaborative rehearsal,** or **rehearsal,** which is the act of analyzing information and relating it to information that is already stored in memory.

To **analyze** is to separate something into its parts for the purpose of studying the parts or understanding how they are related. A great deal of the instruction in *College Study Skills* is designed to help you improve your analytical skills. For example, you analyze information when you make outlines of written material and when you make notes for class lectures or textbooks. Rehearsal also includes relating new information to information stored in memory as, for instance, in rehearsing the following definition:

> *Morphemes* are the smallest meaningful units of language, such as *un-*, *truth,* and *-ful* in *untruthful.*

In rehearsing this statement, you might observe that *un-* is a prefix, *truth* is a word, and *-ful* is a suffix. Then, you might recall other words that consist of these three kinds of morphemes, such as *indirectness* and *retelling,* which contain the prefixes *in-* and *re-,* the words *direct* and *tell,* and the suffixes *-ness* and *-ing.* An analysis such as this used together with recitation is very effective for storing information in memory.

One barrier in using rehearsal is that you may sometimes not have in your memory information to which you can productively relate new information. For instance, you can rehearse the dates of the Boer War (1899–1902) by relating them to the dates of the Spanish American War (1898) and World War I (1914–1918) *only if* the dates of these other wars are in your memory. When college courses are difficult for you, it may be partly because you have insufficient information in your memory to which you can relate the new information you must learn.

Retrieval

In the information-processing model, **retrieval** is the act of recalling or recollecting information stored in memory. You retrieve information when you search your memory for it and recall it. Retrieval is aided by good organization and retrieval cues. Look at the following list of sixteen words:

An Unorganized List of Words

> long, wine, chemistry, pear, algebra, narrow, grape, beer, milk, orange, wide, history, apple, psychology, soda, short

Compare this unorganized list with the following logically organized lists of the same words:

Organized Lists of Words

psychology	orange	wine	long
algebra	apple	milk	short
history	grape	soda	wide
chemistry	pear	beer	narrow

The words in these well-organized lists are the same as the words in the unorganized list, but since they are organized, they are easier to store in memory and they are easier to retrieve.

Retrieval is further facilitated by using **retrieval cues,** which are words or images that help in recalling information. Each of the following lists of words is headed with a retrieval cue:

Subjects	Fruits	Beverages	Dimensions
psychology	orange	wine	long
algebra	apple	milk	short
history	grape	soda	wide
chemistry	pear	beer	narrow

When all these words are stored in memory, each retrieval cue can be used to recall four words. For instance, *fruits* can be used as a cue to retrieve *orange, apple, grape,* and *pear.*

Forgetting

Forgetting occurs very rapidly. Psychologists have documented that we forget about 70 percent of what we learn within two days of learning it! Three main theories have been offered to explain why we forget: decay, interference, and retrieval failure.

Decay theory proposes that if we don't use information stored in memory, we will not be able to retrieve it because it fades away from disuse. It's as though old memories crumble and disappear to make way for new ones. On the surface, this explanation seems reasonable. For instance, I was good at solving algebra problems when I was in high school, but it seems reasonable to me that I've forgotten virtually everything I knew about algebra because I haven't used it since I was a teenager. However, the other two theories about forgetting propose that once information is stored in memory, it remains there even though we may not be able to recall it.

Interference theory advances the idea that information stored in memory sometimes cannot be retrieved because other memories stored there interfere with retrieval. If you imagine your memory as books on a shelf, interference theory suggests that when new books are added, old books fall off the shelf into a place where they cannot be located. This theory is now more highly regarded than decay theory; psychological research seems to support the conclusion that we forget, not so much because memories decay, but because new memories interfere with recalling old memories (and old memories interfere with recalling new ones). According to interference theory, I still remember what I knew about algebra, but other memories interfere with my ability to find my memories about the subject.

Retrieval failure theory holds that when stored memories cannot be recalled, it is because proper retrieval cues are not available. This is a hopeful theory because it suggests what you can do to remember more and forget less. When you store information,

- organize it in a logical manner.
- include an effective retrieval cue.
- use elaborative rehearsal—analyze the information and relate it to other information that is already in your memory.

These are all skills you will improve when you study Chapters 12–20.

ASSIGN

EXERCISE 5.1 Long-Term Memory

According to information-processing theory, the information in this chapter is not stored in your long-term memory unless you expended some effort to store it there. Test this theory by attempting to write the answers to the following questions without referring to the chapter for the answers. After you have attempted this exercise, do Exercise 5.2 before you study the chapter for correct answers.

1. How much information can be stored in (a) sensory memory, (b) short-term memory, and (c) long-term memory?

   a. ______________________________

   b. ______________________________

   c. ______________________________

2. How long is information stored in (a) sensory memory, (b) short-term memory, and (c) long-term memory?

   a. ______________________________

   b. ______________________________

   c. ______________________________

3. What is the main function of sensory memory?

   ____

   ____

   ____

4. What is *encoding*?

   ____

   ____

5. What is a *visual code*?

   ____

   ____

6. What is *automatic processing*?

   ____

   ____

7. What is *elaborative rehearsal*?

____

____

____

8. What are the two aids to *retrieval*?

   a. ____________________________________

   b. ____________________________________

9. What percentage of the information we learn do we forget within two days after we learn it?

____

10. What are the names of the two theories of forgetting that propose that once information is stored in long-term memory, it remains there even though we may not be able to recall it?

   a. ____________________________________

   b. ____________________________________

EXERCISE 5.2 Retrieval Cues

According to information-processing theory, retrieval cues help in retrieving information that is stored in memory. The questions in Exercise 5.1 were written to include no retrieval cues. In contrast, all the following questions contain retrieval cues that may help you retrieve information you remember as a result of reading this chapter. Check the boxes in front of correct answers.

1. How many pieces of information can be stored in short-term memory?
   - ☐ a. one to five
   - ☐ b. three to six
   - ☒ c. five to nine
   - ☐ d. eight to twelve

2. Information is stored in sensory memory for
   - ☒ a. a fraction of a second.
   - ☐ b. one second.
   - ☐ c. twenty seconds.
   - ☐ d. up to a lifetime.

3. Which stage of memory provides a means for connecting bits of incoming information so that we experience them in a smooth, uninterrupted flow?
   - [x] a. sensory memory
   - [ ] b. short-term memory
   - [ ] c. long-term memory
   - [ ] d. both *a* and *b*

4. The process by which information enters memory is called
   - [ ] a. storage.
   - [x] b. encoding.
   - [ ] c. retrieval.
   - [ ] d. automatic processing.

5. A mental image of information or an event is called
   - [ ] a. a daydream.
   - [ ] b. an elaboration.
   - [ ] c. a hallucination.
   - [x] d. a visual code.

6. The effortless transfer of information into memory is called
   - [ ] a. semantic coding.
   - [ ] b. visual coding.
   - [x] c. automatic processing.
   - [ ] d. simplified processing.

7. The storing of information in memory by analyzing it and relating it to information already stored there is called
   - [ ] a. semantic coding
   - [ ] b. visual coding.
   - [ ] c. maintenance rehearsal.
   - [x] d. elaborative rehearsal.

8. The retrieval of information in memory is aided by
   - [ ] a. good organization.
   - [ ] b. retrieval cues.
   - [ ] c. semiautomatic processing.
   - [x] d. both *a* and *b*

9. What percentage of information do we forget within two days after learning it?
   - [ ] a. 80 percent
   - [x] b. 70 percent
   - [ ] c. 30 percent
   - [ ] d. 20 percent

10. Which theory of forgetting proposes that once information is stored in memory it remains there even though we may not be able to recall it?
    - [ ] a. decay theory
    - [ ] b. interference theory
    - [ ] c. retrieval failure theory
    - [x] d. both *b* and *c*

EXERCISE 5.3 Rehearsal

Rehearsal, or elaborative rehearsal, involves analyzing information and relating it to information that is already stored in memory. When you answer the following questions using the information in this chapter, you will engage in rehearsal of that information.

1. What information is registering in your sensory memory at this moment?

____

____

2. You promised a friend that you would meet her in the cafeteria at noon, but you completely forgot that you had made this promise. Why did you forget?

____

____

3. What is your earliest memory from childhood?

____

____

____

4. Name three fairly complicated procedures, such as the ability to ride a bicycle, that are stored in your memory.

   a. ______________________________

   b. ______________________________

   c. ______________________________

5. Describe the room in which you sleep. As you do so, notice whether your memory is mostly in visual images or in some other form.

____

____

____

6. Recollect some of the places you were yesterday. Were those places stored in your memory using automatic processing, recitation, or rehearsal?

____

7. How would recitation help you avoid the embarrassment of forgetting people's names when you are introduced to them?

8. Is there any course you will be required to take that will be difficult because you have little information stored in your memory to which you can relate the new information you must learn? If so, what is the course?

9. If you forgot to take your shopping list with you to the grocery store, what are some retrieval cues you would use to remember the things that were written on your list?

10. Think of a telephone number that you once knew and called often but that you can no longer recall. Why do you believe you are unable to recollect the number now?

6

Understand Your Learning Style

A student came to me one day upset because she had not done well on a test in her psychology course. I was surprised. She was an outstanding study skills student; she knew how to make notes and how to mark her textbooks and had learned all the other study procedures she needed for doing well in her psychology course. I set up an appointment for her to come to my office so we might find the source of her problem.

It was not long into our conference that the reason for her difficulty became obvious. When I opened her psychology textbook, I found no highlighting, underlining, or other marks in it. And, when I asked to see the notes she had made to learn the information in the book, she told me that she hadn't made any notes. Rather, she had tried to learn the information in the book by reading and rereading it, as she had done in high school. Her problem was that her learning style did not include using all the learning strategies she knew!

In case you have never thought about your learning style, this chapter is designed to give you insight into three aspects of it. You will find out about

- the learning strategies you prefer to use.
- your preferences for learning by visual, auditory, or kinesthetic means.
- the environmental conditions under which you prefer to study.

The following discussions and exercises will help you understand your learning style and give you an opportunity to think about whether you want to make any changes in it.

Learning Strategies and Styles

A **learning strategy** is a set of procedures for accomplishing a learning task, such as the procedures that are used to learn information for tests. A **learning style,** on the other hand, is the set of procedures that a particular person *actually uses* to accomplish a learning task.

Students cannot use study strategies that they do not know, but, like my student who failed a psychology test, they sometimes do not use study strategies that they do know. Use Exercises 6.1 and 6.2 to think about and analyze the learning strategies you use.

Three Kinds of Learning

Most of what we learn, we learn through reading, watching, hearing, touching, or moving. When you read or watch, you use your sense of seeing; when you hear, you use your sense of hearing; and when you touch and move, you use your senses of touch and kinesthesia. **Kinesthesia** is the sensory experience that comes from moving muscles, tendons, and joints.

Some teachers provide students with visual, auditory, and kinesthetic learning experiences. For instance, a swimming instructor would probably teach you a new stroke by demonstrating it, explaining it, and having you practice it. You would receive the instruction *visually* by watching the demonstration, *auditorily* by hearing the explanation, and *kinesthetically* by making the movements of the swim stroke.

Though we all learn by these three means, some students have a definite preference for one of them:

- **Visual learners** prefer to learn by reading and watching demonstrations. Since they would rather read a textbook than listen to a lecture, they enjoy lecture courses more when they take many notes to study after class.
- **Auditory learners** prefer to learn by listening and discussing. Since they would rather listen to a lecture than read a textbook, they enjoy reading more *after* they listen to a background lecture on the subject matter.
- **Kinesthetic learners** prefer to learn by being physically involved, such as by doing something or by handling and manipulating things. Since they prefer to learn by experimenting on their own, they benefit most from listening to lectures and reading textbooks when they understand how these activities benefit them in their experimentation.

The primary advantage of knowing your instructional preference is that it will help you in adjusting to the demands of college study. For instance, in a discussion with a student I uncovered that his dissatisfaction with his history professor's lectures was not due to any fault in the lectures, but to the student's preference to learn by reading rather than by listening. He adjusted to the history course by taking more notes and comparing what his teacher said to what was written in course reading material.

Use Exercises 6.3 and 6.4 to analyze whether you prefer to learn visually, auditorily, kinesthetically, or by using a combination of these means.

Environmental Conditions

Over the past twenty-five years, educational psychologists have studied learning style in a variety of ways. For instance, one area of research investigates how students' performance is affected by studying at times they prefer rather than at other times. This branch of research, called chronobiology, has produced clear evidence that students perform much better when they study or take courses at the times of day when they are most alert than when they study at other times.

It used to be commonly believed that everybody learns best when they study in a quiet place, seated at a desk. Today, these assumptions are questioned. Researchers have found that some students study better with the distraction of background music and that others learn just as well when they study sitting in an easy chair as they do when they study sitting at a desk.

Some of the other environmental conditions that affect studying include room temperature and the presence or absence of noise, food, or other people. Exercise 6.5 provides an opportunity for you to think about the environmental conditions under which you prefer to study.

EXERCISE 6.1 Learning Strategy Checklist

Following is a list of fifty-four of the learning strategies that are explained in *College Study Skills.* They are organized into the topics taught in nine chapters of this book. Check the boxes following strategies that *you actually use* and total the boxes you check in each category. You will use the totals when you do Exercise 6.2.

	I use this strategy
A. Basic Strategies (Chapter 2)	
1. At the beginning of each term, I find out exactly what teachers require.	☐
2. I attend all classes unless I'm sick.	☐
3. I purchase all required books and other materials at the beginning of the term.	☐
4. I keep up-to-date with course work.	☐
5. I have all assignments ready on time.	☐
6. I am always prepared for tests.	☐
Total checks	______
B. Time Management (Chapter 10)	
7. I schedule time for doing assignments and preparing for examinations.	☐
8. I keep a daily list of things that I need to do.	☐
9. I keep a record of the assignments for *all* of my courses in *one* convenient place.	☐
10. I set priorities for the order in which I do assignments.	☐
11. I schedule the study of difficult subjects at the time of day when I am most alert.	☐
12. I schedule major projects to complete them a step at a time over as long a period as possible.	☐
Total checks	______

C. Surveying Textbooks (Chapter 15)

13. I know how to determine if a book is sufficiently up-to-date for a specific purpose. ☐
14. I read the table of contents in books to get an overview of the topics in them. ☐
15. I read prefaces and introductions in preparation for studying books. ☐
16. I locate and use appendixes. ☐
17. I locate and use glossaries. ☐
18. I locate and use subject indexes *and* name indexes. ☐

Total checks ______

D. Surveying Chapters (Chapter 16)

19. I use the title, introduction, and headings in a chapter to learn the topics in it. ☐
20. I use learning goals or chapter previews as guides for studying chapters. ☐
21. I study tables, graphs, diagrams, and other visual materials in a chapter *before* reading it. ☐
22. I read a chapter summary *before* reading the chapter. ☐
23. I identify the important terminology introduced in a chapter. ☐
24. I use review questions, exercises, and problems to check my learning. ☐

Total checks ______

E. Class Notes (Chapter 17)

25. I read about topics in textbooks before class lectures on them. ☐
26. I begin each day's notes with a heading that includes the date and lecture topic. ☐
27. I make major thoughts stand out clearly in my notes. ☐
28. I use simplified handwriting and abbreviations to write notes quickly. ☐
29. I review class notes immediately after class. ☐
30. I study class notes thoroughly before tests. ☐

Total checks ______

F. Marking Textbooks (Chapter 18)

31. I underline, highlight, or otherwise mark information I want to learn in a book. ☐
32. I read a section of a book *before* I mark it. ☐
33. I use a variety of techniques to avoid underlining or highlighting too much. ☐
34. I try to mark information in a book that will help me make good notes later. ☐
35. I mark definitions of terminology in books. ☐
36. I mark examples in books. ☐

Total checks ______

G. Making Notes for Books (Chapter 19)

37. I make notes for information I want to learn in my textbooks. ☐
38. I use a variety of formats for notes. ☐
39. I begin notes with a title that accurately describes the information in them. ☐
40. I make major thoughts stand out in notes. ☐
41. I include examples in notes. ☐
42. I make notes in the classification chart or time-line format when appropriate. ☐

Total checks ______

H. Preparing for Tests (Chapter 14)

43. I use class notes as a guide about what to study for tests. ☐
44. When studying for tests, I emphasize information teachers said was important or difficult to learn. ☐
45. I use learning goals and review questions in textbook chapters as a guide in deciding what to learn in them. ☐
46. I always learn the meanings of important terminology in textbooks. ☐
47. I master skills by doing exercises and problems in textbooks. ☐
48. I always attend test reviews when they are offered. ☐

Total checks ______

I. Remembering and Recalling (Chapter 20)

49. I learn information by reciting it over and over. ☐
50. I learn information by analyzing it into its parts to study the parts and understand how they are related. ☐
51. I learn information by relating it to information I already know. ☐
52. I review information to guard against forgetting it. ☐
53. I use effective methods to learn virtually all kinds of information. ☐
54. I use a variety of effective techniques to recall information when I take tests. ☐

Total checks ______

EXERCISE 6.2 Analyzing Your Learning Strategies

Put an X on each line under the number of items you checked in each category in Exercise 6.1. For example, if you checked four of the basic strategies in Exercise 6.1, put an X under "4" for "A. Basic Strategies."

	Number of Checks in Exercise 6.1						
	0	**1**	**2**	**3**	**4**	**5**	**6**
A. Basic Strategies	___	___	___	___	___	___	___
B. Time Management	___	___	___	___	___	___	___
C. Surveying Textbooks	___	___	___	___	___	___	___
D. Surveying Chapters	___	___	___	___	___	___	___
E. Class Notes	___	___	___	___	___	___	___
F. Marking Textbooks	___	___	___	___	___	___	___
G. Making Notes for Books	___	___	___	___	___	___	___
H. Preparing for Tests	___	___	___	___	___	___	___
I. Remembering and Recalling	___	___	___	___	___	___	___

The Xs you placed on the lines create a profile of the strategies you use for studying. The Xs farthest to the right indicate areas of relative strength, and the Xs farthest to the left signify areas of relative weakness. There is room for improvement in any category for which you checked fewer than six items.

EXERCISE 6.3 Auditory and Visual Learning

Check one answer for each question.

1. I prefer to learn by
   - ☐ a. reading a textbook.
   - ☐ b. listening to a lecture.
2. I prefer to learn by
   - ☐ a. watching a demonstration.
   - ☐ b. listening to an explanation.
3. I like to read maps.
   - ☐ a. true
   - ☐ b. false
4. When listening to a lecture
   - ☐ a. I take many notes.
   - ☐ b. I take few notes.
5. I tend to remember people's
   - ☐ a. faces but forget their names.
   - ☐ b. names but forget their faces.

6. I don't mind studying with noise in the background.
   - ☐ a. false
   - ☐ b. true
7. I like a classroom seat from which I can
   - ☐ a. see what's going on.
   - ☐ b. hear what is said.
8. Graphs, charts, and diagrams
   - ☐ a. are interesting to me.
   - ☐ b. confuse me.

The *a* responses are usually checked by visual learners, and the *b* responses are usually checked by auditory learners. If you checked about the same number of visual and auditory responses, you are probably one of the majority who prefer visual and auditory methods of learning about equally.

EXERCISE 6.4 Kinesthetic Learning

Check the boxes in front of statements that describe you or that you believe are true.

- ☐ If I bought a new VCR, I would probably try to figure out how it works by playing with it rather than by reading the owner's manual.
- ☐ I prefer a job that keeps me on my feet, moving from place to place, rather than one that gives me a chance to sit most of the time.
- ☐ The best part of studying sciences is doing experiments in a lab.
- ☐ Engineering and construction work interest me.
- ☐ I usually don't enjoy sitting in a classroom listening to a lecture.
- ☐ I like to cook meals.
- ☐ I get great enjoyment from typing or using a computer.
- ☐ When I was in grade school, I could usually find an excuse to get up and move around the room.
- ☐ When I'm in an airplane, I prefer to sit on the aisle so I can get up when I want rather than to sit by a window so I can see out.
- ☐ When I study, I need to take frequent breaks.

Most students check four or five of these statements; if you checked seven or more of them, you are strongly oriented toward learning kinesthetically.

EXERCISE 6.5 Your Environmental Preferences

Check the answers to the following questions that best describe you. If no answer to a question describes you, write an answer that does describe you.

1. I am most alert for learning difficult subjects
   - ☐ in the morning.
   - ☐ in the afternoon.
   - ☐ in the evening.
2. I study best in a
   - ☐ dormitory room.
   - ☐ bedroom.
   - ☐ living room.
   - ☐ library.
   - ☐ kitchen.
   - ☐ lounge or cafeteria.
3. I prefer to study
   - ☐ at a desk, sitting in a chair.
   - ☐ in an armchair or on a sofa.
4. I like to study in a place with
   - ☐ bright overhead light.
   - ☐ medium light.
   - ☐ dim light.
5. I prefer to study in a room that is
   - ☐ hot.
   - ☐ warm.
   - ☐ cool.
   - ☐ cold.
6. I learn best when I study with
   - ☐ loud background music playing.
   - ☐ soft background music playing.
   - ☐ no background music playing.
7. When I study, the sound of voices or noise
   - ☐ doesn't bother me.
   - ☐ bothers me a little.
   - ☐ makes it impossible for me to study.
8. When studying, I like to
   - ☐ drink a beverage.
   - ☐ smoke.
   - ☐ chew gum.
   - ☐ eat candy.
   - ☐ eat snack food.
   - ☐ eat a meal.
   - ☐ avoid eating or drinking.
9. I prefer to study
   - ☐ by myself.
   - ☐ with one other person.
   - ☐ with a group of people.
10. I study most efficiently when
    - ☐ I am under the pressure of a deadline.
    - ☐ there is no rush to meet a deadline.

Reevaluate the conditions under which you study best from time to time. Some students believe they study best late at night in a hot room under a dim light, only to later find that, in fact, they study more efficiently early in the day in a moderately cool room with bright sunlight flooding through a window. Experiment with a variety of environmental conditions to find the optimum study conditions for yourself.

EXERCISE 6.6 Your Learning Style

See Page 56

Write a description of the procedures that you prefer to use when you study. Include the following:

- A summary of the learning strategies you prefer to use when you study
- An explanation of your preference for visual, auditory, or kinesthetic learning
- A description of your environmental preferences when you study

Use your answers to Exercises 6.1 through 6.5 as the primary source of information in writing your description. Include a discussion of ways you might improve your learning style.

7

Deal with Stress

Stress is the mental or physical strain you experience in response to events that make psychological or physical demands on you. The events or situations that induce stress are called **stressors;** they range from major life changes, such as entering college, to everyday hassles, such as having to deal with an annoying neighbor.

We usually think of stress as being undesirable, but that is not necessarily so. The stress of being in armed combat may be harmful to all who experience it. However, some stress is beneficial for people who adapt to it. For example, in adapting to the stress of entering college, some students are challenged to do better in school than they ever thought they could. On the other hand, those who cannot adapt to the stress created by entering college may be overwhelmed and defeated by it.

As a college student, you will have many opportunities to experience stress. This chapter explains events that may be sources of stress for you, ways you may react to stress, and methods for adapting to and coping with stress. See "Understanding Stress" on page 60.

Sources of Stress

Stress can come from problems at school, at home, at work, or in any other aspect of life. When you experience stress, it will usually arise from one of the following situations:

- You are going through a major change in your life, such as entering college, losing a job, or moving from one place to another.
- You are required to do too much in too little time, such as having only one day to study for a test that requires three days of studying.
- You are involved in a conflict, such as a serious disagreement with a friend, relative, teacher, employer, or coworker.
- You are prevented from getting something you want, such as you are unable to attend college because you don't have enough money for tuition.

OVERHEAD

Understanding Stress

- Stress is mental or physical strain that is experienced in response to psychologically or physically demanding events.
- Stress can arise from things that happen at school, at home, at work, or in any other area of life. For example, having a serious argument can be stressful whether it is with a teacher at school, a relative at home, or an employer at work.
- Reactions to stress can be emotional, behavioral, or physical. Emotional reactions include depression and anxiety; behavioral reactions include eating, drinking, or sleeping too much; physical reactions include headaches, indigestion, and skin problems.
- Some ways of coping with and adapting to stress are to eliminate stressors, to manage time efficiently, to exercise, to eat a nutritious diet, to value one's ability, to not insist on perfection, to turn threats into challenges, to change goals, and to use relaxation techniques.

The "Sources of Stress Checklist" on page 61 lists common experiences students have that cause them stress. Read the stressors on the list and check the ones you are experiencing or have experienced in the past twelve months.

People often react very differently to the same situation; an event that is a stressor for one person may not be a stressor for somebody else. For instance, your roommate may study best under the pressure of having to learn a great deal in a short time, whereas you may "freeze up" and be incapable of learning anything when you are rushed. You may enjoy bungee jumping but become nervous on the dance floor, whereas your best friend loves to go dancing but gets sick to her stomach at the thought of making a bungee jump.

- LOSS OF CONCENTRATION
- APPETITE DISTURBANCE
- SLEEP DISTURBANCE
- RISK TAKING BEHAVIOR
- POOR JUDGEMENT

Reactions to Stress

When you are under stress, you will always react to it. Emotional, behavioral, or physical reactions may alert you that you are experiencing stress or that you are not coping with it effectively.

Emotional Reactions

Depression and anxiety are the most common emotional reactions to stress. Events such as a layoff at work, the death of a loved one, or the breakup of a relationship often bring about depression. Depressed people lose interest in life and feel "down," worthless, tired, and hopeless. Anxious people, on the other hand, tend to be worried, fearful, and uneasy about the future. They also often experience weakness or dizziness and feel irritable, tense, or nervous. Waiting to take a test, visiting a dentist's office, and asking an employer for a pay raise are examples of stressors that cause anxiety for many people.

OVERHEAD

Sources of Stress Checklist

The following situations commonly cause mental or physical strain. Check the items that state something you have experienced in the past year.

School
- ☐ Entered college for first time
- ☐ Transferred to new school
- ☐ Too many courses
- ☐ Too much schoolwork
- ☐ Serious problem with teacher
- ☐ Failed a course
- ☐ Lower grades than expected
- ☐ Missed too many classes
- ☐ Worried about grades
- ☐ Dropped more than one course
- ☐ On academic probation

Family
- ☐ Close relative died
- ☐ Close relative seriously ill or injured
- ☐ Serious problem with close relative
- ☐ Moved and left close relatives
- ☐ Parents divorced
- ☐ Parent lost job

Friends
- ☐ Close friend died
- ☐ Close friend seriously ill or injured
- ☐ Serious problem with close friend
- ☐ Moved and left close friends
- ☐ Not enough friends

Love and Marriage
- ☐ New love interest
- ☐ Became engaged or married
- ☐ Became pregnant
- ☐ Fathered a pregnancy
- ☐ Became a parent
- ☐ Sexual problems
- ☐ Serious problem with partner
- ☐ Trouble with in-laws
- ☐ Divorced or separated
- ☐ Couldn't find desired partner
- ☐ Felt physically unattractive

Work
- ☐ Unemployed
- ☐ Disliked job
- ☐ Serious problem with boss or coworker
- ☐ Fired or laid off
- ☐ Worried about losing job
- ☐ Started new job

Money
- ☐ Not enough money for school
- ☐ Not enough money for food, clothing, or housing
- ☐ Not enough money for car or entertainment
- ☐ Worried about debts
- ☐ Denied credit card or loan
- ☐ Took large loan

Living Place
- ☐ Too many responsibilities
- ☐ Not enough space or privacy
- ☐ Annoying neighbor
- ☐ Bad neighborhood
- ☐ Moved to new place
- ☐ Denied living in desired place
- ☐ Problems with roommate

Health
- ☐ Seriously ill or injured
- ☐ Unable to get needed medical or dental care
- ☐ Abused alcohol or drugs

Behavioral Reactions

When people are under a great deal of stress, they often have difficulty concentrating on their work or studies. They may also have sexual problems or eat too much, drink too much, sleep too much, watch too much television, or spend too much money. Any excessive or self-destructive behavior such as these may be a response to stress.

Physical Reactions

Stress has been identified as a contributing factor in many illnesses, including heart disease, diabetes, hypertension, and cancer. Common reactions to stress also include the following:

- Aches in the neck or lower back
- Tension or migraine headaches
- Frequent colds or other illnesses
- Allergy or asthma attacks
- Excessive perspiration
- Constant feeling of tiredness
- Indigestion, constipation, or diarrhea
- Acne, psoriasis, or other skin problems

If you suffer any of these physical conditions *and* are under a great deal of stress, the ailment could be a symptom of the stress.

Coping with Stress

You may be one of the fortunate people who has a natural talent for managing stress by listening to music, gardening, or engaging in a hobby. However, if you want to improve your stress-coping skills, begin by using the "Sources of Stress Checklist" on page 61 to help in making a list of your stressors. The checklist does not include every source of stress, but the examples in it should help you in listing your stressors. Then, identify how you react to these stressors. Do you become depressed or anxious? Do you eat, drink, or sleep too much? Do you have frequent headaches, colds, or allergy attacks? Or, do you have reactions that are not mentioned on pages 60–62? Finally, use some of the following suggestions to cope with the stress. There is no one best way to manage stress; select from the following stress management methods the ones that you feel are best suited to your personality and the kinds of stress you experience.

Eliminate Stressors

Sometimes it is possible to eliminate a source of stress. For instance, if you are under extreme stress because of difficulty in a college course, you may be able to drop the course and take it later with a different teacher. Or, if you are upset because a neighbor's noise prevents you from getting a good night's sleep, you may be able to figure out a way to get the neighbor to be less noisy or arrange to move to a quieter place.

Manage Your Time

Students who do poorly in college because of their tendency to procrastinate suffer the stress that comes from being underprepared and the embarrassment that comes from doing inferior work. The failure to manage time well is such a widespread problem that Chapter 10 of *College Study Skills* is devoted entirely to this topic. When you study that chapter, you will learn a systematic approach to planning how to make the best use of your time for study, work, and the enjoyment of life.

The natural reluctance to change is a major cause of procrastination; we are naturally attached to the ways that we habitually do things. As a result, many students encounter difficulty when they try to do well in their college courses by using study methods and procedures that helped them "get by" in high school. They are reluctant to give up their accustomed study methods and replace them with procedures that are tailored to the demands of college study.

Seek Help from Others

HANDOUTS

When you are in distress, your greatest source of comfort may be another person who is understanding and can help you deal with your problem. Turn to a friend, relative, teacher, counselor, or other person who might be able to help you in dealing with your problem. See the suggestions on pages 34–35.

Exercise

In addition to its obvious physical benefits, exercise promotes mental and emotional health. Walking and climbing stairs are two forms of exercise that are readily available to students on most college campuses. You should expect to feel an increase in energy and a decrease in fatigue for up to two hours after a brisk walk. Wear comfortable walking shoes and step out smartly; don't stroll. Try to walk one or two miles every day at the rate of at least four miles per hour.

Some people don't exercise because they believe it saps them of their energy and leaves them too tired to meet their other responsibilities. This is a completely false belief. Exercise strengthens you, making you better able to withstand stress and to accomplish the mental and physical tasks that are required of you.

Make exercise an integral part of your life by varying your activity from day to day. For instance, you might stretch your muscles by bicycling on Sunday, walking three miles on Monday, mowing the lawn on Tuesday, shooting hoops on Wednesday, swimming on Thursday, jogging on Friday, and cleaning house on Saturday.

Eat a Nutritious Diet

A nutritious diet promotes well-being and strengthens the body so it can deal more effectively with stress. The key to good nutrition is to eat a variety of foods, emphasizing large quantities of fruit, vegetables, bread, and cereal and small servings of meat, milk, and cheese. Experts also advise not eating too much fat, sodium (salt), and sugar—major ingredients in popular foods such as hamburgers, hot dogs, potato chips, french fries, soft drinks, salad dressings, cookies, muffins, ice cream, and candy.

If you take a health education course, you will learn the fundamentals of good nutrition. Or, you can learn about a healthful diet by reading books that are available in your college library or bookstore.

Sleep Sufficiently

Lack of sleep weakens you and makes you less able to deal effectively with stress. Some medical doctors recommend nine hours of sleep a night; if you sleep less than you need, you may be creating an unnecessary source of stress for yourself.

By keeping track of how long I slept and how well I functioned the next day, I found that I need eight hours of sleep and that I can function for one day with seven hours of sleep and "get by" on six hours of sleep if it is followed by an undemanding day. If you keep similar records, in a week or two you will know whether insufficient sleep is a source of stress for you and how much sleep you need to function at your best.

Value Your Ability

Some people feel that there are certain things they cannot do or subjects that they are incapable of learning. If you feel there is a subject that you cannot learn, ask yourself this question: "Why do I feel that I cannot learn this subject when I know that people *just like me* learn it, and do well in it?" If you answer this question, you may discover that the only thing that is preventing you from learning a subject is your erroneous belief that you cannot learn it.

Don't Insist on Perfection

You do not need to be outstanding in every subject you study in college. If you are majoring in business and receive low grades in your business courses, then you have a serious problem. But if you are majoring in business, you don't need to be outstanding in all courses outside your specialization. Also, keep in mind that you do not need to be outstandingly good at something to enjoy it. For instance, you may have a singing voice that nobody would pay to hear, yet derive great pleasure from singing. The same is true of subjects you study in college. Give yourself permission to enjoy all the subjects you study, even the ones in which you do not excel.

Turn Threats into Challenges

Some stressful situations can be controlled by treating them as challenges. For instance, if you have difficulty with a college subject, develop more effective study strategies rather than dwell on the possibility of failing or doing poorly. A subject that you find difficult to learn may merely require more time than you are devoting to it. Ask yourself this question: "Could I learn this subject if I spent more time studying it?" If so, give the subject the additional time that it requires. You will then have the satisfaction of learning something that you thought you could not learn; you will discover that you can do things that you thought you could not do. This will improve your opinion of yourself and reduce your stress.

Change Your Goals

You may experience stress because you lack the necessary support or ability to achieve a goal. In such instances, you can take pressure off yourself by changing your goal. For example, if you lack the financial support to achieve your goal of graduating from college in four years, you might take a job to earn money and revise your goal to graduate in six years. If you lack the math skills to achieve your goal of becoming a certified public accountant, you might alter your goal to acquire the necessary math skills or to prepare for some other profession. (Chapter 9 of *College Study Skills* explains how to establish and work toward realistic goals.)

Use Relaxation Techniques

Deep muscle relaxation, imagery, and meditation are three relaxation techniques that help the body cope with stress by triggering a calming relaxation response. Instruction in one or more of these methods may be offered by your school's counseling, psychology, or physical education department.

- *Deep muscle relaxation* involves tensing and relaxing each part of your body at least twice, breathing in while tensing and breathing out while relaxing. Begin with your hands and work up to your biceps, shoulders, neck, face, and down to your chest, stomach, buttocks, legs, and feet.
- *Imagery* requires closing your eyes to visualize yourself in a totally relaxed state or performing a difficult task perfectly. For instance, you might relax by imagining yourself sitting on a mountaintop or build confidence by visualizing yourself walking down an aisle in cap and gown to receive your college diploma.
- *Meditation* is a method for telling your mind to be quiet. It requires being in a quiet place, assuming a comfortable position, organizing attention by focusing on something calming (such as your breathing), and allowing your mind to relax without making an effort for it to do so.

Muscle relaxation, imagery, and meditation are all effective in reducing stress. It would be worthwhile to take advantage of relaxation instruction, if it is available at your school. Even if you find that it is inconvenient for you to take time each day to practice a relaxation method, once you master one of the techniques, you will have it as a resource to draw upon when you are under stress.

EXERCISE 7.1 Sources of Stress

Check the stressors in the "Sources of Stress Checklist" on page 61 that you are experiencing or have experienced in the past twelve months. What are the greatest sources of stress for you at this time?

EXERCISE 7.2 Reactions to Stress

Read "Reactions to Stress" on pages 60–62, and then answer the following questions:

1. Are you experiencing any emotional reactions to stress? Are you depressed or anxious, or are you experiencing other emotions, such as anger, shame, or guilt?
2. Is your behavior affected by stress? Are you having difficulty concentrating? Or, are you eating, drinking, or sleeping too much?
3. Do you have physical problems as a result of stress, such as backaches, headaches, indigestion, constipation, or skin disorders?

EXERCISE 7.3 Coping with Stress

Considering your personality and the kinds of stress you experience, which of the stress management strategies described on pages 62–65 do you believe may be helpful to you in reducing stress you are under now or may experience in the future?

8

Use the Library

The library is the center for study and research on most campuses. You will use the library frequently to collect information for papers you write and other projects you do for your courses.

Library Instruction

It is likely that your library offers a service to teach you about its facilities and their proper use. The instruction may be printed in a booklet or in a series of leaflets, it may be recorded on videocassettes or on computer software, or it may be presented by a librarian to small groups of students at various times during the school year. Take advantage of whatever instruction is available. You will enjoy your visits to the library more when you know what is there and how to find it.

Also, when you need help in a library, go to a librarian for assistance. Librarians are highly trained professionals who know about sources of information and library services that you might overlook. Thank the librarians who give you good suggestions, and seek them out when you need help in the future.

How to Begin Research

If your library has an electronic data base that can be accessed by computer (see "Electronic Data Base Searches" on page 68), use the data base to research topics. If an electronic data base is not available in your library, begin your research in the periodical reading room. **Periodicals** include newspapers and magazines, which are the most up-to-date sources of information. Also, the papers you write in college will be closer to the length of articles than to the length of books. As a result, articles are likely to give you some good ideas about the ways you can discuss a topic in a paper for a college course.

Electronic Data Base Searches

In the past, researchers seeking secondary data had no choice but to slowly and systematically search manually through card catalogs and through several years' worth of relevant directories and indexes. They then had to locate the books and periodicals and scan them to determine if they were relevant.

Today, most university libraries and many public libraries can perform computer-assisted data searches. An entire knowledge industry has evolved in which organizations store huge amounts of statistical, financial, and bibliographic information in the memory banks of their mainframe computers or on computer disks and then make this information available to users nationwide for a fee.

An electronic data base is a computer-searchable collection of information on a particular topic. You can access numerous data bases within the broad topics of business, education, psychology, and the like. Electronic data bases are fast: a user can typically collect more data electronically in one hour than would be possible in one day of traditional library research.

In addition, electronic data bases are typically more current than printed data bases; most are updated weekly or monthly. Also, each contains several years' worth of citations, whereas manual indexes require searching through individual annual volumes of indexes. Finally, electronic data bases are extremely flexible. You can use different search terms, combine them, and modify your search at every step.

Popular Magazines

The *Readers' Guide to Periodical Literature* is an index to the articles that appear in about two hundred popular magazines, such as *Newsweek, Time,* and *Consumer Reports.* Articles are listed by subject and author. Figure 8.1 on page 69 contains an excerpt from the *Readers' Guide.* It lists an article about the subject "youth and business," and it informs readers where in the guide to look for articles about "youth and drugs" and "youth and television."

The abbreviations used in the entry in Figure 8.1 are clearly explained on the first pages of each volume of the *Readers' Guide.* By consulting those pages you will learn that in the sequence "38: 121–2," the volume number is printed before the colon and the page numbers are printed after the colon. Months are abbreviated using one or two letters. For example, "O" is the abbreviation for October, but "Je" is used for June and "Jl" is used for July.

When you locate an article that you want to read, make notes of the type in Figure 8.2 on page 69. Include the following information in your notes:

- The title of the article
- The name of the magazine
- The volume number of the magazine
- The pages on which the article is printed
- The month and year the magazine was published

FIGURE 8.1

An Entry from the *Readers' Guide*

Youth and business
Eighteen-year-old financial whiz [owner and founder S. Salter of Continational Financial Corp.] il pors *Ebony* 38:121-2 O '83
Youth and drugs *See* Drugs and youth
Youth and television *See* Television and youth

The *Readers' Guide* and other indexes to periodical literature are published in volumes for various time periods. You may need to consult several volumes of an index. Since your library probably does not subscribe to all magazines that are listed in an index, it may maintain a list or file of all the magazines and newspapers that are part of the collection of the library. This list or file will tell you whether your library has the periodical you want and, if so, for which years it owns the publication. If a periodical you want is not available, a librarian may be able to inform you whether it is in the collection of some other library in your community.

FIGURE 8.2

Notes for the *Readers' Guide* entry in Figure 8.1

"Eighteen-year-old Financial Whiz"
Ebony
Volume 38, pages 121-122
October, 1983

Specialized Periodicals

There are also indexes to periodicals that publish articles about specialized subjects. The *Art Index,* for instance, lists articles about fine arts, architecture, photography, film, and many other related subjects. Other indexes to specialized and professional periodicals include the following:

- *Applied Science and Technology Index*
- *Business Periodicals Index*
- *General Science Index*
- *Humanities Index*
- *Social Science Index*

When you do research for college courses, it is important to consult indexes such as these. For example, if you write a paper for a business course, you should consult the *Business Periodicals Index.*

Newspapers

When you want to find articles in newspapers, consult the *New York Times Index;* it lists all the articles that have appeared in that newspaper since 1851. All issues of the *New York Times,* beginning in 1851, are available on microfilm at most college and university libraries. Also, since news events are printed in most newspapers at about the same time, the *New York Times Index* may be used to locate articles published in other newspapers. For example, if you learn in the index that the *New York Times* published an important news story on May 15, 1994, you may be confident that your local newspaper also published a story about the event on or about May 15, 1994.

Books

Books and other materials owned by a library are located by using an index that lists them by author, title, and subject. The index may be a **card catalog,** in which information is printed on cards that are stored in filing cabinets, or an **on-line catalog,** in which information is stored in a computer and retrieved by typing the author, title, or subject into a computer terminal. Use the following procedure to locate books:

- When you know the author of a book, look for the author's name.
- When you know the title of a book, look for the title.
- When you do not know the author or title of a book, look for the subject that interests you.

When you locate a book you want to examine, list the following information on a piece of paper:

- The call number
- The name of the author
- The title of the book

The letters and numbers typed in the upper left corner of the cards in Figure 8.3 on page 71 are call numbers. **Call numbers** tell where a book is located in a library. Most libraries use the Library of Congress System, in which call numbers begin with capital letters, such as A, B, or C. However, the Dewey Decimal System is also widely used, especially by smaller libraries.

Libraries print leaflets or post signs to guide library users to the locations of books. If you have difficulty locating a book, ask a librarian for assistance.

Reference Books

The collection of a library may include specialized encyclopedias, dictionaries, indexes, and other reference books for art, anthropology, economics, education, and other subjects. Some reference books are helpful for researching the life and accomplishments of a person, and some indexes and digests are useful

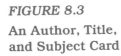

FIGURE 8.3
An Author, Title, and Subject Card

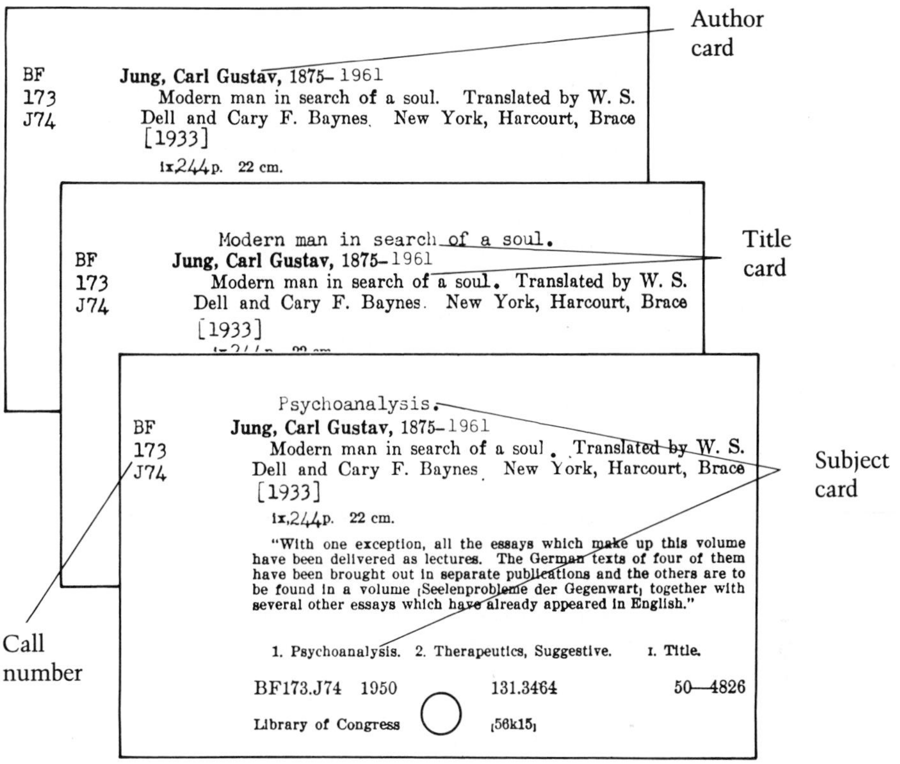

when writing book reports or book reviews. When you do research in a library, ask a reference librarian to suggest specialized reference books that may be helpful to you.

You will usually want to consult at least a general encyclopedia. Articles in encyclopedias may give you good ideas about how you can narrow the topic of a paper, and they sometimes include titles of books or articles that are worthwhile to examine.

The two best-known general encyclopedias are the *Encyclopedia Americana* and the *Encyclopaedia Britannica.* However, some articles in these encyclopedias are written using highly technical language. Therefore, do not overlook *Collier's Encyclopedia, Merit Students Encyclopedia,* and *World Book Encyclopedia.* All three of these are easy-to-read and authoritative encyclopedias.

Borrowing and Photocopying

Library materials may be studied in the library, or they may be borrowed or photocopied. When you find information in a book, borrow the book if it is one that circulates. If it is a reference book, you may want to photocopy the pages that you need to use. For instance, if you find a useful article in an encyclopedia, it may be convenient to have a copy of the article to refer to when you are at your usual study place.

It is also a good idea to photocopy useful magazine and newspaper articles. For a small investment in photocopying, you can analyze the articles in the comfort of your home rather than in the library.

EXERCISE 8.1 Selecting a Topic

Do the following activities to select a topic that you will research in the library.

1. Suppose that you must write a five-page paper about any topic you choose for one of your courses. Which course will you use for this exercise?

   ____

2. Study the table of contents and the index in the textbook for the course you listed above. Select three topics in the book that are especially interesting to you. Write the topics on the following lines together with the page numbers on which the topics are discussed in the book.

   a. ______________________________

   b. ______________________________

   c. ______________________________

3. Read about the three topics in the textbook. Which of the three topics is most interesting to you?

   ____

Do the following exercises using the topic that interests you most.

EXERCISE 8.2 The *Readers' Guide*

In the most recent annual volume of the *Readers' Guide,* look for articles about the topic you are researching. If you don't find any articles listed for your topic, ask a librarian for help. If the librarian cannot help you find articles for your topic, select one of the other topics you listed in Exercise 8.1.

1. How many articles are listed for the topic?______________________________

2. Make notes of the type illustrated on page 69 for three of the articles. Select articles in magazines that your library owns.

   a. ______________________________

   ____

   ____

   b. ______________________________

   ____

   ____

c. ______________________________

____

____

3. Locate the three articles in the library and read them quickly. Which one of the three articles has the most interesting and useful information for writing a five-page paper about your topic?

☐ Article 1 ☐ Article 2 ☐ Article 3

EXERCISE 8.3 The *New York Times Index*

In the most recent annual volume of the *New York Times Index,* look for articles about the topic you are researching. If you do not find any articles listed for your topic, ask a librarian for help.

1. How many articles are listed for your topic?______________

2. If articles are listed, write the title of one of the articles, the date it was published, and the page numbers on which it is printed.

____

____

____

3. What procedure must you use to read articles published in the *New York Times* five years ago?

____

____

EXERCISE 8.4 The Card Catalog

Find subject cards for your topic in the card catalog. Ask a librarian for help if you cannot find them.

1. How many subject cards are there for your topic?______________

2. On the following page, list the call numbers, names of authors, and titles for three books that include information about your topic.

a. ______________________________

____

____

b. ______________________________

____

____

c. ______________________________

____

____

3. Attempt to locate these three books in the library. How many of them did you find?

____

4. Ask a librarian how you can secure a copy of a book when it is not where it is supposed to be in the library. Write the answer on the following lines.

____

____

____

EXERCISE 8.5 An Encyclopedia

Find where your topic is discussed in an encyclopedia.

1. To which encyclopedia did you refer?

____

2. In which volume and on which pages is your topic discussed?

____

PART II

Use Time Wisely

Preview of PART II

Most college students have difficulty in attempting to accomplish all the things they must do during a typical college term. Some students are pressed for time because they have a job, care for a family, or have other responsibilities; others have enough time to do all the things they need to do, but they do not know how to make good use of it. This part of *College Study Skills* examines three ways to make better use of time:

- Chapter 9, "Work Toward Goals," explains how to identify your goals so you can use them to make basic decisions about how you will use your time.
- Chapter 10, "Manage Your Time," describes how to plan and organize your time for studying and achieving your other goals.
- Chapter 11, "Increase Concentration," teaches methods you can use to make better use of study time by keeping your mind focused on studying rather than letting it wander.

When you use time wisely, you will do the things you need to do and have more time to spend with your friends and family and to engage in activities you enjoy.

9

Work Toward Goals

A fundamental way to make good use of your time in college is to prepare an efficient plan for achieving your goals. Your **goals** are the accomplishments you work toward or strive for; they are the things you want enough to spend your time, effort, and money to achieve them. Check the boxes in front of any of the following statements that are goals of yours:

- ☐ To have a more desirable job
- ☐ To be respected in my profession
- ☐ To travel in Europe, Africa, or Asia
- ☐ To be a kind and considerate person
- ☐ To earn a college degree
- ☐ To be a better conversationalist
- ☐ To be healthy and physically fit
- ☐ To always do my best
- ☐ To improve in a sport or athletic event
- ☐ To be married and a parent
- ☐ To live in a more desirable house or apartment

Your goals give your life direction by helping you decide how you will use your resources. For instance, if one of your aims is to earn a college degree, this goal will guide you in making decisions about spending time going to classes, spending effort studying, and spending money on tuition and textbooks.

The emphasis in this chapter is on the goals that lead to success in college. However, the information pertains to all kinds of goals. Use the suggestions given here to also achieve your objectives for general self-improvement, friendship, health, travel, or any other area of interest to you. "Achieving Goals" on page 78 summarizes what this chapter teaches about writing and accomplishing goals.

Achieving Goals

Use the following procedures to achieve goals of the type illustrated in Figure 9.1:

1. Write primary goals first.
2. Make an effective plan for achieving primary goals that is expressed in intermediate and current goals.
3. Use suggestions in Chapter 10 to schedule the exact times you will accomplish your current goals.
4. Write goals that state things you want to achieve.
5. Word goals in ways that make it easy for you to evaluate your success in achieving them.
6. Write goals that
   - you have the ability to achieve.
   - you have enough time to achieve.
   - you will pay the price to achieve.
   - you are in control of the circumstances necessary to achieve.
7. Do not be discouraged by obstacles.
8. Monitor and assess your progress in achieving your goals.
9. Revise your intermediate and current goals when necessary.

Types of Goals

Figure 9.1 on page 79 gives examples of the three basic types of goals: primary, intermediate, and current.

A **primary goal** is something that you hope to achieve in the future. Following are examples of primary goals some students have for their education:

- To earn a college degree
- To graduate with at least a 3.00 grade point average
- To prepare for a specific profession

Primary goals are of special importance because they are used as a guide in establishing intermediate and current goals.

An **intermediate goal** is a goal that helps in accomplishing a primary goal. For example, to successfully complete a college course is an intermediate goal that helps in attaining the primary goal of earning a college degree. A **current goal** is a goal that leads to accomplishing an intermediate goal. To earn a good grade on a test you will take next week is a current goal that helps in attaining the intermediate goal of successfully completing a course you are taking.

FIGURE 9.1
Examples of Goals

Current Goals

Start smoking later in the day.
Smoke only ten cigarettes daily.
Smoke only half of each cigarette.
Drink water rather than smoke.
Chew gum rather than smoke.

↓

Intermediate Goal

Become a nonsmoker.

↓

Primary Goal

Live a healthy lifestyle.

As you come close to achieving primary goals, they usually become intermediate goals. For instance, as you draw near to your primary goal of graduating from college, you may set a new primary goal, such as to have a well-paying job or to be admitted to a graduate school. In so doing, your primary goal of graduating from college becomes an intermediate goal that helps you in attaining your new primary goal.

Writing Goals

Write primary goals first and use them to write your intermediate and current goals. Keep a list of your goals in a special place so you can read them from time to time. The following discussions explain how to write goals that are positive, measurable, and realistic.

Write Positive and Measurable Goals

Positive goals state a behavior you want, whereas negative goals state a behavior you do not want. Compare the following goals:

- I will earn a B average this term.
- I will try to stop wasting my time.

The first goal is positive—it states a behavior a student wants; the second goal is negative—it states a behavior she doesn't want. Pursue positive goals; it is more satisfying to spend time and effort working for the worthwhile things you want than to dwell on behaviors you disapprove of. Positive goals will focus your attention on self-improvement rather than on self-defeat.

The first goal is also measurable; it states exactly what will be accomplished in terms that can be measured. If the student keeps records of the grades she receives on tests, quizzes, and assignments, she can easily monitor the degree of success she has in earning a B average. In contrast, the second goal is not measurable; it is worded in a way that makes it virtually impossible to assess when it is achieved.

Write Realistic Goals

A goal is realistic if it is one that you are able and willing to work toward and over which you have reasonable control. Use the following criteria to decide whether a goal is realistic:

- *You have the abilities that are needed to achieve the goal.* Only a few people have the abilities that are necessary to be a professional football player or to write a best-selling novel, but millions of people have the abilities that are needed to graduate from college and to find a better-paying job. When you lack abilities, you may make it your goal to acquire them. For instance, if you lack the math skills to earn the grade you want in a statistics course, you may make it your goal to improve these skills.
- *You have enough time to achieve the goal.* There are goals for which you may possess the necessary skills but that you are unable to achieve because you don't have enough time. For instance, you may not be able to earn grades of B or higher in all of your courses because work, family, or other responsibilities deprive you of the study time you need to achieve this goal.
- *You are willing to pay the price necessary to achieve the goal.* To achieve an academic goal you may need to spend many hours alone at your desk and away from friends and activities you enjoy. A goal is not realistic for you unless you are willing to make it a priority and to pay whatever price is necessary to achieve it.
- *You are in control of the circumstances necessary to achieve the goal.* I once knew an English composition teacher who gave A's only to students who wrote as well as he did. In his first ten years of teaching he gave only four A's! Students with the goal of earning A's in a composition course taught by this teacher seldom succeeded because of his unreasonably strict grading procedures. To be more in control of earning A's, students needed to identify instructors who were more generous in giving A's and study composition with them. Analyze your goals to make certain that you have reasonable control over the circumstances necessary for you to accomplish them.

Think of something you want very much to accomplish, and use these four criteria to evaluate whether it is a realistic goal for you.

Working Toward Goals

To make steady progress toward a primary goal (1) plan your intermediate and current goals, (2) do not be discouraged by obstacles, (3) monitor and assess your progress, and (4) revise goals when necessary.

Plan Intermediate and Current Goals

A primary goal is achieved by using an effective plan that is expressed in appropriate intermediate and current goals. When the primary goal is to earn a college degree, intermediate goals invariably include satisfactorily completing all courses that lead to the degree. Following is a list of the current goals a student prepared at the beginning of a term to help in earning a grade of at least B in a psychology course:

- I will read required material before each class.
- I will attend all classes and take good notes.
- I will review and revise notes immediately after class.
- I will do library research for the term paper.

He used suggestions given in Chapter 10 to schedule the exact times he would read his psychology textbook, revise class notes, and do library research for his term paper.

Do Not Be Discouraged by Obstacles

The path to a goal is seldom unobstructed; if you are not prepared for hindrances, you may become discouraged and give up. For instance, an unexpected problem at work or home could take your attention away from studying and prevent you from achieving the grade you want on a test. Temporary setbacks are inevitable; prepare yourself for them so that you will not become discouraged. Discouragement is the enemy of persistence, and you must be persistent to accomplish the things you want.

Monitor and Assess Your Progress

If you have written specific and measurable goals, it will be easy for you to monitor and assess the progress you make toward achieving them. Following are some examples of current goals that are easy to monitor:

EVALUATE YOUR PROGRESS

- I will have all assignments completed on time.
- I will schedule time to study for all tests.
- I will participate in all class discussions.

Continually monitor your current goals to assess whether you are accomplishing them.

Also monitor your intermediate goals. For example, a student with the intermediate goal of maintaining a B average assessed his progress toward this goal every few weeks. Following are the grades he estimated he had earned as of the fifth week of a term: English, B+; chemistry, B; history, C; speech, A; and psychology, B. After making these estimates, he realized that he was not achieving his goal in his history course and took measures to raise the grade.

Revise Goals When Necessary

The student who wanted to do better in his history course analyzed why he was falling short of his goal. He determined that he had used ineffective methods in studying the course textbook, that he had not paid sufficient attention to his teacher's study suggestions, and that he had not spent enough time reviewing for tests. He developed a strategy for improvement that he expressed in the following revised current goals:

- I will make complete notes about things to learn in my history textbook (rather than try to learn the information by reading and rereading the textbook).
- I will spend twelve hours (rather than eight hours) reviewing for the next test.
- When I review for my next history test, I will emphasize learning the things the teacher states are important to learn (rather than only the things that interest me most).

These revised goals helped the student earn a B− in his history course.

However, in pursuing a goal you may sometimes find that you were too optimistic about what you could achieve. For instance, in working for a grade of B in a chemistry course, a student found that despite her best efforts she was unable to earn a test grade higher than C+. Since she did not want to delay her progress toward her degree by dropping the course and taking it later, she revised her goal to bring it in line with the C grade that she could realistically earn.

EXERCISE 9.1 Primary, Intermediate, and Current Goals

The following list contains a primary goal, two intermediate goals, and three current goals. On the lines provided, write **P** in front of the primary goal, **I** in front of intermediate goals, and **C** in front of current goals.

______ 1. I will maintain a 3.00 grade point average.

______ 2. I will attend all my classes.

______ 3. I will complete all assignments on time.

______ 4. I will earn a college degree.

______ 5. I will be thoroughly prepared for all tests.

______ 6. I will take all courses required in my program.

The following list contains a primary goal, two intermediate goals, and five current goals. On the lines provided, write **P** in front of the primary goal, **I** in front of intermediate goals, and **C** in front of current goals.

______ 7. I will read books and articles about Mexico.

______ 8. I will save $50 each month from my wages.

_______ 9. I will learn a great deal about Mexico.

_______ 10. I will save the money I receive as gifts.

_______ 11. I will find a better-paying job.

_______ 12. I will spend one month traveling in Mexico.

_______ 13. I will buy a map and guidebook for Mexico.

_______ 14. I will save enough money to make the trip.

EXERCISE 9.2 Writing Goals

COLLECT + GRADE

Practice writing positive, measurable, and realistic goals.

1. Write your primary goal for your education.
2. Write two intermediate goals that will help you achieve your primary goal.
3. Write three current goals that will help you achieve each of your intermediate goals.

EXERCISE 9.3 Monitoring Goals

1. What method will you use to monitor and assess the intermediate goals you wrote for item 2 in Exercise 9.2?
2. What method will you use to monitor and assess the current goals you wrote for item 3 in Exercise 9.2?

EXERCISE 9.4 Your Personal Goals

Use the following questions to stimulate your thinking about your personal goals. Your instructor may conduct a class discussion about this topic.

DISCUSSION

1. Do you want to live in a big city, a small town, the suburbs, or a rural setting?
2. What kind of apartment or house do you want for your home?
3. What kind of car, furniture, and other possessions do you want to own?
4. Do you want to live with a friend, a spouse, or by yourself?
5. Do you want to be a parent? If so, how many children do you want?
6. What profession or occupation do you want to pursue?

7. What annual income do you want to have five years from now?
8. Are good health and long life important to you?
9. Do you want others to regard you as having an attractive appearance?
10. Is hiking, hunting, fishing, bicycling, boating, or some other outdoor activity important to you?
11. Do you want to travel extensively in foreign countries?
12. Do you want to write a book, invent a machine, or make some other unique contribution to society?
13. Do you want to work to relieve the suffering of others?
14. Do you want to be respected by others?
15. Do you want to be known as a kind and loving person?
16. What are some of your personal goals that are not in this list?

10

Manage Your Time

As a college student you will have many demands on your time. In addition to attending classes and studying, you will spend time visiting with your friends and relatives, participating in sports or other activities, and attending to personal matters such as eating, shopping, traveling, and grooming. You may also spend time working at a job.

The problem all college students confront is to find time to attend class, study, and also do all the other things they need or want to do. This is made more difficult by the fact that college study is very demanding—it requires much more time than studying in high school. In a typical term, full-time college students may read five, six, or more textbooks, complete a major project in each course, and take many tests. With a great deal to accomplish in the few weeks of a term, successful college students find it is essential for them to schedule their time to accomplish everything they must do.

"How to Manage Your Time" on page 86 summarizes the procedures that are explained in detail in this chapter. You will learn how to manage your time by using a weekly study schedule, a list of things to do, an activity calendar, and a weekly assignment sheet like those shown on pages 88–90.

CAN'T SAVE TIME — ONLY CAN SPEND IT
SO SPEND IT WISELY

Analyze the Demands on Your Time

Before you try to figure out how to manage your time, you need to analyze the various ways in which you use it.

Some Demands on Your Time

- *School.* In addition to the time you spend in classes, you need time to study for tests and to complete papers and other projects for your courses.
- *Work.* If you have a job, you may need to plan time for traveling to and from your place of employment in addition to the time you actually spend working.
- *Friends and family.* Developing and maintaining good relations with friends and relatives requires spending time with them. You need time for making telephone calls, writing letters, and socializing, and for celebrating birthdays, anniversaries, and holidays.

How to Manage Your Time

Use the following procedures to schedule the time you will spend studying for your college courses:

- **Analyze the demands on your time.** Analyze how you use your time for school, work, friends and family, caring for yourself, and other activities.
- **Decide how much to study.** Figure out how much time you need to study to get the grades you want.
- **Determine how much time you have available for studying.** Use your list of things to do, your calendar, and your analysis of times you can't study because you're engaged in other activities.
- **Decide what you will study first.** Use the records of assignments you keep on a form of the type illustrated on page 90.
- **Decide when you will study.** Schedule short rather than long study sessions at times you are most alert and not engaged in other activities.

- *Activities of special interest to you.* If you have a special interest such as acting, gardening, playing a sport, being an active member of church, or participating in school or local politics, you will need time for this activity.
- *Caring for yourself.* You need time for sleeping, eating, grooming, traveling, paying bills, and caring for your clothing. These activities can be very time consuming if you need to shop for groceries, clean your living place, do your own laundry, or travel to school or work.
- *Caring for others.* If you are responsible for the care of a spouse, children, or parents, this may require many hours each week.

In addition to planning time for the things you need and want to do, you must be prepared to deal with the unexpected. One key to successful time management is to be ready to handle emergencies such as the following:

Common Types of Emergencies

- *Mechanical failure.* You could be delayed in your arrival to school because of the breakdown of an automobile or bus, you could be unable to complete an assignment because a computer went down, or you could be prevented from attending classes because of an electrical or plumbing failure in your home.
- *Illness or injury.* An illness or injury could prevent you from going to school and from completing assignments or preparing for tests.
- *Family and friends.* Someone close to you may need your help or attention suddenly, or the illness or death of a family member or friend could make an unexpected demand on your time.

- *Love interest.* A new romance could take a great deal of your time, or a breakup with your boyfriend or girlfriend could upset you and make it impossible for you to concentrate on schoolwork.
- *Miscalculation.* You could have insufficient time to do an assignment because you underestimated how long it would take you to complete it or because you forgot or overlooked when it was due.

Now and then you will need to adjust your schedule because of emergencies such as these.

Decide How Much to Study

If one of your goals is to earn good grades in your college courses, you will need to decide how much time you will spend studying so you can achieve this goal.

Teachers often tell students that they should spend two hours studying outside of class for each hour they spend in the classroom. For instance, when students take a course that meets for three class hours each week, instructors customarily recommend that they study for six hours each week outside of class. Unfortunately this advice doesn't take into account that some students need to devote more time to studying than others.

There is no way for anybody but you to know how long it will take you to do any particular assignment; you should study for as long as it takes you to achieve the goals you have set for yourself and to learn whatever it is you want to learn. An assignment that takes you two hours may take another student five hours, and an assignment that takes you five hours may take someone else two hours.

One way to find out how much *you* must study is to keep records of how long it actually takes you to study for your courses. For example, when you read a textbook, write the time in pencil on the page where you begin. After you have finished reading, write the time again. Then count the number of pages you read and figure out the average time it took you to read each page. If you do this a few times with each book you are studying, you will soon be able to estimate very accurately how long it takes you to read ten, twenty-five, or fifty pages in any book you are studying. Use this information to help in deciding how much time you will spend studying.

Determine Time Available for Study

Use the following three steps to determine how many hours each week are available to you for studying.

1. **Enter in your schedule all the times you have specific obligations, such as attending class, working, traveling, or engaging in other activities that you cannot change.** Use one of the study schedules printed on the last pages of this book. In Figure 10.1 on page 88 these types of obligations are shaded in light blue. "Free" indicates time that may be used for exercise, leisure activities, or additional studying.

FIGURE 10.1

A Weekly Study Schedule

The student cannot study during the hours shaded in blue because she is in class, working, or engaged in other activities.

	SAT	SUN	MON	TUE	WED	THU	FRI
	Oct. 7	Oct. 8	Oct. 9	Oct. 10	Oct. 11	Oct. 12	Oct. 13
8-9	Eng – Revise +	Free	Chem –	Psych – Read Ch. 9	Math – Odd	Psych – Read Ch 10	Chem – Ex 12.1,
9-10	type paper	Free	Ex 11.1–11.5	Prep to discuss ques 1, 4, & 6	problems 1–19, PP 187–188	Prep to discuss ques 1–7	12.3, 12.7–12.9
10-11	Hist – Read	Chem –	X	X	X	X	X
11-12	Ch. 8, pp 231–252	Read Ch. 11	X	X	X	X	X
12-1	X	↑	X	X	X	X	X
1-2	Hist – Work on	Lunch and movie	Hist – Read	Math – Prep for	Hist – Answer	Eng – Research	X
2-3	paper (Library)	with George	Ch. 8, pp 253–279	quiz on Ch. 4–6	ques 1–12, pp 280–281	for paper (Library)	Hist – Work on
3-4	X	↓	X	Eng – Outline	X	X	Paper (Library)
4-5	X	– Do Laundry	Math – Odd	for paper (Library)	X	X	↓
5-6	X	– Wash Car	problems 20–39, pp 172–174	Free	X	Free	X
6-7	Free	– Plan dinner	X	Free	X	Free	X
7-8	Free	for Oct. 14	X	X	X	X	Free
8-9	Free	Math – Odd problems	Free	Chem –	↑	Chem – Read	Free
9-10	Free	1–19, pp 171–172	Free	Ex 11.6–11.11	Photography Club	Ch. 12	Free
10-11	Free	X	X	X	↓	X	Free

2. **Keep a list of chores and other things that you have to do each week.** The study schedule in Figure 10.1 above, includes the items in the following list.

<u>Things to do</u>
Wash the car
Do the laundry
Plan dinner for Sat. (10/14)
Buy birthday present for Mom
Lose five pounds

3. **Prepare a calendar of social activities and other important dates.** Some of the activities shown in the following calendar are included in the study schedule in Figure 10.1.

OCTOBER

Sunday	Monday	Tuesday	Wednesday	Thursday	Friday	Saturday
1	2	3 Psych Quiz	4	5	6	7 Jane's party 9 PM
8 Lunch/movie with George	9	10	11 Photography Club 8 PM	12	13	14 Friends for dinner 7 PM
15	16	17	18 History paper due	19 Football game 2 PM	20	21
22	23 Mom's birthday	24	25	26 Chemistry test	27	28 Rita visits campus
29	30	31 Halloween party 9 PM				

When you analyze how much time you have for studying, you may find that you don't have enough time to study because you devote a great deal of time to work, sports, family responsibilities, or some other activity. If you are so busy with another activity that it interferes with your ability to do well in college, you may need to reduce the number of courses you take each term, or you may need to spend less time engaging in the conflicting activity (see pages 35–37).

Set Priorities for What to Study

Students sometimes make the mistake of studying first for the courses for which they *prefer* to study rather than for the courses for which they *need* to study. One secret of success is to do now the things that must be done now. Begin each day by looking over your assignments to decide which of them must absolutely, positively be done today, and do those assignments now. This decision is easier to make if you keep your assignments in the format illustrated in Figure 10.2 on page 90.

FIGURE 10.2
A Method for Keeping Assignments

COURSE	MON Oct 9	TUE Oct 10	WED Oct 11	THU Oct 12	FRI Oct 13
English	Revise the two-page paper Type neatly		Bring outline for research paper		Bring list of references for research paper (at least 10)
Math	Odd problems 1-19, pp. 171-172	Odd problems 20-39, pp. 172-174	Quiz on chapters 4-6	Odd problems 1-19, pp. 187-188	
Chemistry	Read Ch. 11 Do Ex. 11.1-11.5 (Test Oct 26)		Do Ex. 11.6-11.11		Read Ch. 12 Do Ex. 12.1, 12.3, + 12.7-12.9
History	Read Ch. 8, pp. 231-252 (Paper due Oct 18)	Read Ch. 8, pp. 253-279		Write answers to questions 1-12, pp 280-281	
Psychology		Read Ch. 9 Prepare for discussion questions 1, 4, + 6		Read Ch. 10 Prepare for discussion questions 1-7	

The record of assignments in Figure 10.2 was used to prepare the study schedule in Figure 10.1 on page 88. For example, compare Figure 10.2 with Figure 10.1 to notice that the student plans to complete Thursday's assignments on Wednesday and Thursday.

At the back of this book there are forms that you may use to keep records of your assignments. Make photocopies of one of the forms, punch holes in the copies, and put them in the assignment section of your ring binder.

You may sometimes find that you are so busy that it is impossible for you to do all your assignments as thoroughly as you would like. If this happens, use the following questions to help in deciding how much of your available time to spend working on an assignment or preparing for a test:

- *Will the assignment help me master a skill that is important to my long-term goals?* A business student may give priority to English composition assignments because he knows the ability to write well will be important to his success in business.

- *How will my grade for the assignment or test affect my final course grade?* A student of electrical technology may give priority to written assignments in her electrical technology courses because her instructors use assignment grades to compute final course grades.
- *How important is my grade in the course to help me achieve my goals?* A student at a school in Florida wants high grades in all of her courses so she can transfer credits for the courses she takes in Florida to a school in Illinois.

You probably want to do your best in each course you take. However, when you have insufficient time to study as much as you want, establish your priorities by spending your study time in the ways that will benefit you most in the future.

Decide When to Study

Some students try to study when they are taking a sunbath, watching television, or when they are overly tired, hungry, or under too much stress. Unfortunately, studying at times such as these is not likely to be very effective. Rather, use the following suggestions as a guide in deciding the actual times you will study for your various courses.

REFER TO LEARNING STYLE + ENVIRONMENTAL PREFERENCES

1. **Study at the time you are most alert.** Observe yourself when you study to determine whether you are most alert early in the morning, in the afternoon, in the evening, or late at night. Use what you learn to schedule study periods at the time of day you concentrate best.
2. **Study about lecture topics immediately before class.** By reading about the lecture topic just before class, you will have the material fresh in your mind when you listen to the lecture.
3. **Review and correct class notes immediately after class.** If you don't understand your notes right after class, you won't understand them later when you study them to prepare for a test; therefore, review your notes as soon after class as possible.
4. **Try learning information just before you go to sleep.** There is evidence that we remember more information when it is learned just before sleep than when it is learned at other times.

   JUST AFTER EXERCISE +
5. **Schedule many short study sessions rather than a few long ones.** For example, when you schedule six hours to study for a test, plan six one-hour study sessions rather than one six-hour or two three-hour study sessions. Short study sessions are more effective than long ones because it is tiring to study for long periods, and we do not learn well when we are tired.
6. **When you must study a subject for several consecutive hours, take a five- or ten-minute break every hour.** You can make these breaks productive by using them to do things you need or want to do—make a short telephone call, go for a brief walk, shoot a few baskets, read the baby a bedtime story, make a pot of coffee, or put clothes in the washer.

It is necessary to revise study schedules often to accommodate changing school, social, and other obligations. Also, some weeks have holidays that offer uninterrupted stretches of time for working on major projects and preparing for examinations. There are study schedule forms at the back of the book; you may photocopy one of them if you want. You may want to make one copy for each week of the term because no two weeks are exactly alike.

Make Better Use of Time

If you analyze how you spend your time, you may find that you waste time each day that you could use studying and doing other things you need to do. One way you can make better use of your time is to combine activities by doing two things at once, as suggested in the following list:

Some Ways to Do Two Things at Once

- As you drive friends or children from place to place, have them quiz you on material in your notes.
- Write material on 3-by-5-inch cards and study the information while you walk from place to place or ride on a bus.
- Think about what you will do during your next study session while you are walking, driving, or doing routine chores.
- Record material you want to learn on an audiocassette and listen to the cassette while you are driving or doing household chores.
- Study while you wash clothes, while you wait for a favorite television program to start, or while you wait for a friend to arrive.

A second way to accomplish more is to make use of short periods that you now may waste doing nothing of importance. Following are some suggestions:

How to Use Short Periods

- *Five minutes.* In five minutes you could review words you are learning, revise your list of things to do, plan your next study session, do some sit-ups or pushups, take out the garbage, put clothes in the washer, or clean the bathroom sink.
- *Fifteen minutes.* In fifteen minutes you could pay a bill, review notes, survey a chapter, wash dishes, solve a math problem, pick the topic for a paper, balance a checkbook, pay some bills, or work out on exercise equipment.
- *Thirty minutes.* In thirty minutes you could run an errand, write a letter, locate material in the library, review notes, read five pages in a textbook, buy birthday cards, or jog three miles.

Give some thought to how you might make better use of your time. One of my students saved time by using the telephone. He avoided unnecessary trips to the library by calling first to find out whether books he wanted were available; he also avoided time-consuming shopping trips by using catalogs and toll-free numbers to do much of his shopping by telephone. Another of my students taught her nine- and ten-year-old children to do laundry and other household chores so that she would have more time to play with them and help them with their homework. The best time-saving strategies are the ones that you devise to suit your particular circumstances.

EXERCISE 10.1 Decide How Much to Study

List the courses you are taking, the grade you want for each course, and the number of hours per week you will need to study for each course to earn the grade you want.

Courses	Grades I Want	Hours I Need to Study
______________________	__________	________
______________________	__________	________
______________________	__________	________
______________________	__________	________
______________________	__________	________
______________________	__________	________

What is the total number of hours you will study each week? __________

EXERCISE 10.2 Make a Calendar for the Term

Make a calendar for the entire term.

1. Use a calendar of the type illustrated on page 89 (they are sometimes available free in bookstores and card shops).
2. Consult your school's catalog for the dates of holidays, vacations, final examinations, and other important dates in your school's academic calendar.
3. Use syllabuses, outlines, and other materials your instructors give you to find the dates of tests and the dates papers and other course projects are due.
4. Use the school newspaper or other student government publications to find the dates of important athletic and social events you want to attend.
5. Use your personal records as the source of information about the dates of weddings, birthdays, anniversaries, and other important events you will observe with your relatives and friends.

Include these and other important dates in your calendar.

EXERCISE 10.3 Prepare a List of Things to Do

Prepare a list of the things you need to do next week. Include chores, social obligations, and other things you want to accomplish. Entitle your list "Things to Do Next Week."

EXERCISE 10.4 Determine Time Available for Study

Referring to your list of things to do, your calendar, and your class schedule, use one of the forms at the back of this book to analyze how many hours you have available *next* week that you can use for studying. Cross out the times when you cannot study because you are attending class, working, traveling, eating meals, or engaging in other activities. Be certain to cross out enough time for each activity. If it takes you an hour each morning to get dressed and eat breakfast, cross out an hour, not half an hour. Also, be certain to allow enough time for meals and relaxation; they are essential to your enjoyment of life and your physical and mental well-being.

How many hours do you have available for studying *next* week? ________

If you have fewer hours than you need for studying, figure out how you can make more time available or consider whether you overestimated the number of hours you will need for studying when you did Exercise 10.1.

EXERCISE 10.5 Decide What to Study First

Use one of the assignment forms in the back of this book to list the assignments you must do next week. Also, on the following lines, list days tests will be given and the days reports are due.

Tests and Reports

____

____

____

____

____

EXERCISE 10.6 Decide When to Study

Referring to the materials you prepared when you did Exercise 10.5, enter in your study schedule the exact times you will study for each of your courses next week.

11

Increase Concentration

To make the best use of your study time, you must be able to focus your thought and attention on studying during the time you set aside for this purpose. Yet you may find that you are unable to concentrate for long stretches of time. Some students report that their minds begin to wander after as few as five minutes of reading. Others complain that their minds can't concentrate on studying for more than ten or fifteen minutes.

This chapter explains strategies for increasing concentration, which are summarized in "How to Increase Concentration for Studying" on page 97. In addition, when you study Chapters 14–20 of *College Study Skills,* you will learn methods that will keep your mind active and less likely to wander when you read and study.

Accommodate Your Preferences

Use your answers to Exercise 6.5 on page 58 as a guide for providing yourself with a study environment in which you are likely to concentrate best. For instance, study at the time of day you are most alert. Also, take into account your preferences for conditions, such as the place you study, the kind of desk and chair you use, the brightness or dimness of light on your study surface, the temperature of the room, and whether you prefer to study while music is playing or while other people are present.

Select a Specific Place to Study

Try to always study in the same place, and avoid using your study place for other purposes, such as watching television or socializing. In this way, when you go to your study place, you will sense your purpose for being there, and your mind will prepare itself to concentrate on studying.

Eliminate Interruptions

You will probably find that it is difficult for you to concentrate if you must constantly deal with interruptions. Therefore, if you have roommates, agree with them about the hours that will be devoted to study each day. Also, explain to friends and relatives that you do not want to be disturbed while you are studying because it will interrupt your concentration. You may devise a method to signal that you are studying. One of my students uses a silk rose to indicate that she doesn't want to be disturbed; when her husband and children see her seated at the kitchen table wearing the pink rose they know that she is studying, and they don't bother her.

If you have friends who insist on interrupting you while you are studying, try to replace them with more considerate companions. You deserve friends who respect your study time and who want you to do well in college.

Keep Records of Concentration

When you begin to study, make a note of the time. Then, when you first become aware that your attention is not focused on studying, record the time again. Compare the two times and make a note of how many minutes you studied before you lost your concentration. Next, spend a few minutes doing something other than studying; you might stand up and stretch or look out the window. When you begin to study again, make another note of how long you concentrate.

Continue in this way until you are satisfied with the length of time you are able to concentrate. Many students report that keeping this kind of record helps them to double or triple their attention span very quickly.

Use Your List of Things to Do

Your list of things to do, explained on page 88, provides a handy method for dealing with distracting thoughts, such as "Do the laundry," "Telephone Dad," and "Photocopy the report for history." When you study, keep your list of things to do handy and add items to it as they come into your mind. By writing the things you want to do in the place they belong, you free your mind to concentrate on studying rather than on keeping track of other responsibilities.

Decide That You Want to Study

Once your mind drifts off, you are no longer studying. You might be thinking about something that happened earlier in the day, something that is worrying you, or something that you would rather be doing—but you are not studying!

If you want to make the best use of your study time, decide that you *want* to study rather than daydream, listen to music, watch television, or do other things you enjoy. If you don't decide that you really want to spend your study time studying, you may become resentful and grow to feel that studying is a punishment. If you feel that you are being punished when you study, your thoughts will be about your suffering. When you think about your suffering, you cannot concentrate on reading or studying.

How to Increase Concentration for Studying

Use these strategies to improve your ability to concentrate on studying for longer periods.

- Accommodate your preferences for the conditions under which you study, such as the place, temperature, and presence or absence of music, food, or other people.
- Always study in the same place.
- Explain to your friends and relatives that you do not want to be interrupted while you are studying.
- Keep records of how long you concentrate when you study and try to concentrate longer the next time you study.
- Keep your list of things to do handy and add items to it as they come into your mind while you are studying.
- Decide that you want to study rather than do something else.
- Begin study sessions by doing routine or easy tasks.
- Do large tasks a bit at a time.
- Accept that you must do difficult tasks to achieve your goal of getting a college education.
- Reward yourself for studying.

In addition, use the study methods that are explained in Chapters 14–20 of *College Study Skills.*

Do Routine Tasks First

Keep a list of your assignments, arranged in the sequence they must be completed, and start each study session by examining the list to do first what is either most routine or easiest (see Exercise 10.5 on page 94). If it is equally important to proofread a draft of a paper for an English course and to study for a chemistry test, do first whichever of the assignments is easiest for you.

Another way to begin a study session is to review things you have studied previously. For instance, before trying to solve a new type of problem for a mathematics course, spend a few minutes solving a kind of problem you already know how to do. You will provide yourself with the review practice you need, and you will put yourself in the right frame of mind for learning how to solve the new type of problem.

Do Large Tasks a Bit at a Time

It is sometimes difficult to concentrate on a task that seems impossible to accomplish. For instance, the thought of reading and learning everything in a six-hundred-page textbook can be overwhelming. However, reading and learning the information in a textbook is accomplished one step at a time using methods that are explained in following chapters of *College Study Skills*. Similarly, English handbooks explain how to do the small tasks that make it possible to write long term papers.

Mathematics, science, technology, and foreign language courses are among the ones for which information must be learned a bit at a time. If you do not keep up-to-date with the work in courses such as these, you may find it is extremely difficult to catch up.

Accept Difficult Tasks

When your mind is focused on the thought that a task is difficult or unpleasant, it cannot concentrate on accomplishing the task. Replace the thought "I don't want to do this difficult task" with the thought "To achieve a worthwhile goal, I accept that I must do this and other difficult tasks."

Those who achieve important goals do difficult or unpleasant things they would not do *except* for the fact that they are intent on attaining their objectives. For example, if you are determined to own an expensive automobile, you may work long hours at a difficult or unpleasant job that you would not work at *except* that you are determined to have the car you want. In the same way, if your goal is to earn a college degree, you may have to do difficult or unpleasant tasks that you would rather not do *except* that you are determined to have the benefits of a college education.

Reward Yourself for Studying

You can motivate yourself to concentrate by arranging your schedule so that studying is followed by something pleasant to do. Before you begin to study, plan that after an hour or two you will telephone a friend, read a magazine, go jogging, or engage in some other activity that you enjoy. When you study on a Saturday afternoon, plan that in the evening you will visit a friend, go to a movie, or do something else that entertains you.

Study followed by a reward is usually productive. If you know that you have only three hours to study because you've scheduled some fun for yourself, you may be inspired to make the best use of the three hours that you set aside for studying.

EXERCISE 11.1 Accommodating Your Environmental Preferences

Refer to your answers to Exercise 6.5 on page 58 to write a description of the environment in which you prefer to study. Include all ten conditions mentioned in the ten questions in Exercise 6.5.

EXERCISE 11.2 Keeping Records of Concentration

When you begin to read for a college course, make a note of the time in pencil at the place where you begin reading. Then, when you detect that your attention is not focused on reading, record the time again. Compare the two times and make a note of how many minutes you read before you lost your concentration. Continue in this way, striving each time to concentrate longer than you did the time before.

Determine how many minutes it now takes you to read ten pages in four textbooks you are studying for courses you are taking this term.

1. It takes me ______ minutes to read ten pages of the textbook for my ____________________ course.
2. It takes me ______ minutes to read ten pages of the textbook for my ____________________ course.
3. It takes me ______ minutes to read ten pages of the textbook for my ____________________ course.
4. It takes me ______ minutes to read ten pages of the textbook for my ____________________ course.

EXERCISE 11.3 Do Routine Tasks First

1. Refer to Exercise 10.5 on page 94 and copy on the following lines the first two assignments you will do next week.

   ____

   ____

   Decide which of these two assignments is easier, more routine, or more interesting, and do it first.

2. Decide for which of your courses is it appropriate to begin a study session by reviewing things you have studied previously.

   ____

   ____

EXERCISE 11.4 Unpleasant or Difficult Tasks

List the most unpleasant or difficult tasks you must do this term.

1. ______________________________

2. ______________________________

3. ______________________________

4. ______________________________

5. ______________________________

Is your education important enough to you that you are willing to do these unpleasant or difficult tasks?

PART III

Learn Organizational Skills

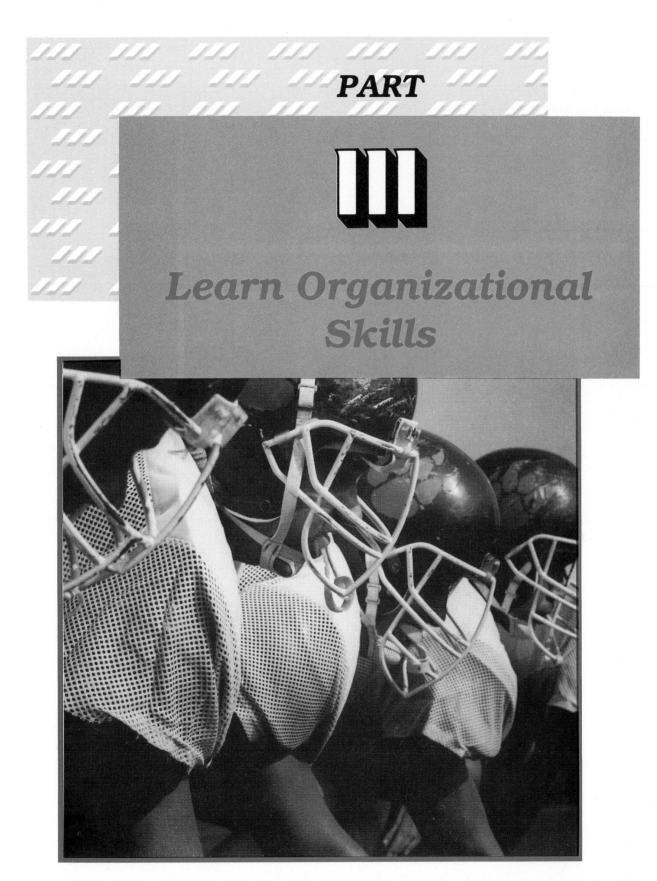

Preview of PART III

This part of *College Study Skills* will help you to develop understandings and abilities that are necessary for taking good class notes, underlining books accurately, and doing many other study tasks efficiently.

- Chapter 12, "Learn to Label Outlines," teaches how to use Roman numerals, capital letters, and Arabic numerals to make notes in the traditional outline format.
- Chapter 13, "Make Well-organized Outlines," provides instruction and practice for making notes in the traditional outline format.

The things you learn in Chapter 12 and Chapter 13 will provide you with the foundation you need to benefit most when you study how to take good class notes (Chapter 17), mark textbooks (Chapter 18), and make notes for textbooks (Chapter 19).

12

Learn to Label Outlines

In this chapter and in Chapter 13, you will learn how to use Roman numerals, capital letters, and Arabic numerals to make notes in the traditional **outline** format, which is illustrated in "Fast Food Restaurants," below.

To make outlines you must analyze written material—you must study it to understand how statements in it are related. Analysis, you may recall, is an essential step for effectively storing information in memory (see page 44). Thus, the abilities you will develop by learning to make outlines are the ones you will use to take good class notes, to select what to underline in your textbooks, to make well-organized notes for learning information in books, and to store information in your memory.

Major Thoughts and Details

In an outline, major thoughts are labeled with Roman numerals and listed under titles, and details are labeled with capital letters and listed under major thoughts.

Fast Food Restaurants

I. McDonald's
   A. Big Mac
   B. French fries
   C. Apple pie
   D. Chocolate shake
II. Burger King
   A. Whopper
   B. Onion rings
   C. Vanilla shake
III. Dairy Queen
   A. Big Brazier
   B. Fiesta sundae

This outline is organized to show that McDonald's, Burger King, and Dairy Queen are three fast food restaurants and to identify some of the foods each restaurant serves.

FIGURE 12.1
Logical Subordination of Details

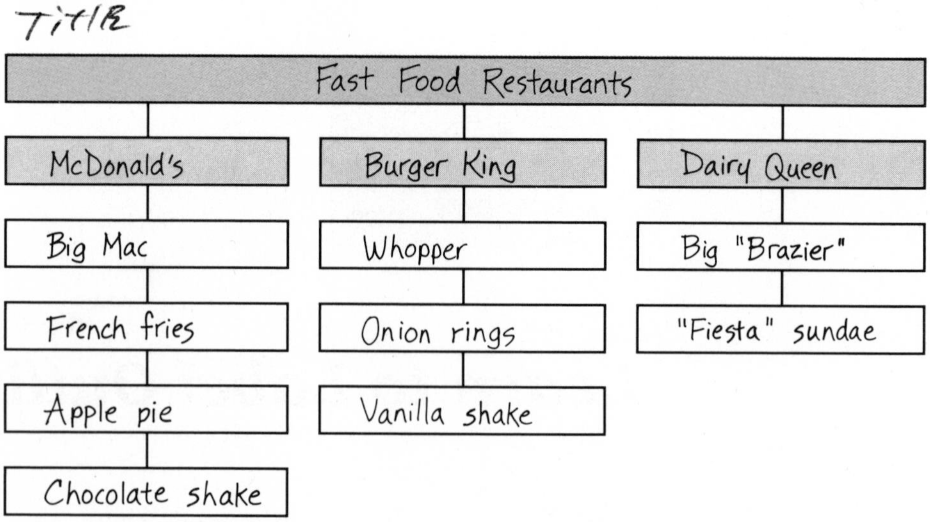

The diagram in Figure 12.1 above illustrates how to check whether the information in an outline is logically organized. Notice in Figure 12.1 that "McDonald's," "Burger King," and "Dairy Queen" logically belong under "Fast Food Restaurants" because they are three fast food restaurants. Also, observe that the various types of food are logically organized under the names of the restaurants that serve them. For instance, "Big Mac" is under "McDonald's," and "Whopper" is under "Burger King." When information is logically organized in this way, it is said to be logically subordinated.

The exercises for outlines in *College Study Skills* are prepared so you will learn to make outlines in which all statements are logically subordinated and logically coordinated.

Coordination in Outlines

Statements in outlines must be logically subordinated *and* logically coordinated. To coordinate is to put together things that belong together. For instance, when you wear two brown socks, your socks are coordinated. However, if you wear a brown sock and a white one, your socks are not coordinated. Cross out any items that you believe are *not* logically coordinated in the following outline.

My Summer Vacation

I. California
   A. Los Angeles
   B. Uncle Joe
   C. San Francisco

II. Washington
   A. Swimming
   B. Sailing
   C. Mt. Rainier
   D. Hiking

III. Yellowstone National Park

IV. Oregon
   A. Crater Lake

You should have made the outline coordinate by crossing out the italicized items in the following list:

- *III. Yellowstone National Park* is not coordinate with the other items following Roman numerals; they are states.
- *B. Uncle Joe* is not coordinate with the other items in the list; they are cities.
- *C. Mt. Rainier* is not coordinate with the other items in the list; they are sporting activities.
- *A. Crater Lake* is not coordinate because there must be at least two items under any category to coordinate.

There must be coordination *within* the lists of an outline, but there need not be coordination *between* the lists of an outline. In the corrected outline entitled "My Summer Vacation," the items under "California" are coordinate; they are both cities. Also, the items under "Washington" are coordinate; they are sporting activities.

Minor Details

When minor details are added to outlines, they are labeled with Arabic numerals. Minor details in the following outline are the names of college courses.

Social Science and Science Courses

I. Social Science
   A. Sociology
      1. Sociology of the Family
      2. Women in Society
   B. Psychology
      1. Abnormal Psychology
      2. Human Development
      3. The Psychology of Aging
II. Science
   A. Biology
      1. Evolution of Humankind
      2. Anatomy and Physiology
   B. Chemistry
      1. Fundamentals of Chemistry
      2. Inorganic and Analytic Chemistry
   C. Physics
      1. Principles of the Physical Environment
      2. Physics of Life Processes
      3. Basic Atomic and Nuclear Physics

Some exercises at the end of this chapter provide practice for labeling outlines that include minor details.

How to Label Outlines

Use the following procedures when you label the outlines in the exercises at the end of this chapter:

- Always use at least two Roman numerals in an outline (**I** and **II**). Enter Roman numerals before you enter any capital letters.
- If you use capital letters under a Roman numeral, always use at least two (**A** and **B**). Enter capital letters before you enter any Arabic numerals.
- If you use Arabic numerals under a capital letter, always use at least two (**1** and **2**). Enter Arabic numerals last.

If you follow these suggestions, you will make coordinate outlines. All the exercises in *College Study Skills* are prepared to help you learn to make coordinate outlines.

The following exercises are arranged to help you acquire skill in writing titles for outlines and in labeling statements in outlines with Roman numerals, capital letters, and Arabic numerals. You should find the first exercises very easy to do; they are included to prepare you for other exercises that are more challenging.

EXERCISE 12.1 Major Thoughts in Lists

Check the word in each list that is the major thought. For instance, check *Coins* in the first list because pennies, nickels, dimes, and quarters are all coins.

1. ☐ Pennies
   ☐ Nickels
   ☐ Dimes
   ☒ Coins
   ☐ Quarters

2. ☐ Hate
   ☒ Emotion
   ☐ Envy
   ☐ Fear
   ☐ Love

3. ☒ Store
   ☐ Grocery
   ☐ Bakery
   ☐ Pharmacy
   ☐ Florist

4. ☒ Entertainment
   ☐ Television
   ☐ Movies
   ☐ Circuses
   ☐ Theater

5. ☐ Letter
   ☒ Writing
   ☐ Newspaper
   ☐ Magazine
   ☐ Book

6. ☐ Steam
   ☒ Energy
   ☐ Atomic
   ☐ Electric
   ☐ Gasoline

7. ☐ May
   ☐ June
   ☒ Women
   ☐ April
   ☐ Mary

8. ☐ Second
   ☐ Minute
   ☐ Day
   ☒ Time
   ☐ Hour

9. ☐ Beef
   ☒ Meat
   ☐ Lamb
   ☐ Pork
   ☐ Veal

10. ☐ Milk
    ☐ Coffee
    ☒ Beverage
    ☐ Soda
    ☐ Tea

11. ☒ Fowl
    ☐ Chicken
    ☐ Turkey
    ☐ Duck
    ☐ Quail

12. ☐ Car
    ☐ Airplane
    ☐ Train
    ☐ Bus
    ☒ Transportation

13. ☐ Hat
    ☐ Shoes
    ☐ Shirt
    ☐ Pants
    ☒ Clothes

14. ☐ Ballet
    ☐ Sculpture
    ☒ Arts
    ☐ Painting
    ☐ Opera

15. ☐ Eyes
    ☐ Lips
    ☐ Nose
    ☒ Face
    ☐ Chin

16. ☐ Novel
    ☐ Poem
    ☐ Essay
    ☐ Drama
    ☒ Literature

17. ☐ Seattle
    ☐ Boston
    ☐ Chicago
    ☒ Cities
    ☐ Indianapolis

18. ☐ Spain
    ☒ Europe
    ☐ Germany
    ☐ France
    ☐ Italy

EXERCISE 12.2 Major Thoughts and Titles

Check the major thoughts and write titles for the lists. For instance, check *Short* and *Long* in the first list and write "Measures of Time" as a title for it.

1. ______________________

- ☐ Short
- ☐ Second
- ☐ Minute
- ☐ Long
- ☐ Week
- ☐ Month
- ☐ Year

2. ______________________

- ☐ Feet
- ☐ Socks
- ☐ Shoes
- ☐ Torso
- ☐ Shirt
- ☐ Sweater
- ☐ Vest
- ☐ Jacket

3. ______________________

- ☐ Africa
- ☐ Nile
- ☐ Congo
- ☐ United States
- ☐ Mississippi
- ☐ Columbia
- ☐ Hudson
- ☐ Missouri
- ☐ Delaware

4. ______________________

- ☐ Vegetables
- ☐ Potatoes
- ☐ Onions
- ☐ Tomatoes
- ☐ Lettuce
- ☐ Beans
- ☐ Fruit
- ☐ Apples
- ☐ Oranges
- ☐ Bananas
- ☐ Lemons

5. ______________________

- ☐ California
- ☐ Los Angeles
- ☐ San Francisco
- ☐ Sacramento
- ☐ Illinois
- ☐ Chicago
- ☐ Decatur

6. ______________________

- ☐ Theater
- ☐ Opera
- ☐ Ballet
- ☐ Drama
- ☐ Musical
- ☐ Museums
- ☐ Paintings
- ☐ Sculpture

7. ______________________

- ☐ Mammal
- ☐ Beef
- ☐ Pork
- ☐ Lamb
- ☐ Veal
- ☐ Bird
- ☐ Chicken
- ☐ Turkey
- ☐ Duck

8. ______________________

- ☐ Arm
- ☐ Wrist
- ☐ Elbow
- ☐ Shoulder
- ☐ Leg
- ☐ Ankle
- ☐ Knee
- ☐ Thigh
- ☐ Hand
- ☐ Fingers
- ☐ Palm

EXERCISE 12.3 Labeling Outlines

Write titles for the following lists and label the items in them with Roman numerals and capital letters. See the example in Figure 12.2 below and read "How to Label Outlines" on page 106.

1. Arm, Wrist, Elbow, Leg, Thigh, Knee, Shin

2. Bird, Cuckoo, Gull, Dog, Greyhound, Terrier, Spaniel, Snake, Asp, Python, Boa Constrictor

3. Length, Inch, Foot, Yard, Mile, Volume, Ounce, Cup, Pint, Quart, Gallon

FIGURE 12.2

Example of How to Do Exercises 12.3–12.5

Study Equipment

I. Furniture
   - A. Desk
   - B. Chair
   - C. Bookcase

II. Paper products
   - A. Notebook paper
   - B. Typing paper
   - C. Index cards
   - D. File folders

III. Miscellaneous
   - A. Rubber bands
   - B. Paper clips

EXERCISE 12.4 Labeling Outlines

Write titles for the following lists and label the items in them with Roman numerals and capital letters. See the example in Figure 12.2 on page 109 and read "How to Label Outlines" on page 106.

1. Individual, Hiking, Swimming, Bicycling, Jogging, Javelin, Two-person, Tennis, Badminton, Ping-Pong, Handball, Boxing, Wrestling, Team, Baseball, Football, Basketball, Volleyball, Soccer, Hockey
2. String, Violin, Cello, Viola, Woodwind, Piccolo, Oboe, Flute, Clarinet, Saxophone, Brass, Trumpet, Trombone, Tuba, Percussion, Xylophone, Bass drum, Kettledrum, Snare drum, Tambourine, Castanets

EXERCISE 12.5 Labeling Outlines

Write titles for the following lists and label the items in them with Roman numerals and capital letters. See the example in Figure 12.2 on page 109 and read "How to Label Outlines" on page 106.

1. Sex, Male, Female, Marital status, Single, Married, Divorced, Age, Weight, Height, Address, Street, City, State, Zip code, Education, High school, College, Previous jobs
2. Office, Secretary, Typist, Clerk, Manager, Hospital, Nurse, Doctor, Dietician, Library, School, Principal, Teacher, Custodian, Factory, Store, Buyer, Salesperson, Stock person

EXERCISE 12.6 Labeling Outlines

Write titles for the following lists and label the items in them with Roman numerals, capital letters, and Arabic numerals. See the example in Figure 12.3 on page 111 and read "How to Label Outlines" on page 106.

1. Restaurant, Dining room, Host, Waiters, Dish carrier, Kitchen, Chef, Baker, Dishwasher, Store, Sales floor, Salespeople, Cashiers, Back room, Wrappers, Stock people, Cleaning staff, Hospital, Doctors, Nurses, Lab technicians
2. Individual, Water, Swimming, Diving, Surfing, Land, Hiking, Jogging, Bicycling, Two-person, Table, Ping-Pong, Pool/billiards, Court, Tennis, Handball, Team, Baseball, Football, Basketball, Soccer

EXERCISE 12.7 Labeling Outlines

Write titles for the following lists and label the items in them with Roman numerals, capital letters, and Arabic numerals. See the example in Figure 12.3 below and read "How to Label Outlines" on page 106.

1. Produce, Fruit, Apples, Bananas, Grapefruit, Vegetables, Potatoes, Lettuce, Onions, Dairy, Eggs, Cheese, Swiss, American, Cheddar, Milk, Meat, Beef, Hamburger, Chuck steak, Pork
2. Nonalcoholic, Milk, Skim, Whole, Buttermilk, Fruit juice, Orange, Grape, Apple, Soda, Cola, Ginger ale, Alcoholic, Beer, Wine, Californian, French, Liquor, Gin, Vodka, Scotch

FIGURE 12.3

Example of How to Do Exercises 12.6–12.10

Celebrities' Birth Years

I. Born in the 1950s
   A. Men
      1. Kevin Costner, 1955
      2. Prince, 1958
   B. Women
      1. Debbie Allen, 1951
      2. Kim Basinger, 1953
      3. Madonna, 1958

II. Born in the 1960s
   A. Men
      1. Sean Penn, 1960
      2. Eddie Murphy, 1961
      3. Tom Cruise, 1962
      4. John Cusack, 1966
   B. Women
      1. Demi Moore, 1962
      2. Paula Abdul, 1962

EXERCISE 12.8 Labeling Outlines

Write titles for the following lists and label the items in them with Roman numerals, capital letters, and Arabic numerals. See the example in Figure 12.3 on page 111 and read "How to Label Outlines" on page 106.

1. Hot, Cereal, Oatmeal, Cream of Wheat, Eggs, Fried, Scrambled, Meat, Bacon, Ham, Beverages, Coffee, Cocoa, Cold, Cereal, Cornflakes, Shredded Wheat, Raisin bran, Juice, Orange, Apple
2. Grooming aids, Mouth, Toothpaste, Mouthwash, Hair, Shampoo, Conditioner, Body, Soap, Deodorant, Drugs, Aspirin, Laxative, Iodine, Beauty aids, Face, Lipstick, Cheek blush, Hands, Nail polish, Hand cream

EXERCISE 12.9 Labeling Outlines

Write titles for the following lists and label the items in them with Roman numerals, capital letters, and Arabic numerals. See the example in Figure 12.3 on page 111 and read "How to Label Outlines" on page 106.

1. Field, Baseball, Football, Soccer, Table, Card, Poker, Gin, Rummy, Boxed, Scrabble, Monopoly, Court, Racket, Tennis, Badminton, Nonracket, Volleyball, Handball
2. Fall–winter, November, Veterans Day, Thanksgiving Day, December–January, Christmas, New Year's Day, Martin Luther King Day, February, Presidents' Day, Valentine's Day, Spring, Easter, Mother's Day, Memorial Day, Summer, Father's Day, Independence Day, Labor Day

EXERCISE 12.10 Labeling Outlines

Write titles for the following lists and label the items in them with Roman numerals, capital letters, and Arabic numerals. See the example in Figure 12.3 on page 111 and read "How to Label Outlines" on page 106.

1. Pie, Fruit, Apple, Cherry, Cream, Banana, Chocolate, Cake, Pound, Angel food, Fruit, Jell-O, Fruit, Ice cream, Sundae, Chocolate, Butterscotch, Strawberry, Soda, Shake
2. Furniture, Seats, Sofas, Chairs, Benches, Tables, Dining, Coffee, End, Bookcases, Beds, Dressers, Accessories, Walls, Pictures, Mirrors, Table tops, Lamps, Plants, Figurines

13

Make Well-organized Outlines

If you have done the exercises in Chapter 12, you know the traditional method for labeling major thoughts, details, and minor details in outlines. This chapter provides additional information and practice that will help you learn how to make outlines of textbook selections. As you do the exercises in this chapter, keep in mind that you are doing them to develop skills you will use when you take class notes, mark textbooks, make notes about information you want to learn in textbooks, and store information in your memory.

Topic and Sentence Outlines

Outlines are of two basic types: topic outlines and sentence outlines. The outline in Figure 13.1 on page 114 is a topic outline; the statements in it are all phrases. The following outline is a sentence outline; the statements in it are all sentences.

Outlines

I. Outlines have two basic characteristics.
   A. They are accurate summaries of information.
   B. They are organized to show how ideas are related.
II. Outlines are written in a specific format.
   A. They begin with titles.
   B. Statements are labeled with numbers and letters.
      1. Roman numerals label major thoughts.
      2. Capital letters label details.
      3. Arabic numerals label minor details.

When you submit an outline to a teacher for a paper you will write or a speech you will give, the statements in it should be all phrases or all sentences. However, when you prepare outlines for your own purposes, you may use a combination of phrases and sentences.

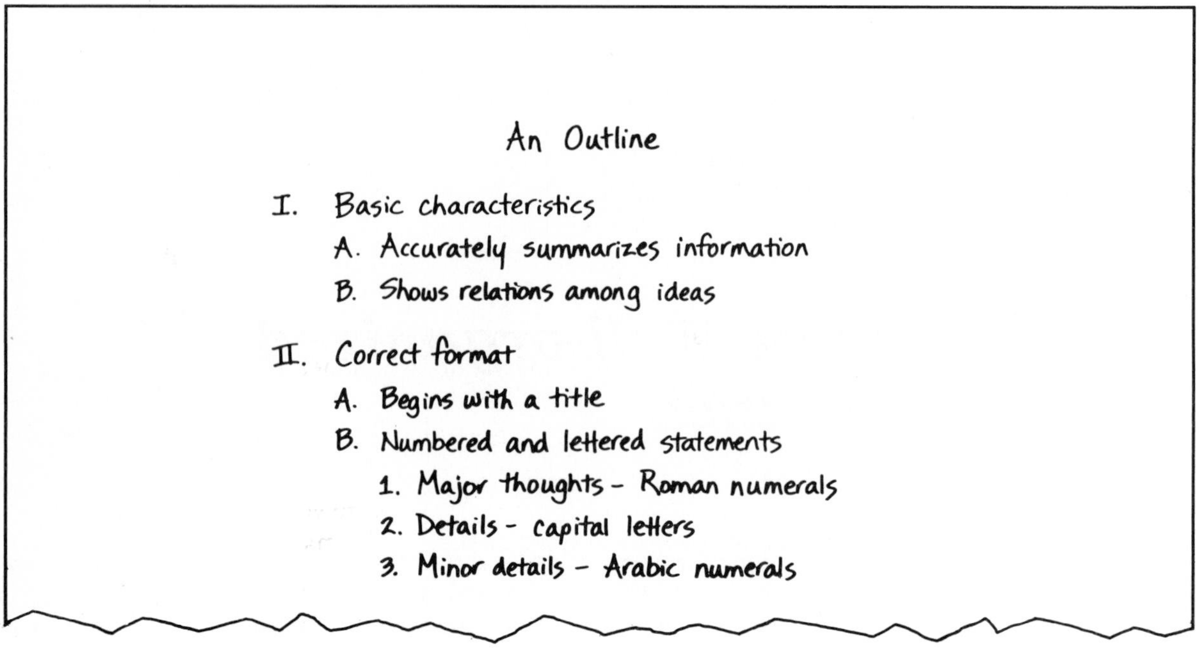
An Outline
I. Basic characteristics
A. Accurately summarizes information
B. Shows relations among ideas
II. Correct format
A. Begins with a title
B. Numbered and lettered statements
1. Major thoughts - Roman numerals
2. Details - capital letters
3. Minor details - Arabic numerals

FIGURE 13.1
A Topic Outline

How to Make Outlines

Use the following procedures to make outlines for the exercises at the end of this chapter.

1. Make coordinate outlines.
   - Always use at least two Roman numerals (**I** and **II**).
   - If you use capital letters under a Roman numeral, always use at least two (**A** and **B**).
   - If you use Arabic numerals under a capital letter, always use at least two (**1** and **2**).
2. Always subordinate items if they can be subordinated.
3. Outline information in the order in which it is written in a passage (rather than rearrange the sequence).
4. Write titles for your outlines that summarize the information in the passage.

All the exercises in *College Study Skills* are designed to help you learn how to make coordinate outlines. If you prepare an outline with an **I** but no **II,** an **A** but not **B,** or a **1** but no **2,** you know that you have made a mistake. Also, one of the purposes of the exercises in this chapter is to give you practice subordinating items in outlines. Therefore, practice subordinating at every opportunity. If you can write an outline that includes Arabic numerals *or* an outline that includes no Arabic numerals, write the one that includes Arabic numerals.

When you are dissatisfied with an outline you make, refer to these directions; they will help you to make better outlines in the future.

Evaluation of Outlines

Figure 13.2 shows an example of a model outline like ones your instructor may give you to score and evaluate the outlines you make. If your instructor makes these models available to you, use the following procedures to score your outlines.

1. Score 10 points if you write a title that summarizes the information in a passage.
2. Score 30 points if you have the same number of Roman numerals as a model *and* the information next to your Roman numerals is essentially the same as the information in a model.
3. Score the points shown for each set of capital letters or Arabic numerals when you have the same number of capital letters or Arabic numerals as shown in a model *and* the information next to your capital letters or Arabic numerals is essentially the same as the information in a model.

In the models, the points for sets of details and minor details are distributed so that the maximum score for an outline is always 100.

FIGURE 13.2

A Model for the Outline in Figure 13.1

10 [Outlines

30 [
I. Have two basic characteristics
20 [
A. Accurate summaries of information
B. Organized to show how ideas are related

II. Are prepared in a specific format]
20 [
A. Begin with a title
B. Have statements correctly labeled
20 [
1. Roman numerals for major thoughts
2. Capital letters for details
3. Arabic numerals for minor details

EXERCISE 13.1 Advertising

Outline the following passage using the procedures explained in "How to Make Outlines" on page 114. Do not outline the first sentence, which is the introduction. Use the following numbers and letters: I, A, B, C, II, A, B, III, A, B.

There are three basic types of advertising: selective, primary demand, and institutional.

I *Selective advertising* promotes the sale of specific brand name products, such as Bayer aspirin, Ford automobiles, and Maxwell House coffee.

II *Primary demand advertising*, on the other hand, encourages the total demand for a product without promoting any single brand. For example, advertisements of the Wool Bureau attempt to convince consumers to purchase clothing made of wool rather than synthetic fibers. Similarly, the American Dairy Association advises us to "Drink More Milk."

III The third type, *institutional advertising*, has as its purpose to create good will toward the advertiser. When a utility company runs an ad that explains how to save money on electric bills or when an insurance company sponsors a television commercial that explains how to maintain good health, it uses institutional advertising. Any advertisement designed to make you think well of a company or organization, and that does not request you to make a purchase, is an example of institutional advertising.

EXERCISE 13.2 News Stories

Outline the following passage using the procedures explained in "How to Make Outlines" on page 114. Do not outline the first sentence, which is the introduction. Use only Roman numerals in your outline.

Doris A. Graber has argued that five criteria are used most often for choosing news stories, and all are related to popular appeal rather than political significance.[1] First, the content of stories must have a *high impact* on the audience. The kidnapping of a local child will usually be more interesting than the deaths of many unknown persons far away. Second, interest will be heightened if a story deals with "natural or man-made *violence, conflict, disaster,* or *scandal.*"[2] People find events of this sort endlessly fascinating in real life as well as in the world of fiction.

Familiarity is the third element of newsworthiness. The more the public knows about famous people and institutions, the more they want to know. Thus, established politicians and celebrities receive more coverage than persons who have not yet found a way to public prominence. Fourth, the public likes *novel* and *up-to-date* stories. Interest can wane quickly. Finally, *local events* are generally more newsworthy than stories from far away. As Graber points out, this kind of interest is what keeps small-town newspapers and local television alive. *Local* can be an elastic term, however. Washington and Hollywood have become so familiar that they may seem local to the regular TV viewer.

References

1. These factors are discussed in Doris Graber, *Mass Media and American Politics*, 2nd ed. (Washington, D.C.: Congressional Quarterly Press, 1984), pp. 78–79.
2. Graber, *Mass Media*, p. 78.

EXERCISE 13.3 Property

Outline the following passage using the procedure explained in "How to Make Outlines" on page 114. Do not outline the first sentence of the first paragraph or the first sentence of the second paragraph, which are introductions. Begin your outline as follows: I, A, 1, 2, 3, 4, 5, 6, B.

Property is of two basic types: real property and personal property. **Real property** includes land, buildings on the land, mineral deposits beneath the land, bodies of water on the land, anything attached to the land (such as fences and oil wells), and the air above the land. By contrast, furniture, clothing, money, automobiles, books, and other property not attached to land is **personal property.**

Property may be acquired by inheritance, legacy, or accession. **Inheritance** refers to ancestry and the acquisition of property under laws of inheritance, which specify who will receive the property of a person who dies leaving no will and who may not be excluded from receiving such property. Property is acquired by **legacy** when it is so specified in a properly executed will. You acquire property by **accession** when there is an increase in something you already own. If your rosebush blooms or your cat has a litter, the roses and kittens are yours by right of accession.

EXERCISE 13.4 Misspellings

Outline the following passage using the procedures explained in "How to Make Outlines" on page 114. Do not underline the first paragraph, which is the introduction. Use the following numbers and letters: I, A, B, 1, 2, C, II, A, B, 1, 2, C, III.

Among the most frequently misspelled English words are *two, too, to, they're, there,* and *their.* If you confuse the spellings of these words, you should benefit from the observations made here.

The confusion among *two, too,* and *to* may be overcome by remembering three things. First, use *two* only when counting (as in "*two* heads are better than one"). Second, use *too* when you intend to say "also" or "overly." For example:

"I hope you will come *too* (also)."
"She is *too* (overly) kind."

Third, use *to* when you cannot use *too* or *two*!

Problems with *they're, there,* and *their* may also be solved rather easily. Use *they're* only when you wish to say "they are," as in "they're going to the party." Use *there* when you wish to say "at or in that place"—for example, "over *there*" or "it's *there.*" Then use *their* when you cannot use *they're* or *there.*

If you have difficulty with the spellings of any of these words, you will probably be interested to know that *a lot* is two words, not one word.

EXERCISE 13.5 Families

Outline the following passage using the procedures explained in "How to Make Outlines" on page 114. Do not outline the first sentence, which is the introduction. Use Roman numerals, capital letters, and Arabic numerals in your outline.

There are several ways in which sociologists may view families.

A **nuclear family** consists of parents and their children. Most people are born into a nuclear family—their family of orientation—and then go on to establish a nuclear family of their own—their family of procreation. The only possible members of a *family of orientation* are a mother, father, brothers, and sisters. Your *family of procreation* may include your spouse, sons, and daughters.

The **extended family** is another term sociologists use to describe family relationships. Exactly who is considered a member of an extended family differs from country to country, but in the United States the extended family is usually considered to include children, parents, and other relatives who live with them in the same house or very near by.

Families may also be viewed in terms of the number of partners in a marriage. In our country we have **monogamous families**—there is only one husband and one wife in a marriage partnership. In some societies, though, there are **polygamous families** with more than two marriage partners. Polygyny is the form of polygamy in which there is one husband and two or more wives; polyandry is the form in which one wife has two or more husbands.

EXERCISE 13.6 Tests

Outline the following passage using the procedures explained in "How to Make Outlines" on page 114. Do not outline the first sentence, which is the introduction. Begin your outline as follows: I, A, 1, 2, B, 1, 2.

Some educators believe that multiple-choice and true-false tests are fairer to students than essay tests.

Critics claim that essay tests have three disadvantages. First, they say, the reader of an essay test may be unduly influenced by the writing talent of the test takers. As a result, students with good writing ability may get high grades although they may not have mastered course content, and students with poor writing ability may get low grades even though they have an excellent grasp of what they were supposed to learn. The second major problem, critics argue, is that the "halo effect" sometimes operates when essay tests are graded. For example, a teacher who has the notion that a student is below average might let this idea influence the grading of the student's essay and give the student's good essay a low mark. On the other hand, an instructor who has the impression that a student is capable of superior work might give the student's poor essay a higher grade than it deserves. Finally, teachers are known to vary in their opinions, and, as a result, the same answer to an essay question might be graded high by one instructor and low by another.

Those who favor the use of multiple-choice and true-false tests say that their primary advantage is that they do not require students to be graded on writing ability. Also, the halo effect has no chance to operate because an instructor's opinion of a student does not enter into the grading of the student's test in any way. Finally, since multiple-choice and true-false tests are graded using an answer key, teachers' judgments of students' scores on a test cannot vary if the answer key is used correctly.

EXERCISE 13.7 Products

Outline the following passage using the procedures explained in "How to Make Outlines" on page 114. Do not outline the first sentence, which is the introduction. Use Roman numerals and capital letters in your outline.

The names for products come from a great variety of sources. Many famous brand names such as *Arrow, Carnation,* and *Bumble Bee* were chosen by studying the pages of a dictionary. Coined, or invented, words are another major source of brand names. *Vaseline, Kodak,* and *Kleenex* are a few of the well-known words in our vocabulary that did not exist until they were coined to name products. *Elizabeth Arden* and *John Hancock* are examples of brand names that come from the names of real people; *Pittsburgh* paint and *Olympia* beer are two of the many products that took their names from geographical locations. Even initials and numbers have been used: *IBM, Heinz 57,* and *A-1,* for example.

EXERCISE 13.8 Spelling

Outline the following passage using the procedures explained in "How to Make Outlines" on page 114. Do not outline the first sentence, which is the introduction. Use Roman numerals, capital letters, and Arabic numerals in your outline.

There are two important spelling rules that many writers of English never master. Many people are not certain when to drop a final silent *e* before adding a suffix to an English root word and when not to drop it. The final *e* is almost always dropped before a suffix that begins with a vowel. For example, the final *e* in *care* is dropped before *-ing* is added to spell *caring,* and the final *e* in *cure* is dropped before *-able* is added to spell *curable.* The final *e* is not dropped before endings that begin with consonants. Thus, the final *e* in *care* is not dropped before *-ful* is added to spell *careful,* and the final *e* in *white* is not dropped before *-ness* is added to spell *whiteness.*

Confusion also exists about when to change a final *y* to *i* before adding a suffix to an English root word and when not to change it. There are, however, only two simple rules to remember. First, *y* is usually changed to *i* before any suffix if there is a consonant in front of the *y.* Examples are *beauty* and *beautiful, happy* and *happier,* and *silly* and *silliness.* Second, *y* is not changed to *i* when there is a vowel in front of the *y.* Examples are *destroy* and *destroyer, pay* and *payable,* and *annoy* and *annoyance.*

EXERCISE 13.9 Behavior Disorders

Outline the following passage using the procedures explained in "How to Make Outlines" on page 114. Do not outline the first paragraph, which is the introduction. Use Roman numerals, capital letters, and Arabic numerals in your outline.

Exam

Neuroses are relatively mild behavior disorders. However, they are sometimes sufficiently disturbing that it is necessary for individuals showing the symptoms of neuroses to seek professional help.

Anxiety reactions, constituting the most common neurosis, are found in people who have much more tension than average people have. Sometimes people who suffer from this neurosis are overtaken by the strong feeling that something unfortunate is about to happen. This feeling may be accompanied by physical responses, such as weakness, fast breathing, or the desire to vomit.

There are two basic types of **obsessive-compulsive reactions:** obsessive thoughts and compulsive acts. *Obsessive thoughts* are unwelcome thoughts that crowd the neurotic's mind to the extent that they interfere with normal activity. The person may, for example, have recurring thoughts of killing a spouse, jumping out a window, or committing a crime. *Compulsive acts* often serve the purpose of making a person feel better about obsessive thoughts. A man who has continual thoughts of killing his wife may call her several times a day to check on her well-being; people who have the obsessive thought that they will say something "dirty" may brush their teeth many times a day.

Phobic reactions are uncontrollable fears about dangers that do not exist, or fears that are too great in relation to the danger that actually exists. Acrophobia and claustrophobia are two of the many phobic reactions. *Acrophobia* is the excessive fear of height. A person who cannot look out the window of a skyscraper or cannot cross a bridge without extreme discomfort may be suffering from acrophobia. *Claustrophobia* is the fear of being in small, closed places. A person who cannot enter an elevator or walk into a large closet without experiencing great distress may be a victim of claustrophobia.

PART

IV

Study for Tests

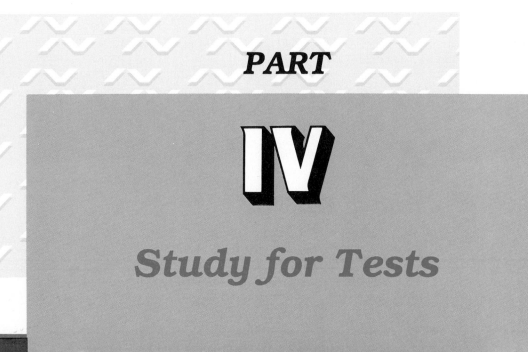

Preview of PART IV

Some students have difficulty when they take tests because they prepare for them by reading rather than by studying. **Reading** is the process we use to understand information presented in writing, but **studying** is the process that is used to learn and remember information. Studying calls for using procedures such as the following:

- Take good class notes.
- Use study aids provided in textbooks.
- Mark your textbooks.
- Make notes for information in textbooks.
- Anticipate test questions.
- Recite, rehearse, and review from notes.

These and other study procedures are explained in the next seven chapters. Several chapters in Part I and Part II of *College Study Skills* explain additional study procedures, especially Chapters 2, 5, 6, 10, and 11.

14

Use Effective Study Methods

Studying involves identifying the information you want to learn, organizing it for easy learning, and using effective methods to remember and recall it. The procedures for effective study have been stated in a variety of ways, including the well-known SQ3R study formula, which is summarized in Exercise 14.1 on page 129. SQ3R represents five study steps: Survey, Question, Read, Recite, and Review.

About twenty years ago I developed the SOAR study formula to emphasize the importance of organization for efficient learning. Following is a slightly revised version of the SOAR study procedure:

The SOAR Study Formula

1. **Survey** before you read.
   - Survey textbooks (see Chapter 15).
   - Survey chapters (see Chapter 16).
2. **Organize** information in lectures and books.
   - Take good class notes (see Chapter 17).
   - Mark your textbooks (see Chapter 18).
   - Make notes for textbooks (see Chapter 19).
3. **Anticipate** test questions (see pages 125–127).
4. **Remember and recall** information (see Chapter 20).

The four steps in this formula are represented by SOAR: Survey, Organize, Anticipate, and Remember and Recall. This chapter gives an overview of the procedures for effective study that are summarized in the SOAR study formula and explained in detail in Chapters 15–20.

Survey Before You Read

For most of your courses, you will need to learn information in textbooks. **Textbooks** are books that summarize information taught in college courses, such as the books teachers assign for psychology, business, and chemistry courses.

FIGURE 14.1
An Example of Highlighting

Conflict

We encounter conflict when we must choose between two or more alternatives. There are three basic types of conflict: approach-approach, avoidance-avoidance, and approach-avoidance.

The **approach-approach conflict** is the need to choose between two attractive alternatives. The need to choose between vacationing in England or France is an example of an approach-approach conflict. This type of conflict is resolved when one possibility becomes more attractive than the other. If a vacation in England will include visits with friends and the trip to France will not, then England may become the more attractive choice.

The **avoidance-avoidance conflict** exists when you must choose between two *un*attractive alternatives. An example is the need to decide whether you will have a tooth pulled or have root canal work done on it. This type of conflict is resolved when one possibility becomes more *un*attractive than the other. If having a tooth pulled becomes more unattractive, you may choose to have root canal work done on the tooth.

The **approach-avoidance conflict** is present when one possibility or goal is both attractive and unattractive. The pursuit of a college degree is an approach-avoidance conflict for many students. It is attractive because a college degree may lead to better job opportunities in the future. But it is unattractive because it requires students to study hard and to take courses that they may prefer not to take. This type of conflict is often resolved unsatisfactorily. For instance, many students resolve their conflict about college study by dropping out of college. Later many of these people regret that they did not stay in school and earn a college degree.

Survey your books when you purchase them at the beginning of each term, and survey the chapters in your textbooks before you read them. A **survey of a book** includes reading the preface, introduction, and table of contents to learn how the book is organized and what its major features are. A **survey of a chapter** involves reading the introduction, headings, and closing summary. It takes only a few minutes to survey a chapter, but this is time well spent because it provides background information that increases reading comprehension. The methods for surveying are explained in Chapters 15 and 16.

Organize What You Read

One of the best-known facts about human learning is that information is easier to learn when it is organized in a meaningful way. Begin by taking well-organized class notes.

It is essential for you to have good notes about what your teachers say in your classes. During class meetings your teachers will explain information in required course reading material that they know is difficult for many students to understand, and they will provide important information that is not printed in course textbooks. They will also give hints about what you should study

FIGURE 14.2
Notes for the Passage in Figure 14.1

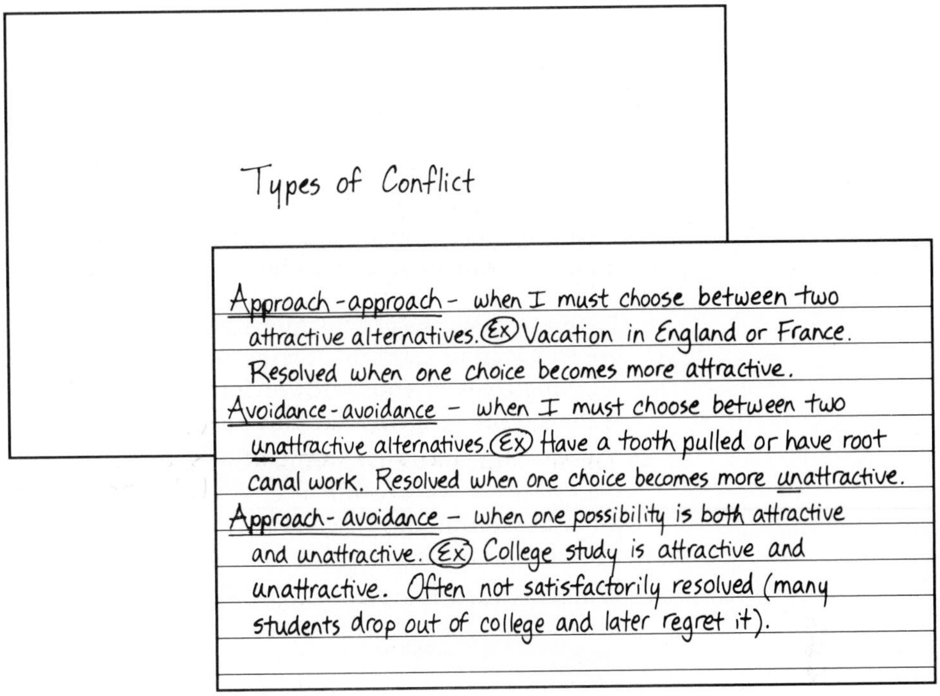
Types of Conflict
Approach-approach - when I must choose between two attractive alternatives. (Ex) Vacation in England or France. Resolved when one choice becomes more attractive.
Avoidance-avoidance - when I must choose between two unattractive alternatives. (Ex) Have a tooth pulled or have root canal work. Resolved when one choice becomes more unattractive.
Approach-avoidance - when one possibility is both attractive and unattractive. (Ex) College study is attractive and unattractive. Often not satisfactorily resolved (many students drop out of college and later regret it).

when you prepare for tests. You need records of these kinds of information if you want to do your best when you take tests. Chapter 17 explains how to take complete and well-organized class notes.

Also, organize the information in your textbooks. Figure 14.1 on page 124 and Figure 14.2 above illustrate how to organize information in a textbook by marking it and summarizing it in well-organized notes. The skills you developed when you studied Chapters 12 and 13 will help you learn how to take good class notes, mark books, and make notes for textbooks when you study Chapters 17–19.

Anticipate Test Questions

The questions that appear on college tests tend to emphasize the information that is most important for students to know. Therefore, if you anticipate test questions, you will study the things that are most important for you to learn, and you will also be more likely to earn good test grades.

Use Class Notes as a Guide

Most college teachers use class time to help students understand the things that are important for them to learn. As a result, the notes you take in class will usually be your best source of information about test questions. When you study your notes, be certain to give special attention to the following:

- Information you copy from the chalkboard
- Information teachers said is important or difficult to learn
- Information teachers stated while reading directly from their notes
- Information about topics that are also discussed in required course reading material

Mark these four types of information so that you don't overlook them when you study. You might draw a star or write *Important* in the margin next to the information, or you might mark it with yellow highlighting ink so it will stand out in your notes when you prepare for tests.

Use Textbook Helps

Use learning goals, review questions, lists of terminology, and exercises and problems in your textbooks to help you anticipate test questions.

- **Learning goals** and **review questions** give information about what students are expected to learn in a textbook. Therefore, when a chapter begins with learning goals or ends with review questions, make certain that you have achieved the goals or that you can answer the questions.
- The meaning of course **terminology** is usually tested in many questions on college tests. As a result, it is essential that you make certain you know all of the terminology that is listed at the end of chapters or that is printed in italics or boldface within chapters.
- When instructors assign you to do **exercises** or solve **problems** in a textbook, they will also usually require you to do similar exercises or to solve similar problems on tests. Therefore, when you take a test, be prepared to do any kinds of exercises or to solve any types of problems that are in the course textbook.

These features of textbooks are explained in Chapter 16.

Attend Test Reviews

If your instructors give test reviews, attend them, take complete notes, and learn everything that you are told to learn. Teachers who give reviews want to help you do your best. Use the "Test Review Checklist" on page 127 to be certain you are well informed about each test you take.

Talk with Teachers' Former Students

If at all possible, ask former students of your teachers how to study for tests. Teachers' testing methods seldom change much from year to year. As a result, students who studied with your teachers in the past have answered test questions very much like the ones you will answer. Students who received good grades for the courses you are taking know things that may be very useful to you. They may be eager to explain the methods that they used to earn good grades.

Examine Teachers' Past Tests

Some teachers give students tests to keep, and some schools place tests on file for students to examine. Ask your teachers' former students if they have copies of tests you may examine, and if your teachers' tests are on file, locate them and study them.

Also, analyze the questions on the first test you take for a course; they will give you hints about the types of things to learn for subsequent tests. For instance, if the questions on a first test are mostly about little facts in a textbook, that teacher's other tests are also likely to focus on the same kinds of facts—study them for the next test.

Test Review Checklist

Before you take a test you should know the answers to all the questions in this checklist so that you can prepare for the test properly. Write checks in pencil so you can erase them and reuse the checklist before each test you take.

- ☐ What material will be covered on the test?
- ☐ Will equal importance be given to information in the textbook, class notes, and handouts or will greater importance be given to one of these?
- ☐ What specific suggestions does the teacher have about what you should study in preparation for the test?
- ☐ Will you be allowed to refer to any books, notes, or handouts during the test?
- ☐ Will you be allowed to use a calculator or other equipment during the test?
- ☐ Must you bring any material or equipment to the test?
- ☐ What kinds of problems, if any, will you be required to solve?
- ☐ Will you answer true-false, multiple-choice, matching, fill-in, essay, or some other kind of questions?
- ☐ How many minutes long will the test be?
- ☐ Where will the test be given?
- ☐ Will the test be similar to earlier tests the teacher gave?

Try to find the answers to any questions in this list that you did not check.

Learn "Easy" Information

Some students believe incorrectly that if information is easy for them to understand, they know it. However, the difference between understanding and knowing is the difference between reading and studying. Reading is done to understand information; studying is done to remember and recall it.

You have no doubt understood everything you have read about how to study in *College Study Skills*. However, you cannot recall most of the information in this book unless you have studied it. For instance, when you read Chapter 11, you understood the methods listed there for increasing your concentration; however, you cannot recall all the methods unless you studied them. Without looking back at Chapter 11, list the methods it suggests you use to concentrate for longer periods. Unless you studied Chapter 11, or looked back at it, you were probably not able to list accurately the ten suggestions it gives for increasing concentration.

When you study for tests, make certain that you learn easy-to-understand information. It is extremely disappointing to lose points on tests for failure to learn information that you could have learned easily.

Remember and Recall

Many students try to learn information in books and notes by reading and rereading it. These students believe incorrectly that reading and studying are the same process.

It is true that books must be read to study them; however, books may be read *without* studying them! **Reading** is the process that is used to understand information that is presented in writing. It involves such activities as locating the major thoughts and the details that are related to them. **Studying,** on the other hand, is the process that is used to decide what to learn, to organize it, and to use effective methods to remember and recall it.

Most information stays in your memory only about twenty seconds unless you do something to store it there (see Chapter 5). When you want to remember and recall information, you must recite it, rehearse it, and review it.

- **Recitation** is the act of repeating information silently or aloud until you can recall it without reading it.
- **Rehearsal** is the act of analyzing information and relating it to information that is already stored in memory.
- **Review** is the repetition of recitation and rehearsal that makes it possible to retrieve information quickly when it is needed.

Much of what we learn is difficult to retrieve unless we review it. If you find that you have difficulty recalling information you studied for tests, you probably did not review sufficiently. You will remember best what you review most. Chapter 20 explains how to recite, rehearse, and review.

EXERCISE 14.1 Your Study Procedures

Write a description of the study procedures you use, comparing them to the SOAR study procedure outlined in this chapter and the SQ3R study method described in the following passage.

The SQ3R Study Method

An excellent set of suggestions for effective studying is to be found in the *SQ3R Study Method* designed by Francis Robinson at Ohio State University. The five steps are *Survey, Question, Read, Recite,* and *Review.* Each is described briefly here.

Survey To survey a chapter, begin by reading the various headings and subheadings. In this way you learn generally what the chapter is about, and you know what to expect. Skim some of the first sentences and look at any pictures, tables, or graphs. If there is a summary, read it as part of your survey, because it will give you the important points of the chapter. The survey technique increases your ability to understand and learn new material.

Question Some textbooks have lists of questions at the beginning or end of each chapter. If a book has them, use them and try to answer them. Try to think about the material and ask yourself questions about it. Asking questions is a way of actively taking part in the learning process. Active participation is a key to learning. Questions also are ways of testing yourself to see what you have learned.

Read The next step is to read. Read carefully and try to answer the questions that you have asked yourself. Make sure that you read everything—tables, graphs, and captions as well as the main text. Students often say, "I forget what I read as soon as I put the book down." So read to remember by telling yourself to remember. Notice particularly any words or phrases that are italicized, because authors use italics to point out important terms, concepts, and principles.

Recite Recitation is an important part of effective studying. Recite, not just in class periods, but to yourself by recalling what you have read. Recitation takes a lot of effort, for it is easy just to read and put the book away. Try to recall main headings and main ideas. For example, what does SQ3R stand for? As you read, stop several times and recite to yourself the major points that are being presented in the text. Recitation is important because it helps prevent forgetting by forcing you to keep your attention on the task.

Review The fifth step in the SQ3R technique is to review. Review is important for remembering. The best times for review are right after first studying and again just before a test. Most good students try to get one or two reviews in between. These reviews include rereading and recitation.

EXERCISE 14.2 Anticipating Test Questions

Write the name of the most difficult course you are taking on the line.

____

Check the items in the following list that are sources of help for you in anticipating test questions for this course.

- ☐ The teacher writes important information on the chalkboard.
- ☐ The teacher sometimes mentions that specific information is important or difficult to learn.
- ☐ The teacher covers topics in class that are also discussed in the textbook.
- ☐ There are learning goals at the beginning of textbook chapters.
- ☐ Terminology is listed at the end of textbook chapters or it is printed in italics or boldface in the chapters.
- ☐ There are review questions or problems at the end of textbook chapters.
- ☐ The teacher gives test reviews.
- ☐ I know some of the teacher's former students who can tell me how to study for the teacher's tests.
- ☐ Tests the teacher gave in the past are available for me to examine.
- ☐ I have already taken one of the teacher's tests and examined it to figure out what kinds of questions might be on the teacher's next test.

EXERCISE 14.3 Anticipating Test Questions

Write the name of another difficult course on the line below.

____

Check the items in the following list that are sources of help for you in anticipating test questions for this course.

- ☐ The teacher writes important information on the chalkboard.
- ☐ The teacher sometimes mentions that specific information is important or difficult to learn.
- ☐ The teacher covers topics in class that are also discussed in the textbook.
- ☐ There are learning goals at the beginning of textbook chapters.
- ☐ Terminology is listed at the end of textbook chapters or it is printed in italics or boldface in the chapters.
- ☐ There are review questions or problems at the end of textbook chapters.
- ☐ The teacher gives test reviews.
- ☐ I know some of the teacher's former students who can tell me how to study for the teacher's tests.
- ☐ Tests the teacher gave in the past are available for me to examine.
- ☐ I have already taken one of the teacher's tests and examined it to figure out what kinds of questions might be on the teacher's next test.

15

Survey Textbooks

If you are a full-time college student, you will usually need to read, study, and learn the information in five or more textbooks each term. This may seem to be an impossible task, but it isn't—thousands of college students do it every year. The first step in studying your textbooks is to survey them soon after you purchase them.

Read "How to Survey a Textbook" on page 132 before you read the discussions that follow.

The Title Page

Begin a survey by reading the **title page.** It gives exact information about the title of a book, the author or authors, the publisher, and the city in which the book was published. The title page is usually the second or third page in a book. When the title of a book is not followed by an edition number, it is the first edition; and when more than one city is listed on a title page, the book was published in the first city listed. There is a title page in Exercise 15.1 on page 134.

The Copyright Page

After you have read the title page, read the page that follows it—the copyright page. A **copyright page** tells when a book was published. When more than one year is listed in the copyright information, the book was published in the most recent year listed. For example, if the years 1994, 1990, and 1986 are listed, the book was published in 1994. The years 1990 and 1988 refer to earlier editions of the book.

The copyright year tells you whether the information in a book is sufficiently up-to-date for your purposes. For instance, if you want to learn about the current tax laws of the United States, you will want to read a book with a very recent copyright date. On the other hand, if you want to learn how to give a speech, a book published ten years ago may give information that is sufficiently up-to-date for this purpose. There is information from a copyright page in Exercise 15.2 on page 135.

How to Survey a Textbook

Before you read a textbook, examine the features in the front and back of the book.

1. Survey the front of the book.
   - Read the **title page** to learn the title, author (or authors), and publisher of the book.
   - Read the **copyright page** to find out the year the book was published.
   - Read the **table of contents** to get an overview of the organization of the book and the major topics discussed in it.
   - Read the **preface** or **introduction** to find out whether it describes special features that are provided in the book to help students learn.
2. Survey the back of the book.
   - Determine whether the last chapter is followed by an **appendix;** if it is, find out what is in the appendix.
   - Check to see if there is a **glossary** at the end of the book or if there are short glossaries in each chapter.
   - Determine whether **references** are listed at the end of the book or at the end of each chapter.
   - Determine whether there is an **index** at the end of the book or if the book has a subject index *and* a name index.

The Table of Contents

Continue your survey by reading the **table of contents,** which provides an overview of the organization of a book and the major topics discussed in it. When a table of contents does not follow the copyright page, look for it following the preface or introduction. There is part of a table of contents in Exercise 15.3 on page 136.

The Preface or Introduction

A **preface** or an **introduction** explains why a book was written; it usually presents information about the purpose, philosophy, or contents of a book, and it often describes special features that are provided to help students learn information in the book. These opening remarks are usually located on pages following the table of contents, but sometimes they appear before the table of contents. Most books have either a preface or an introduction; some books have both. Part of a preface appears in Exercise 15.4 on page 137.

The Appendix

An **appendix,** which contains supplementary material, is usually located immediately after the last chapter. An appendix in a chemistry textbook may present an overview of the mathematics that is important to know in chemistry, and an appendix in an English textbook may explain how to punctuate and capitalize when writing. However, many textbooks have no appendix. There is part of an appendix in Exercise 15.5 on page 138.

The Glossary

A **glossary** is an alphabetically arranged list of important words and their definitions. When a glossary is included in a book, it is usually located after the last chapter or after the appendix. A textbook that has no glossary at the end may have short glossaries at the end of each chapter. There is part of a glossary in Exercise 15.6 on page 139.

The References

The **references,** a **bibliography,** or **notes** are lists of publications and other sources that an author quotes or refers to in a book. References are usually listed at the end of a textbook, following the glossary or last chapter. When they are not at the end of a book, they may be listed at the end of each chapter. Textbooks for subjects such as English, speech, and mathematics usually have no references. There are references in Exercise 15.7 on page 140.

The Index

An **index** is an alphabetically arranged list of subjects and the numbers of the pages on which the subjects are discussed in a book. When an index is included in a book, it is on the very last pages.

Some books have two indexes: a **subject index** and a **name index,** or author index. When a name index (or author index) is included in a book, it is located before the subject index. If you do not find the name of a person in an index, look to see if the book has a name index. For instance, if you do not find Sigmund Freud listed in the index of a psychology textbook, look for his name in the name index or author index. There is a part of a name index in Exercise 15.8 on page 141 and part of a subject index in Exercise 15.9 on page 142.

 NAME ______________________ DATE __________

EXERCISE 15.1 Title Page

Answer the questions that follow the title page.

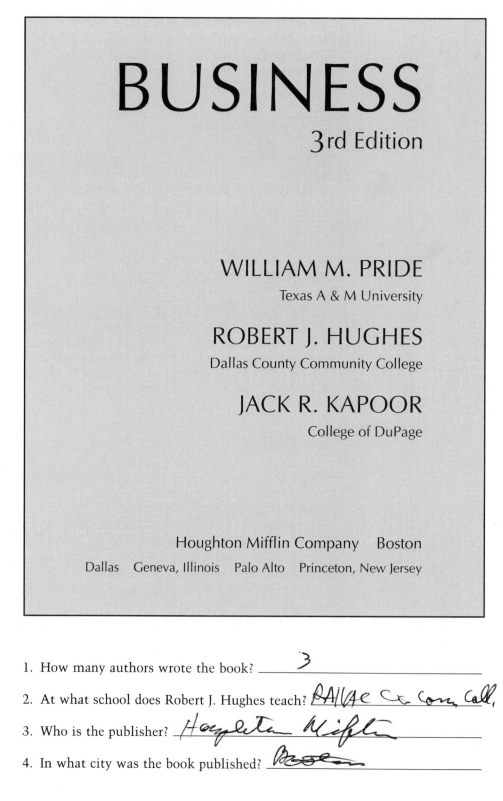

BUSINESS

3rd Edition

WILLIAM M. PRIDE
Texas A & M University

ROBERT J. HUGHES
Dallas County Community College

JACK R. KAPOOR
College of DuPage

Houghton Mifflin Company Boston
Dallas Geneva, Illinois Palo Alto Princeton, New Jersey

1. How many authors wrote the book? 3
2. At what school does Robert J. Hughes teach? Dallas Co. Com. Coll.
3. Who is the publisher? Houghton Mifflin
4. In what city was the book published? Boston

EXERCISE 15.2 Copyright Page

Answer the questions that follow the copyright information from *Business.*

> Copyright © 1991 by Houghton Mifflin Company. All rights reserved.
>
> No part of this work may be reproduced or transmitted in any form or by any means, electronic or mechanical, including photocopying and recording, or by any information storage or retrieval system without the prior written permission of Houghton Mifflin Company unless such copying is expressly permitted by federal copyright law. Address inquiries to College Permissions, Houghton Mifflin Company, One Beacon Street, Boston, MA 02108
>
> Printed in the U.S.A.
>
> Library of Congress Catalog Card Number: 90-83039
>
> ISBN: 0-395-47308-X

1. In what year was the book published? 1991

2. If people want permission to reproduce passages in *Business,* to what address should they write to request the permission?

____

____

____

 NAME ______________________________ DATE ____________

EXERCISE 15.3 Table of Contents

Answer the questions that follow part of the table of contents from *Business.*

CONTENTS

1. What is the title of the first chapter? Foundations of Business

2. On what page is there a summary of Chapter 1? 29

EXERCISE 15.4 Preface

Answer the questions that follow part of the preface of *Business.*

PREFACE

The American system of business is no mere abstraction. It's a network of real people—millions of individuals seeking challenges, opportunities, and excitement through participation in business. Professors and students of business are an important part of this network. The time they invest jointly in examining the business system today bears directly on the success of the business system tomorrow.

Accordingly, we believe that professors and students deserve the best textbook available, one that is current, dynamic, and interesting—just like business itself. We have developed *Business, Third Edition,* to meet this challenge. Along with its comprehensive instructional package, *Business* provides instructors with the opportunity to present business fundamentals effectively and efficiently. For their part, students will enjoy the *Business* experience and will be well prepared for further study in a variety of business fields.

The third edition of *Business* covers new topics, presents expanded coverage of important issues, focuses on small as well as large businesses, provides thorough career information, and contains numerous pedagogical aids. The comprehensive ancillary package includes a computerized study guide and the *Video Resource Manual,* which accompanies *Business Video File,* a free series of twenty-four videos—one for each chapter and the Appendix. Here are several distinctive features of *Business, Third Edition,* and the instructional package that accompanies it.

1. What challenge was the book developed to meet? ____________________

____

2. List three of the five features of the third edition of *Business* that are stated in the third paragraph.

____

____

____

EXERCISE 15.5 Appendix

Answer the questions that follow part of the appendix from *Business.*

APPENDIX

As you look ahead to your own career, you should consider the effects that the trends described below will have on employment and employment opportunities.

- ▶ Jobs in service industries will account for an increasing proportion of total employment.
- ▶ Training—and retraining—will become increasingly important, as firms require their employees to understand and utilize the latest technology. Good jobs will require strong educational qualifications.
- ▶ Automation of factories and offices will create new types of jobs. Many of these will be computer-related. In some cases, employees will be able to complete assignments at home on remote computer terminals.
- ▶ The number of women in the work force, of two-income families, and of older workers will increase. There will be a greater emphasis on job sharing, flexible hours, and other innovative work practices to accommodate employees' special circumstances.

Where will the jobs be? A 1989 survey by *Monthly Labor Review* indicates that paralegals will be in greatest demand, followed closely by medical assistants. Those college graduates with majors in computer science, accounting, business, marketing, and economics will also be in high demand, according to human resources experts. There will be fewer manufacturing jobs, and those that remain will require high-tech skills.

1. Why will the retraining of employees become increasingly important?

   ____

   ____

2. Which two occupations are expected to be in greatest demand in the future? ________________________________

   ____

EXERCISE 15.6 Glossary

Answer the questions that follow part of the glossary from *Business.*

GLOSSARY

absolute advantage the ability to produce a specific product more efficiently than any other nation (23)

accessory equipment standardized equipment used in a variety of ways in a firm's production or office activities (12)

account executive (or **stock broker**) an individual who buys or sells securities for clients (19)

accountability the obligation of a subordinate to accomplish an assigned job or task (6)

accounting equation the basis for the accounting process: Assets = liabilities + owners' equity (16)

accounting the process of systematically collecting, analyzing, and reporting financial information (16)

accounts payable short-term obligations that arise as a result of making credit purchases (16)

accounts receivable turnover a financial ratio that is calculated by dividing net sales by accounts receivable; measures the number of times a firm collects its accounts receivable in one year (16)

accounts receivable amounts that are owed to a firm by its customers (18)

acid-test ratio a financial ratio that is calculated by dividing the sum of cash, marketable securities, accounts receivable, and notes receivable by current liabilities (16)

Active Corps of Executives (ACE) a group of active managers who counsel small-business owners on a volunteer basis (4)

ad hoc committee a committee created for a specific short-term purpose (6)

administrative law the regulations created by government agencies that have been established by legislative bodies (21)

administrative manager a manager who is not associated with any specific functional area but who provides overall administrative guidance and leadership (5)

advertising media the various forms of communication through which advertising reaches its audience (14)

affirmative action program a plan designed to increase the number of minority employees at all levels within an organization (2)

agency a business relationship in which one party (called the principal) appoints a second party (called the agent) to act on behalf of the principal (21)

agency shop a workplace in which employees can choose not to join the union but must pay dues to the union anyway (10)

agent a middleman that facilitates exchanges, represents a buyer or a seller, and often is hired permanently on a commission basis (13)

1. What term has the same meaning as *account executive*?

____

2. What is an *ad hoc committee*? ______________________________

____

3. Must the employees of an *agency shop* join a union?

____

EXERCISE 15.7 References

Answer the questions that follow notes from *Business.*

NOTES

CHAPTER 1

[1] Based on information from Christopher Knowlton, "How Disney Keeps the Magic Going," *Fortune*, December 4, 1989, pp. 111–112, 114, 116, 120, 124, 128, 132; Susan Spillman, "Animation Draws on its Storied Past," *USA Today*, November 15, 1989, pp. 1D, 2D; Richard Turner, "Kermit the Frog Jumps to Walt Disney as Company Buys Henson Associates," *Wall Street Journal*, August 29, 1989, p. 1B. [2] *Fortune*, September 29, 1986, p. 7. [3] Adapted from "The Origins of Enterprise in America," Exxon U.S.A., third quarter 1976, pp. 8–11.

CHAPTER 2

[1] Based on information from Sharon Begley, "Smothering the Waters," *Newsweek*, April 10, 1989, pp. 54–57; Geoffrey Cowley, "Dead Otters, Silent Ducks," *Newsweek*, April 24, 1989, p. 70; Claudia H. Deutsch, "The Giant with a Black Eye," *New York Times*, April 2, 1989, pp. 3-1, 3-8; Stuart Elliot, "Public Angry at Slow Action on Oil Spill," *USA Today*, pp. B1–B2; Philip Shabecoff, "Ship Runs Aground Off Alaska, Causing Largest U.S. Tanker Spill," *New York Times*, March 25, 1989, pp. 1, 19; Michael Satchell, "Tug of War Over Oil Drilling," *U.S. News & World Report*, April 10, 1989, pp. 47–48; Kenneth R. Sheets, "Would You Believe $16.67 an Hour to Scrub Rocks?" *U.S. News & World Report*, April 17, 1989, p. 48; and Rae Tyson, " 'We've Done All We Can Do' On Spill," *USA Today*, April 24, 1989, pp. 1A–2A. [2] CNN poll conducted by the Roper Center of Public Opinion Research, *U.S. News & World Report*, February 23, 1987. [3] O. C. Ferrell and Larry G. Gresham, "A Contingency Framework for Understanding Ethical Decision Making in Marketing," *Journal of Marketing*, Summer 1985, pp. 87–96. [4] "Engineers' Duty to Speak Out," The Nation, June 28, 1986, p. 880. [5] "Ozone Standards," *Environment*, March 1989, p. 24; and Merrill McLoughlin, "Our Dirty Air," *U.S. News & World Report*, June 12, 1989, pp. 48–54. [6] Merrill McLoughlin, "Our Dirty Air," *U.S. News & World Report*, June 12, 1989, pp. 48–54. [7] Dan Morse, "What's Wrong with the Superfund?," *Civil Engineering*, April 1989, pp. 40–43. [8] "Acid Rain Affects Coastal Waters Too," *Environment*, June 1988, p. 22. [9] Merrill McLoughlin, "Our Dirty Air," *U.S. News & World Report*, June 12, 1989, p. 54. [10] "A Biodegradable Recyclable Future," *The Economist*, January 7, 1989, pp. 61–62. [11] Faye Rice, "Where Will We Put All That Garbage?" *Fortune*, April 11, 1988, pp. 96–100. [12] "A Biodegradable Recyclable Future," *The Economist*, January 7, 1989, pp. 61–62. [13] "A Biodegradable Recyclable Future," *The Economist*, January 7, 1989, pp. 61–62. [14] David Landis, "Tighter Rules Put Squeeze on Firms," *USA Today*, May 26, 1989, pp. B-1, B-2.

CHAPTER 3

[1] Based on information from "The Kitchens that Don't Miss a Beat," *Business Week*, June 1989, pp. 45, 49; Erik Larson, "The Man with the Golden Touch," *Inc.*, October 1988, pp. 66–68, 70, 75–76; Stephen Michaelides, "Rich Melman Wears Gym Shoes," *Restaurant Hospitality*, May 1987, pp. 97–102. [2] "The Top 100 Industrial/Service Companies," *Black Entrepreneur*, June 1988, p. 121. [3] Cindy Skrzycki, "Why Nonprofit Businesses Are Booming," *U.S. News & World Report*, January 16, 1984, p. 65. [4] John DuMont, "Swallowing Competition," *Maclean's*, November 7, 1988, p. 42. [5] Ibid. [6] Frank Lichtenberg, "Productivity Improvements from Changes in Ownership," *Mergers and Acquisitions*, September/October 1988, pp. 48–50.

1. Who published the article referred to in the third note for Chapter 1?

______

2. What are the titles of the first three publications referred to in the first note for Chapter 2? ______

______

3. Who wrote the article referred to in the sixth note for Chapter 3?

______

EXERCISE 15.8 Name Index

Answer the questions that follow part of the name index of *Business*.

NAME INDEX

1. On what pages are there references to the Avis car rental company? ______

____

2. On what page is there a reference to Howard Aiken? ______________

3. On what pages are there references to AT&T? ______________________

____

EXERCISE 15.9 Subject Index

Answer the questions that follow part of the subject index of *Business.*

SUBJECT INDEX

1. On what page is *ad hoc committee* explained? ____________

2. On what page is *manufacturer's agent* discussed? ____________

3. On what page is *outdoor advertising* mentioned? ____________

EXERCISE 15.10 Survey of a Textbook

When you do this exercise, use a textbook you are studying for another course; however, if you have no other textbook, answer the questions referring to *College Study Skills.*

1. Title ______________________________
2. Author(s) ______________________________
3. Publisher ______________________________
4. Date of publication ______________________________

Check the items that pertain to the textbook you are surveying.

Table of Contents

☐ It provides an outline of the topics in the textbook.
☐ It shows that the book is divided into parts or sections.

Preface or Introduction

☐ It states for whom the book is intended.
☐ It describes special features that are provided to help students learn.

Appendix

☐ It contains useful or interesting information.
☐ There is no appendix.

Glossary

☐ It is at the end of the book.
☐ There is a short glossary in each chapter.
☐ There is no glossary.

References, Bibliography, or Notes

☐ They are listed at the end of the book.
☐ They are listed at the end of each chapter.
☐ There are no references, bibliography, or notes.

Index

☐ There is a subject index *and* a name (or author) index.
☐ There is only one index.
☐ There is no index.

EXERCISE 15.11 Survey of a Textbook

When you do this exercise, use a textbook other than the one you used when you did Exercise 15.10.

1. Title ______________________
2. Author(s) ______________________
3. Publisher ______________________
4. Date of publication ______________________

Check the items that pertain to the textbook you are surveying.

Table of Contents

☐ It provides an outline of the topics in the textbook.
☐ It shows that the book is divided into parts or sections.

Preface or Introduction

☐ It states for whom the book is intended.
☐ It describes special features that are provided to help students learn.

Appendix

☐ It contains useful or interesting information.
☐ There is no appendix.

Glossary

☐ It is at the end of the book.
☐ There is a short glossary in each chapter.
☐ There is no glossary.

References, Bibliography, or Notes

☐ They are listed at the end of the book.
☐ They are listed at the end of each chapter.
☐ There are no references, bibliography, or notes.

Index

☐ There is a subject index *and* a name (or author) index.
☐ There is only one index.
☐ There is no index.

16

Survey Chapters

Most students read a chapter in a textbook by turning to the first page and reading it through to the last page. This is *not* an efficient way to read and study the chapters in textbooks. Experienced students know that it is more effective to survey a chapter before reading it. When you survey a chapter, you learn things that make it possible for you to read the chapter with greater understanding. Read "How to Survey a Chapter" on page 146 and scan the sample textbook chapter on pages 286–309 of the appendix before you read the discussions that follow.

Title and Introduction

Begin a survey by reading the chapter title and the introduction to the chapter. The title and introduction should summarize what the chapter is about, and an introduction may state the main purpose of the chapter. Whether an introduction to a chapter is short or long, read it carefully as part of your survey.

Learning Goals

Textbook chapters sometimes begin with a list that explains what you should learn as you read and study them. The list may have a heading such as "Learning Goals," "Learning Objectives," "Performance Goals," "Study Guides," or "Chapter Preview." When a chapter begins with **learning goals,** read them as part of your survey, and make certain you have achieved the goals in the list before you take a test on the chapter. When you study chapters using learning goals as a guide, your attention will be focused on learning what you are supposed to learn.

Headings

Continue a chapter survey by reading the **headings** to learn what topics are discussed in the chapter. Textbook designers use a variety of methods to show the relationships between headings.

How to Survey a Chapter

Use the following steps to survey a chapter before you read and study it:

1. Survey the beginning of a chapter.
   - Read the **title** and **introduction** to learn the topic and purpose of the chapter.
   - If there are **learning goals** at the beginning of the chapter, read them to find out what you are supposed to learn when you study the chapter.
2. Survey the body of the chapter.
   - Read the **headings** throughout the chapter to find out what topics are discussed in it.
   - Examine graphs, diagrams, pictures, cartoons, and other **visual material** in the chapter.
   - Scan any **inserts** or **marginal notes.**
3. Survey the end of the chapter.
   - If there is an easy-to-understand **summary** at the end of the chapter, read it to get a quick overview of the important information or ideas discussed in the chapter.
   - If **terminology** is listed at the end of the chapter, read it to find out what new words you are supposed to learn when you study the chapter.
   - If there are **review questions** at the end of the chapter, read them to get an idea of the types of questions you may have to answer about chapter content when you take a test.
   - If there are **exercises** or **problems** at the end of the chapter, read them to understand what skills you are expected to learn when you study the chapter.

- The size of a heading indicates its importance; the larger the heading, the more important it is.
- A heading in boldface or a special color (such as red) is more important than a heading of the same size that is not in boldface or a special color.
- A heading printed above a paragraph is more important than a heading printed on the first line of a paragraph.

Textbooks often have headings in addition to major headings and subheadings. The hints in this list will help you to understand the relative importance of headings in books that have three or four types of headings.

A Kiss Is but a Kiss

A city worker stares at a controversial poster on an elevated train station in Chicago. Part of a national AIDS awareness campaign, this advertisement was intended to show that AIDS is not transmitted through kissing. Public officials and clergy who tried to ban the ad found that they could not because it was neither untruthful nor obscene; it simply conveyed unconventional images of a conventional act.

Visual Materials

Textbooks for natural sciences, social sciences, business, and many other college subjects include photographs, graphs, and diagrams to summarize or illustrate information.

Photographs

Photographs are usually included in textbooks for one or more of the following purposes:

- To show the characteristics of something
- To illustrate or elaborate on a point made in the text
- To arouse an emotional response

Interpret a photograph by studying it to understand what it depicts and to experience whether it arouses an emotional response in you. Then, read the **caption** to learn additional information about whatever is depicted in the photograph or to learn why the photograph was included in your book.

The photograph above is used in an American government textbook. What does the photograph depict? What emotional response does it arouse in you? What point is the photograph used to illustrate in the American government textbook?

Cartoons

A **cartoon** is a drawing depicting a humorous situation, often accompanied by a caption. Textbook authors use cartoons to make amusing comments or to provoke thought about topics in their books. Interpret a cartoon by studying the drawing and reading the caption to decide whether it is amusing to you. Then try to figure out how the cartoon is related to a topic in the text. Is the cartoon below amusing to you? How is it related to the topic of this text?

Roger crams for his microbiology midterm.

Diagrams

A **diagram** is a drawing that explains something by depicting its characteristics or by outlining its parts and showing the relations between them. The diagram in Figure 16.1 on page 149 illustrates how water is recycled through the processes of transpiration, evaporation, condensation, and precipitation. The diagram provides an easy-to-understand summary of a long and rather complicated explanation in a meteorology textbook.

Graphs

Graphs in college textbooks are usually line graphs or bar graphs. A **line graph** is a drawing in which lines are used to show increases or decreases in amounts. The line graph in Figure 16.2 on page 150 shows that females in the labor force will increase from 37 percent in 1960 to 61 percent in 1995 and that men in the labor force will decrease from 83 percent in 1960 to 75 percent in 1995.

A **bar graph** is a drawing in which the lengths of parallel bars are used to show differences in amounts. Use the following steps to interpret the information in the bar graph in Figure 16.3 on page 150.

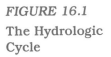

FIGURE 16.1
The Hydrologic Cycle

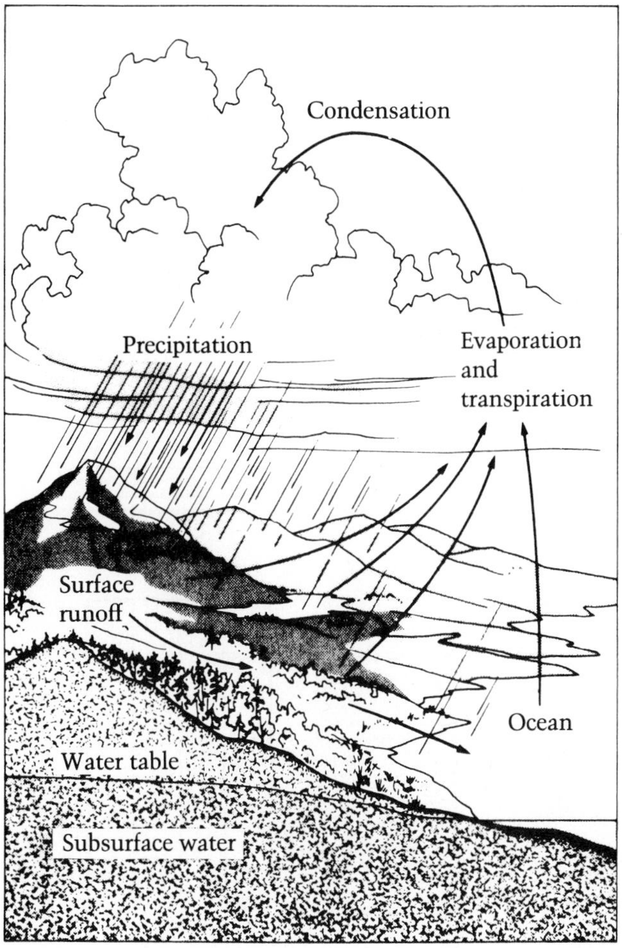

1. **Read the title.** What information is presented in Figure 16.3?
2. **Read the labels.** What information is presented from top to bottom on the left side of the graph *and* from left to right across the bottom of the graph?
3. **Compare the data.** How much greater is the median income for families in which the head of household has thirteen to fifteen years of education than for families in which the head of household has nine to eleven years of education?
4. **Decide the important point.** What is the important point made by the data in the bar graph?

The answers to the questions are (1) median income of families by education of the head of household, (2) amount of education *and* income in thousands of dollars, (3) about $8,000, and (4) median family income is related to the number of years of education of the head of household.

Textbooks also sometimes include circle graphs. A **circle graph** (or pie graph) is a drawing in which a circle is divided into segments to show the sizes of the parts that make up a whole. The segments of the circle (or pieces of the pie) are usually given different colors or designs. The circle graph on page 192 shows what proportion of the money spent on advertising is paid for advertising in newspapers, magazines, and other media.

FIGURE 16.2

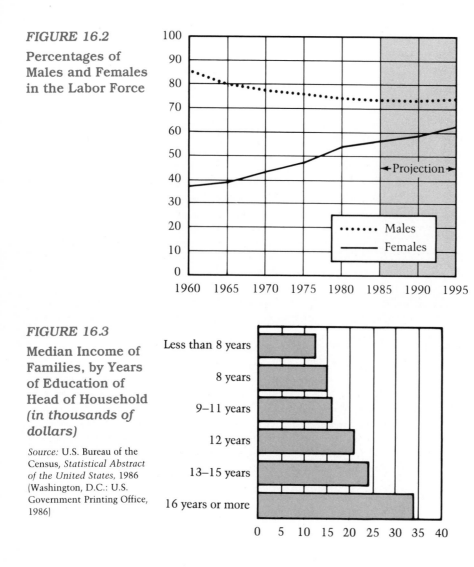

Percentages of Males and Females in the Labor Force

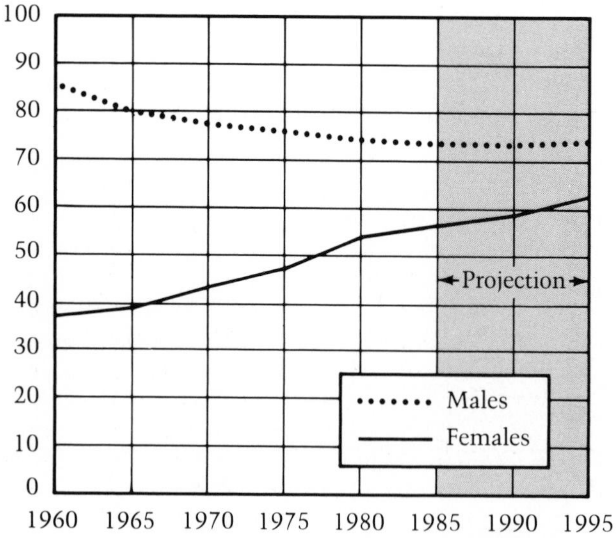

FIGURE 16.3

Median Income of Families, by Years of Education of Head of Household *(in thousands of dollars)*

Source: U.S. Bureau of the Census, *Statistical Abstract of the United States*, 1986 (Washington, D.C.: U.S. Government Printing Office, 1986)

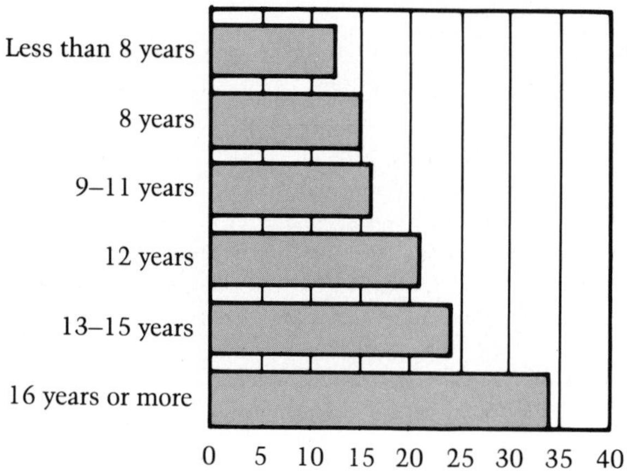

Inserts

An **insert** is material set off from the rest of the information in a textbook by lines or by a shaded background of light blue, yellow, gray, or some other color. Inserts serve a variety of purposes: for example, they may discuss timely issues, explain ways information in a text may be put to practical use, or provide students with opportunities to test themselves. "How to Survey a Chapter" on page 146 is an example of an insert.

Marginal Notes

Some textbooks print definitions of terms and other information in the margins of the text. Figure 16.4 shows a portion of a business textbook with a learning objective and the definition of a term printed in the margin. The term *market* is defined in the margin next to the place where it is first used in the book, and *Learning Objective 3* is printed next to the information that is needed to achieve the objective.

Markets and Their Classification

market *a group of individuals, organizations, or both who have needs for products in a given category and who have the ability, willingness, and authority to purchase such products*

Learning Objective 3
Know what markets are and how they are classified

A **market** is a group of individuals, organizations, or both who have needs for products in a given category and who have the ability, willingness, and authority to purchase such products. The people or organizations must require the product. They must be able to purchase the product with money, goods, or services that can be exchanged for the product. They must be willing to use their buying power. Finally, they must be socially and legally authorized to purchase the product.

Markets are classified as consumer, industrial, or reseller markets. These classifications are based on the characteristics of the individuals and organizations within each market. Because marketing efforts vary depending on the intended market, marketers should understand the general characteristics of these three groups.

Consumer markets consist of purchasers and/or individual household members who intend to consume or benefit from the purchased products and who do not buy products to make a profit.

Industrial markets are grouped broadly into producer, governmental, and institutional categories. These markets purchase specific kinds of products for use either in day-to-day operations or in making other products for profit. *Producer markets* consist of individuals and business organizations that intend to make a profit by buying certain products to use in the manufacture of other products. *Governmental markets* comprise federal, state, county, and local governments. They buy goods and services to maintain internal operations and to provide citizens with such products as highways, education, water, energy, and national defense. Their pur-

FIGURE 16.4
Marginal Notes in a Textbook

Summary

A chapter summary provides a quick overview of the information that is explained in the chapter; therefore, when a textbook chapter ends with a summary, read the summary *before* you read the chapter. The only time it is not helpful to read a summary before reading a chapter is when it is difficult to understand because it includes many technical words whose meanings you will not know until you read the chapter.

Terminology

At the end of chapters there is often a list of the important **terminology,** or words, used in the chapter. Terminology may be listed under a heading such as "Key Terms," "Important Words," "Key Concepts," or "Terms Used in This Chapter." When there is a list of terminology at the end of a chapter, study it before you read the chapter. Also, learn the meanings of *all* the words in the list before you take a test on the chapter; in many college courses a majority of test questions directly or indirectly test students' understanding of subject terminology.

If there is no list of terms at the beginning or end of a chapter, scan the pages of the chapter to locate important words introduced in it; they are likely to be printed in italics, boldface, or a special color (such as red). In *College Study Skills,* terminology is printed in boldface, and it is defined in a glossary at the back of the book.

Review Questions

A chapter may end with a list of questions that summarizes what you should learn in the chapter. This list may have a heading such as "Questions," "Exercises," "Discussion Questions," or "Review Questions." When there are review questions at the end of a chapter, read them before you read the chapter. Also, make certain that you can answer the questions before you take a test on the chapter.

Exercises and Problems

Some textbooks provide exercises or problems to help in learning **skills,** which are abilities acquired through practice. Writing error-free prose, solving mathematical problems, speaking foreign languages, and performing scientific experiments are a few of the skills taught in colleges.

It is often necessary to do more exercises or problems than a teacher requests. For instance, when a mathematics textbook provides forty problems of a specific type, a teacher may assign only twenty of them. However, some students may need to do twenty-five, thirty, or all forty problems.

If you are an accomplished athlete, musician, dancer, or writer, you know that long hours of practice are necessary to acquire a skill. Do the exercises and problems in your textbooks to give yourself the practice you need to develop the abilities taught in mathematics, science, foreign languages, and other courses that teach skills.

EXERCISE 16.1 Surveying a Chapter in Your Textbook

When you do this exercise, use a textbook you are studying for another course you are taking or have taken.

1. Textbook title ______________________________

2. Chapter title ______________________________

3. Number of pages in the chapter ______________________________

4. Check the statements that are true about the chapter.

- ☐ The **title** states what the chapter is about.
- ☐ The **introduction** states the purpose of the chapter.
- ☐ There are **learning goals** at the beginning of the chapter.
- ☐ **Headings** summarize the topics that are discussed in the chapter.
- ☐ There are bar **graphs** or line graphs in the chapter.
- ☐ There are diagrams, cartoons, or other drawings in the chapter.
- ☐ There are photographs in the chapter.
- ☐ There is a **summary** at the end of the chapter.
- ☐ The summary is easy to read and understand.
- ☐ There is a list of **terminology** at the end of the chapter.
- ☐ Terminology is printed in boldface, italics, or a special color in the chapter.
- ☐ There are **review questions** at the end of the chapter.
- ☐ There are **exercises** or **problems** at the end of the chapter.

EXERCISE 16.2 Surveying a Chapter in Your Textbook

When you do this exercise, use a textbook other than the one you used for Exercise 16.1.

1. Textbook title ______________________

2. Chapter title ______________________

3. Number of pages in the chapter ______________________

4. Check the statements that are true about the chapter.

- ☐ The **title** states what the chapter is about.
- ☐ The **introduction** states the purpose of the chapter.
- ☐ There are **learning goals** at the beginning of the chapter.
- ☐ **Headings** summarize the topics that are discussed in the chapter.
- ☐ There are bar **graphs** or line graphs in the chapter.
- ☐ There are diagrams, cartoons, or other drawings in the chapter.
- ☐ There are photographs in the chapter.
- ☐ There is a **summary** at the end of the chapter.
- ☐ The summary is easy to read and understand.
- ☐ There is a list of **terminology** at the end of the chapter.
- ☐ Terminology is printed in boldface, italics, or a special color in the chapter.
- ☐ There are **review questions** at the end of the chapter.
- ☐ There are **exercises** or **problems** at the end of the chapter.

[Do in class-discussion]

EXERCISE 16.3 "The Power of Positive Impressions"

This is the first of five exercises for applying study skills to the sample textbook chapter on pages 286–309 of the appendix. The other exercises are for marking books (Exercise 18.10), making notes (Exercise 19.8), reciting and rehearsing (Exercise 20.4), and test taking (Exercise 21.3).

Surveying a Chapter

Survey the sample textbook chapter on pages 286–309 of the appendix by removing this page from the book and answering the following questions.

1. What is the **title** of the chapter?

   ____

2. **Learning goals** are listed under the heading "Chapter Preview." What is the sixth learning goal?

   ____

3. According to the introduction on page 287, what are two important goals of the chapter?

   a. ______________________________

   b. ______________________________

4. There are two major headings in the chapter. The first major heading is "Making a Good Impression." What is the other major heading in the chapter?

   ____

5. "The Primacy Effect" is the first subheading following "Making a Good Impression" (page 287). Beginning on page 289, check the headings in the list that have the same level of importance as "The Primacy Effect."

   - ☐ "The First Few Minutes"
   - ☐ "Thinking/Learning Starters"
   - ☐ "First Impressions in a Work Setting"
   - ☐ "Total Person Insight"
   - ☐ "Assumptions Versus Facts"
   - ☐ "The Image You Project"
   - ☐ "Surface Language"
   - ☐ "Thinking/Learning Starter"
   - ☐ "Selecting Your Career Apparel"
   - ☐ "Products and Services Offered"
   - ☐ "Type of Person Served"
   - ☐ "Desired Image Projected by the Organization"
   - ☐ "Region"
   - ☐ "Thinking/Learning Starter"
   - ☐ "Wardrobe Engineering"

- ☐ "Your Facial Expression"
- ☐ "Your Entrance and Carriage"
- ☐ "Your Voice"
- ☐ "Your Handshake"
- ☐ "Total Person Insight"
- ☐ "Your Manners"

6. Write an answer to the "Thinking/Learning Starter" **insert** on page 294.

____

____

____

____

7. In your opinion, what image of the Chrysler Corporation is projected by the **photograph** on page 297?

____

____

8. How is the **cartoon** on page 299 related to the topic discussed on pages 298–300?

____

____

9. Read the **summary** on pages 304–305. Does it provide an easy-to-understand overview of the content of the chapter?

____

10. How many **key terms** are listed on page 305? ______________

What is the definition of *wardrobe engineering* given on page 298?

____

____

11. Read the review questions on page 305 and answer the sixth question.

a. ______________________________

b. ______________________________

c. ______________________________

d. ______________________________

17

Take Good Class Notes

Within two days after a lecture you will have forgotten about three-fourths of what you heard, and within a week you will have forgotten virtually all that was said during the lecture. If you don't have written records of what your teachers say in class, you will not be able to prepare for tests by studying what they taught you during class meetings.

Class notes usually include explanations about complicated course material, important facts that are not stated in required reading material, and hints about what to study for tests. Thus, they are usually the best source of help for understanding course subject matter and for deciding what to study for tests. Attend classes faithfully to take complete and well-organized notes about the explanations, facts, and hints you will need when you take examinations.

Use an Appropriate Notebook

It is essential that you have a notebook that makes it easy for you to keep notes for each class completely separate from the notes for your other classes. For example, notes for a biology course, a math course, and an English course should be kept in three separate sections of a notebook. If you mix your notes for one class with your notes for another class, your notes will not be properly organized when you study them to prepare for tests.

There are suggestions for purchasing a notebook on page 16, and "How to Organize Class Notes" on page 158 includes advice for organizing notebooks.

Improve Your Listening

Suggestions for improving your ability to listen to lectures are summarized in "How to Improve Listening" on page 159. The first suggestion in the list is to read or skim information about the lecture topic in the course textbook immediately before class. It is especially important to use this suggestion when teachers tell you to read about lecture topics before class and when you have difficulty understanding what teachers say during lectures. If at all possible, do the reading just before class so it will be fresh in your mind as you listen to the lecture.

How to Organize Class Notes

These are methods that you should definitely use:

- Take notes on 8½- by 11-inch notebook paper so that all the information about topics is usually on one page rather than on two or three pages.
- Write your name, address, and telephone number in the front of your notebook so it can be easily returned to you if you lose it.
- Keep assignments for all classes in a special assignment section of your notebook so when you study you'll be less likely to overlook assignments buried in notes.
- Start each day's notes on a new sheet of paper, and begin them with a heading that includes the date and course name or course number. The date is essential for putting notes back in correct sequence when they become mixed up, for verifying that notes are complete, and for finding where to begin studying when teachers announce that tests cover material in notes beginning on a particular date.
- Leave at least one blank line before each main idea.
- Make diagrams and other drawings large, and skip lines before and after them.

You may also find that these strategies are helpful:

- Keep notes in a ring binder and use dividers to separate the notes for each class.
- Punch holes in papers instructors hand out and insert them in your ring binder for safekeeping.
- Write only on one side of each piece of paper so you can see all your notes when you spread them out on a desk to study them.
- Number each page so you can easily put notes back in correct order if you remove them from your ring binder.

In addition, before you go to a class, take care of any physical needs that may become sources of discomfort and interfere with your concentration. You may need to use the rest room, have a drink of water, or eat something if you are likely to become hungry before class is over. Dress so you can remove clothes if a classroom is too warm or put on clothes if it is too cold. If you wear a shirt or blouse under a sweater or jacket, you can take off the sweater if you become too warm or put on the jacket if you become too cold.

Sit where you can see your teachers clearly because their gestures, facial expressions, and eye movements may often convey important information.

How to Improve Listening

Use these suggestions when you listen to classroom lectures:

1. Just before class, read or skim the information about the lecture topic in the course textbook.
2. Eliminate distractions:
   - Sit where you have a good view of the teacher and where you can't see out a window.
   - Don't sit near students who distract you.
   - Keep only paper, pen, and other essential materials on your desk.
   - Eat before class so you won't be hungry during class.
   - Dress in layers so you can remove clothing if you become warm or put on clothing if you become cold.
3. Keep your eyes on the teacher as he or she speaks because gestures, facial expressions, and eye movements may often convey important information.
4. Sit using good posture.
5. Listen to find the answers to the following questions and use the answers to make good notes:
   - What topic should I use as the heading for my notes?
   - In what format should I record notes?
   - What major thought should I write in my notes?
   - How many details should I list?
6. Ask the teacher for clarification when you are not certain you understood what was said.

- *A gesture may supplement words.* For instance, an instructor may point at the chalkboard to emphasize something written there that she wants you to understand or know.
- *A facial expression may contradict words.* An instructor may say, "This is easy," but a playful expression on his face may suggest that he is teasing and wants you to understand the opposite—"This is very difficult."
- *A gesture or facial expression may suggest what you are to do.* A teacher may stop talking and raise her eyebrows, suggesting that she is ready to answer your questions, or she may purse her lips or give some other signal when opening a book of poetry to indicate that she wants complete silence before she reads aloud from the book.
- *Eye movements may indicate important information is being given.* When instructors glance at their notes as they make a statement, this often indicates that the point is especially important.

When a classroom is very large, try to sit in the front and center of the room. In any event, select a seat from which you can't see out a window and that is away from any student who distracts you.

Finally, avoid worrying and daydreaming during lectures—these activities will distract you from listening. There is nothing you can do about a problem while you are in a classroom listening to a lecture; worrying will not solve the problem, but it will prevent you from taking good lecture notes. Therefore, when a problem comes into your mind, write it in your list of things to do, tell yourself to stop worrying and to pay attention to the lecture, and deal with the problem after class.

There are additional suggestions for improving listening on pages 184–185.

Take Well-organized Class Notes

Take well-organized class notes by using the format illustrated in Figure 17.1 on page 161 or any of the note-taking methods illustrated on pages 205–210. The suggestions in "How to Organize Class Notes" on page 158 apply no matter what note-taking method you use.

Notice that the class notes illustrated in Figure 17.1 on page 161 emphasize the relations between major thoughts and details:

- *Major thoughts stand out clearly.* In Figure 17.1, major thoughts are preceded by a line with no writing on it, they are written to the left side of the page, and they are underlined.
- *Details are listed under major thoughts in an orderly fashion.* In Figure 17.1, some details are preceded by numbers and others are preceded by stars.

Of course, the notes you take under pressure during a class are not likely to be as neatly written and tidy as the notes in Figure 17.1.

Many experienced students favor the Cornell System, which is a variation of the traditional note-taking format. To use the Cornell System, draw or crease a vertical line two and a half inches from the left edge of each sheet of notebook paper, as illustrated below.

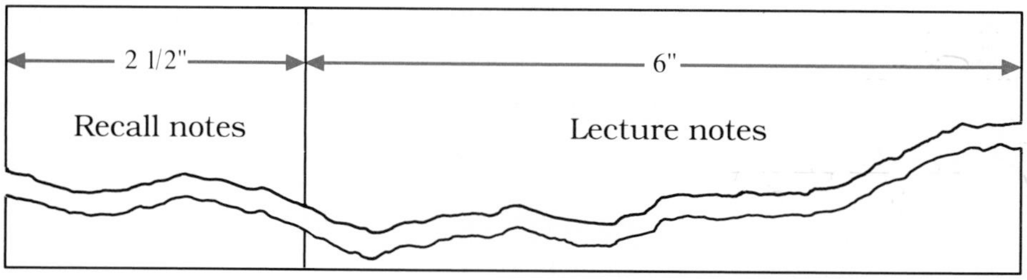

Record class notes in the space to the right of the vertical line, and write words, phrases, or questions to assist you in learning the information in your notes in the space to the left of the vertical line. The Cornell note-taking system is explained in detail by Walter Pauk in *How to Study in College,* 5th ed. (Boston: Houghton Mifflin Company, 1993).

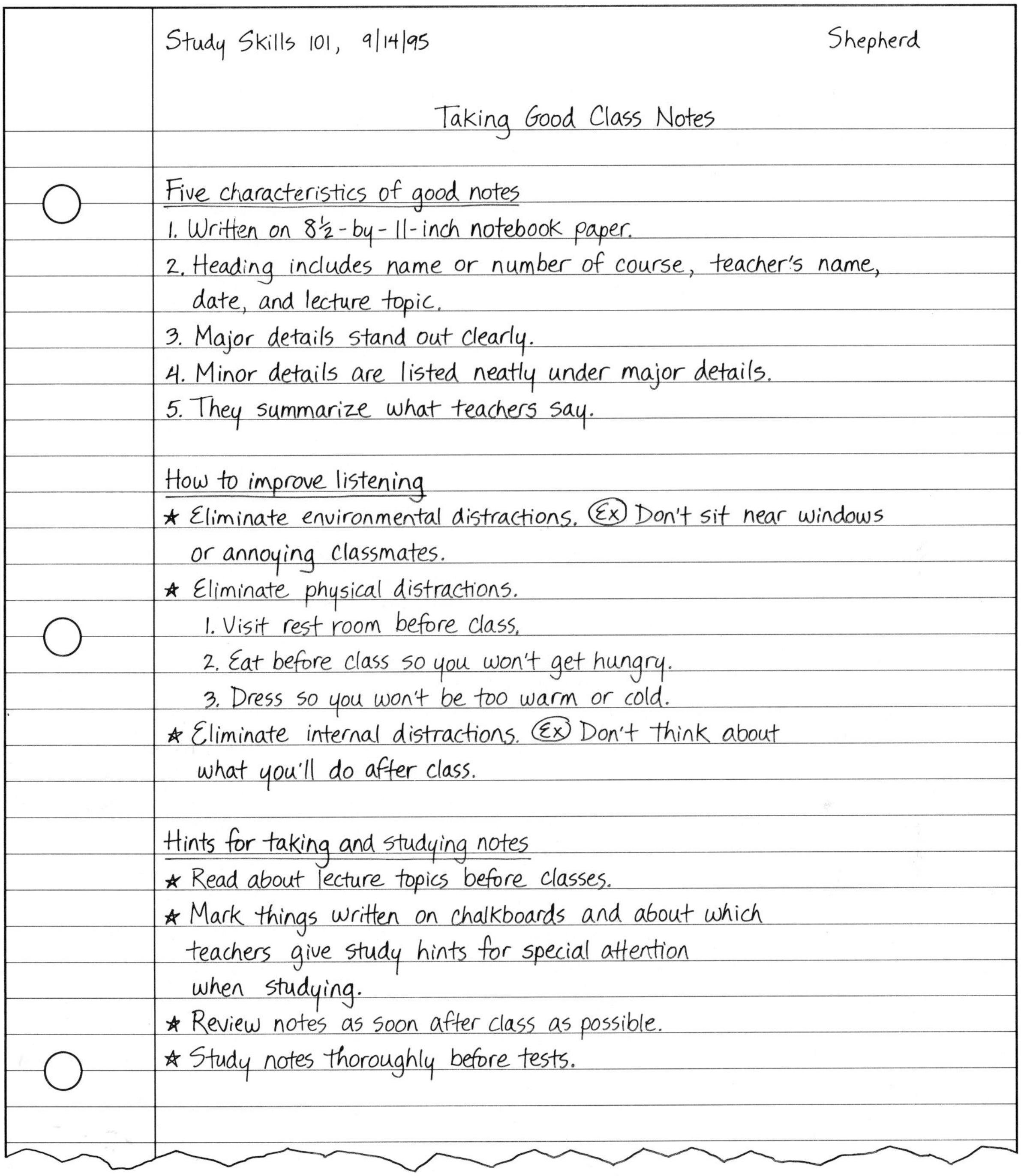
Study Skills 101, 9/14/95
Shepherd
Taking Good Class Notes
Five characteristics of good notes
1. Written on 8½-by-11-inch notebook paper.
2. Heading includes name or number of course, teacher's name, date, and lecture topic.
3. Major details stand out clearly.
4. Minor details are listed neatly under major details.
5. They summarize what teachers say.
How to improve listening
★ Eliminate environmental distractions. (Ex) Don't sit near windows or annoying classmates.
★ Eliminate physical distractions.
1. Visit rest room before class.
2. Eat before class so you won't get hungry.
3. Dress so you won't be too warm or cold.
★ Eliminate internal distractions. (Ex) Don't think about what you'll do after class.
Hints for taking and studying notes
★ Read about lecture topics before classes.
★ Mark things written on chalkboards and about which teachers give study hints for special attention when studying.
★ Review notes as soon after class as possible.
★ Study notes thoroughly before tests.

FIGURE 17.1
Well-organized Class Notes

Summarize What Teachers Say

When you take class notes, summarize what teachers say; do not attempt to write down what they say word for word. It is impossible to record teachers' words exactly because they usually speak at the rate of about 125 to 150 words per minute, but you can probably write no more than 25 to 30 words a minute. Therefore, you must learn to summarize what teachers say in your own words.

Adapt to Each Teacher

The suggestions in this chapter pertain to teachers who give well-organized notes; however, some teachers give disorganized lectures, some ramble from topic to topic, and some refer to the course textbook while they lecture.

- When you have teachers who give *disorganized* lectures, leave the left pages of your notebook blank and after class rewrite notes on the blank left pages.
- When you have teachers who *ramble* from topic to topic without explaining how the topics are related, take the most complete notes you can about each topic they discuss.
- When you have teachers who *read* from the course textbook, follow along in your copy of the textbook; mark the points they emphasize and cross out the information they tell you is not important.

It is your responsibility as a student to adapt to the instructional methods your teachers use.

Listen for Major Thoughts

During lectures, make it your goal to find major thoughts and to make them stand out clearly in your notes. Some teachers directly state important thoughts by using phrases such as "Now I'm going to discuss . . ." and "My next point is. . . ." Instructors also use pauses and repetition to emphasize major thoughts in their lectures. If they pause while lecturing, this is often a clue that you should write down what they said just before the pause or what they will say after it. When teachers repeat statements, it is usually a definite hint that you should record the repeated information in your class notes.

Listen for Details

Many lecturers make it clear how many details to list under major thoughts by making statements such as the following:

- Sociologists identify *four* types of families.
- There are *five* steps in the selling process.
- Let's examine *three* tragic effects of the Civil War.

When instructors make statements such as these, it is clear exactly how many details to list.

In other instances, teachers make it clear that students should list details, but not how many of them to list. For instance, an instructor may say, "I'm going to talk about some of the problems involved in starting a small business." In this case, students should write "Problems with starting a small business" as a major thought in notes and prepare to list the problems. However, they will not know how many problems there are until the teacher states them.

Details in class notes are often of the following kinds of information:

causes	criteria	theories	characteristics
effects	purposes	categories	kinds
reasons	factors	advantages	differences
functions	types	disadvantages	similarities

When teachers use these and similar words during lectures, they are hints about the kinds of details to list in your notes.

Watch the Chalkboard

All of your teachers have been students, and as students they learned that the information their teachers wrote on chalkboards was very often used as the basis for test questions. Many of your teachers assume that you also have figured out that you should copy and learn anything written on the board. Many of them believe that they are announcing a test question to you whenever they write on a chalkboard.

Therefore, include in class notes everything that your teachers write on the chalkboard and mark it for special attention when you study. You might draw a star or write *Important* in the margin next to the information, or you can mark it with yellow or pink highlighting ink so you will not overlook it when you study for a test.

Following are some of the types of information that instructors write on chalkboards:

- Tables, charts, and diagrams
- Mathematical formulas
- Important terminology
- People's names and dates

Make diagrams and other drawings large and set them off in notes with plenty of space before and after them.

Listen for Study Hints

Instructors often inform students about what is especially important to learn by making statements such as the following:

- This is very important.
- I'll probably ask a test question about this.
- You must be able to do these kinds of problems.
- This confuses some students—don't let it confuse you.

When teachers make such statements, write them in your notes and mark the information to which they pertain for special attention in the same way you mark the information you copy from chalkboards.

How to Take Complete Class Notes

- Attend *all* lectures.
- Be ready to take notes the minute class begins.
- Include everything that teachers write on the board and mark it for special attention when you study.
- Include everything that teachers say after glancing at their notes.
- Mark for special attention material in notes teachers say is important or difficult to learn.
- Record examples exactly as they are given so you will recognize them if they show up in test questions.
- Include all definitions of terminology; in many subjects a large portion of test questions directly or indirectly test students' knowledge of terminology.
- When you miss information, leave a blank space for it in your notes. After class find out what you missed and write it in your notes where it belongs.
- Take notes until the very end of class. Instructors often rush to cover a great deal of information during the last few minutes of a class session.
- Build note-taking speed by using simplified handwriting and abbreviations.
- Avoid recopying your notes; it is easy to make errors and lose information when you recopy notes.
- Copy notes from a classmate if you must be absent.

Some of your instructors will give reviews for tests during class or at special times outside of class. Attend reviews, take complete notes, and learn everything that you are told to learn. Teachers who give reviews want to focus your attention on learning what is most important. When instructors don't give test reviews, ask them what to study; it is reasonable for you to assume that your teachers want you to know what you should learn.

Take Complete Notes

When you are aware that you have missed information during a lecture, leave a blank space in your notes. Also place a question mark (?) or some other symbol in the margin next to information that you do not understand or that you believe you may have recorded incorrectly. When the time is appropriate, raise your hand and ask the question that will help you to make your notes complete or accurate. Do not be reluctant to ask questions—skillful instructors depend on students' questions to know what is not clear. You can also improve your notes after class by talking with the teacher, by talking with a classmate who takes good notes, or by studying required reading material.

It is extremely important for you to attend all of your classes so you will have a complete set of notes. If you are absent from a class, you have no alternative but to copy the notes taken by one of your classmates. Unfortunately, though, the notes that are useful to your fellow students may not be very helpful to you. Therefore, when you copy notes, make certain you completely understand them by having the person who took them carefully explain what they mean.

Copy notes before or after class, not during it. Students who copy notes during class miss two lectures—the one they are copying and the one their teacher gives while they are copying.

"How to Take Complete Class Notes" on page 164 summarizes procedures that ensure that notes are complete.

Review Notes After Class

Notes taken in September may contain information that you need to learn for a test in November. If you don't understand your notes in September, you won't understand them in November when you study for a test. Therefore, during the first free time you have following a lecture, reread your notes to make certain that you understand them and that they are complete.

Change your notes in any way that makes them easier to understand. Correct misspelled words, fill in missing information, and make other changes that improve them.

Study Notes Before Tests

It is almost always essential to study class notes thoroughly before tests. If your class notes do not help you do well on tests, either you took poor notes, or your instructor did not give helpful lectures. Improve your note taking by following the suggestions in this chapter and the ones about how to study class notes on page 216.

Build Note-taking Speed

Lecturers usually speak at the rate of about 125 to 150 words per minute, but students take notes at the rate of only about 25 to 30 words per minute. Therefore good class notes are summaries rather than word-for-word records of teachers' statements.

Note taking requires the ability to write quickly and neatly, but there are very few first-year college students who use a fast, neat method for writing class notes. If you want to write notes more quickly and neatly, you may benefit from an experience reported by Walter Pauk in *How to Study in College:*

> The breakthrough in my own notetaking came when I saw an instructor write on a blackboard using a modified printing style. Her writing was not only surprisingly rapid, but also amazingly clear. I immediately began to write in a similar style—without needing practice at all. I believe anyone can adopt this style, and use it to write neatly and clearly.

Here is how the individual letters are formed in this modified printing style:

a b c d e f g h i j k l m n o p q r s t u v w x y z

And here is the style as used in two paragraphs:

There are four advantages to using this modified printing style. First, it is faster than cursive writing; second, it is far neater, permitting easy and direct comprehension; third, it saves time by precluding rewriting or typing; and fourth, it permits easy and clear reforming of letters that are ill-formed due to haste.

Even today, I almost always write this way because the style is the easiest, swiftest, and neatest of any I've tried.

Practice writing class notes more neatly and rapidly by using Professor Pauk's simplified method of handwriting. You may also write faster by using symbols of the type listed in "Symbols for Building Note-taking Speed" on page 167 and abbreviations of the following kinds:

1. Use standard abbreviations: *pp.* (pages), *etc.* (and so on), *e.g.* (for example), *i.e.* (that is).
2. Use standard abbreviations without periods: *NY* (New York), *ex* (example), *mph* (miles per hour), *p* (page).
3. Use first letters of words: *subj* (subject), *psy* (psychology), *chap* (chapter), *ques* (question).
4. Omit vowels: *bldg* (building), *hdbk* (handbook), *wk* (week), *yr* (year).
5. Add *s* to abbreviations to form the plural: *subjs* (subjects), *hdbks* (handbooks), *chaps* (chapters), *yrs* (years).
6. Use Arabic numerals: *7/4/1776* (July 4, 1776), *2* (two), *4th* (fourth), *$15 million* (fifteen million dollars).

The best abbreviations for you to use in class notes are the ones you understand. Be careful not to use an abbreviation such as *comp* and later find yourself unable to remember whether it stands for *companion, comparative, compensation, complete, compose, composition, compound, comprehensive,* or one of the many other words that begin with *comp.*

Finally, do not slow yourself down by worrying a great deal about spelling when you take class notes. You are the only one who reads your notes; you can correct misspelled words after class.

Symbols for Building Note-taking Speed

Symbol	Meaning	Example of Its Use
&	and	Bring a pen & pencil.
#	number	He gave his S.S. #.
%	percent	Only 41% voted for him.
$	money	She earns a lot of $.
@	at	He bought 2 shirts @ $20 each.
?	question	The ? was never answered.
′	feet	There are 5,280′ in a mile.
″	inches	She's 5′ 6½″ tall.
×	by	The room is 10′ × 14′.
=	equals	A kilo = 2.2 pounds.
≠	not equal to	He's ≠ to the task.
∴	therefore	I think, ∴ I am.
∵	because	She smiles ∵ she's happy.
. . .	and so on	We ate, sang, danced . . .
>	greater than	His taxes are > than hers.
<	less than	His income is < than hers.
w/	with	Wine improves w/age.
w/o	without	He's never w/o a kind word.

EXERCISE 17.1 Abbreviations and Symbols

Rewrite the following sentences using abbreviations and symbols for the words printed in boldface. If you do not know the standard abbreviation, make up an abbreviation of your own.

1. **Seventy-five percent** of the students earned **less than one hundred dollars** last month.

   ____

2. He **could not answer** the **professor's question.**

   ____

3. She is **five feet four and one-half inches** tall.

   ____

4. They lived **two thousand years before the birth of Christ.**

   ____

5. We drove **fifteen miles north** of **New York City.**

____

6. Read the **first twenty pages** of **Chapter Ten.**

____

7. His acting was **without equal.**

____

8. Our debts are **greater than** our income.

____

9. The dance floor measures **twenty feet by forty-five feet.**

____

10. The **United States of America** entered **World War II** on **December 8, 1941.**

____

EXERCISE 17.2 Abbreviations

Write abbreviations for the following common words. If you do not know a standard abbreviation, make up an abbreviation of your own.

1. Mister	________	11. following	________
2. miles per hour	________	12. company	________
3. Senior	________	13. incorporated	________
4. Junior	________	14. corporation	________
5. Doctor	________	15. chapter	________
6. Professor	________	16. without	________
7. pages	________	17. equal	________
8. for example	________	18. number	________
9. page	________	19. money	________
10. handbook	________	20. second	________

EXERCISE 17.3 Summarizing

Write summaries of the following statements. For instance, you might summarize the first problem in the following way: "Write notes on 8½" × 11" paper."

1. Write class notes on paper that measures 8½ by 11 inches rather than on paper of a smaller size, such as 5-by-8-inch paper.

 ____

2. Major thoughts should stand out clearly in notes, and details should be listed neatly under them; however, they need not be labeled with Roman numerals, capital letters, and Arabic numerals in the traditional outline format.

 ____

 ____

3. Each day's notes should have a heading that includes the name or number of the course, the date, the teacher's name, and the lecture topic. For example, a heading might include the following: Introduction to Psychology; September 22, 1996; Professor Martin; Freud's Theory of Personality.

 ____

 ____

4. All your teachers have been students, and as students they learned that the information *their* teachers wrote on chalkboards was very often used as the basis for test questions. Many of your teachers assume that you also have figured out that you should copy and learn anything written on the board. Many of them believe that they are announcing a test question whenever they write on a chalkboard. Therefore, include in class notes everything that your teachers write on chalkboards and mark it for special attention when you study.

 ____

 ____

5. If you believe you write too slowly, you can increase the speed with which you take class notes by using fewer lines, curves, and flourishes in your writing and by using abbreviations (such as *eq* for *equation*) and symbols (such as % for *percent*).

 ____

 ____

EXERCISE 17.4 Summarizing

Write summaries of the following statements, as you did for Exercise 17.3.

1. Teachers ordinarily explain course requirements during the first few days of classes. When course requirements are presented orally, take accurate and complete notes; when they are distributed on printed pages, keep them in a safe place. In either case, understand them completely and follow them exactly.

   ____

   ____

2. Be certain that you arrive at your classes on time. When students arrive late to class, they interrupt their teacher and classmates, and they create the impression that they are disorganized or irresponsible. Don't be rude or create an unfavorable impression of yourself; arrive at your classes on time.

   ____

3. College terms start out slowly. They gradually get busier and busier, reaching a peak of activity at final examination time. If you fall behind in the work for a course, you will find yourself trying to catch up at the time when you are very busy with all of your other courses. Don't fall behind—keep up-to-date with course work.

   ____

4. Always keep photocopies of papers you write for college credit so you will have accurate records of what you wrote in case a teacher loses or misplaces one of your papers. In addition, you may find that the photocopy of a paper you wrote for one of your courses contains references or other information that will be helpful to you in the future.

   ____

   ____

5. If you have difficulty with a course, turn to a teacher, counselor, or adviser for help. These people usually know if study groups, tutors, or other sources of help are available. If they do not, they can suggest where to look further for help. They may advise visiting the office of the department that offers the course that is giving you a problem. Or they may suggest visiting an office of academic skills, a learning center, a tutorial service, or some other department or service on campus.

   ____

   ____

EXERCISE 17.5 Rating Lectures

Write the names of two of your lecture courses above the columns on the right. Then rate lecturers in each category, using 100 (perfect), 90-99 (excellent), 80-89 (good), 70-79 (satisfactory), 60-69 (poor), 0-59 (unacceptable).

	1. ________	2. ________
1. Gives well-organized lectures	________	________
2. States main ideas clearly	________	________
3. Usually identifies the number of minor details to include in a list	________	________
4. Pauses to give me time to write	________	________
5. Repeats important statements so I can get them in my notes	________	________
6. Makes me feel free to ask questions so my notes will be complete	________	________
7. Makes good use of the chalkboard	________	________
8. Informs me what is most important to learn	________	________
9. Seems very interested in the subject matter of the course	________	________
10. Explains difficult ideas and concepts so they are easy for me to understand	________	________
Totals	________	________
Divide totals by 10 to find averages.		
Averages	________	________

EXERCISE 17.6 Rating Class Notes

Write the names of the same lecture courses you wrote in Exercise 17.5 above the columns on the right. Then rate your notes for the courses in each category, using 100 (perfect), 90-99 (excellent), 80-89 (good), 70-79 (satisfactory), 60-69 (poor), 0-59 (unacceptable).

	1. ________	2. ________
1. I read about lecture topics before class when lectures are difficult to understand.	________	________
2. I begin each day's notes with a complete heading.	________	________
3. Main ideas stand out clearly.	________	________
4. Minor details are listed under main ideas, and they are often numbered.	________	________
5. My notes summarize rather than repeat word for word what the teacher said.	________	________
6. My notes include everything written on the chalkboard, marked for special attention when I study for tests.	________	________
7. My notes include study hints, and the information to which they pertain is marked for special attention when I study for tests.	________	________
8. I ask questions when I need to make my notes complete.	________	________
9. I practice new ways to write faster when I take notes.	________	________
10. I review my notes as soon after class as possible.	________	________
Totals	________	________
Divide totals by 10 to find averages.		
Averages	________	________

Compare your ratings for lecturers in Exercise 17.5 with those for your notes to determine whether there are relationships between them. For instance, if you rated a lecturer for a course high, did you rate your class notes for the course high also?

18

Mark Your Books

As you learned when you read about memory in Chapter 5, it is easier to store information in memory when it is well organized. Most successful college students mark information they want to learn in their textbooks and then use their marks as a guide for summarizing the information into organized study notes.

Figures 18.1 and 18.2 on pages 174 and 175 illustrate how markings are used as a guide in making notes.

Reasons for Marking Books

If you were told in high school that you must not write in books, you may wonder why marking textbooks is an essential skill for efficient college study. The main reason is that when you mark a book in the way explained in this chapter, you make a permanent record of the information you want to learn. On the other hand, when you do not mark a book as you read it, you must reread it to find the information you need to learn.

Some students resist writing in their books because they cannot, or fear they cannot, resell marked books. This is a foolish way to economize. Textbooks are expensive, but they are a small part of the cost of attending college in comparison to tuition, housing, food, transportation, and other expenses. Virtually all successful students mark their books because it saves them valuable study time.

The only students who do not need to mark their books are the ones who make good notes as they read. If you make well-organized summaries of the information in your books as you read, you do not need to underline, highlight, or write in your books.

Underline or Highlight

To **underline** is simply to draw lines under words; it is usually done with a pen, using a ruler as a guide. Many students prefer to highlight rather than underline because highlighting can be done neatly without using a ruler. To **highlight** is to mark words using a felt-tipped pen that contains watercolor

FIGURE 18.1
A Highlighted Textbook Passage

Steps in the Selling Process

Many businesses have as their primary function the selling of a product or service; selling may be viewed as a four-step process.

First, **the selling business wants to find buyers.** Buyers are attracted to a product or service through advertising, the availability of the product or service, or the efforts of salespeople. Department stores find buyers by advertising and by being located where customers shop. Encyclopedias are often sold through advertising and the efforts of salespeople.

After potential buyers have been found, **a product or service must be presented in the most attractive and convincing way possible.** Expensive perfume is offered for sale in attractive and expensive-looking bottles. Low-cost vacation trips are sold in offices that convince customers they will receive a bargain; it would not be convincing to sell low-cost travel in an office that is decorated with rare objects of art and expensive furniture.

Once buyers have been found and the product or service has been presented in an attractive and convincing way, **the salesperson must create the customer's desire to buy.** This is usually achieved by persuading customers that their lives will be better when they make a purchase. Another technique salespeople use is to establish rapport with customers so they buy because they like the salesperson rather than because they need or want what they purchase.

The final step in the selling process is to **close the sale.** Once the customer has the desire to buy, the salesperson will do something to motivate the customer to put out money for a purchase. A clothing salesperson might ask, "Will you take the brown sweater or the blue one?" A travel salesperson might close a sale by asking, "Shall I book you hotel rooms in London, Paris, and Rome, or have you decided not to stop in Paris?"

ink. Yellow and pink are the most popular colors. In this book I use *underline* to mean "underline" or "highlight." Light blue is used to indicate highlighting in the passage above.

When you use the guidelines that are summarized in "How to Mark Books" on page 176, you may find that it sometimes seems impossible to follow the second guideline—"Do not mark too much." However, there are at least three ways to avoid excessive underlining. First, it is sometimes better to underline only key words that identify major details than to underline information about major details. For instance, if a page in a human anatomy textbook describes all the bones in the hand and arm, underline the names of the bones but not the information about them. Later, use the underlining as a guide for making notes. You may also use numbers and vertical lines to reduce the amount of underlining in your books.

FIGURE 18.2

Notes for the Passage in Figure 18.1

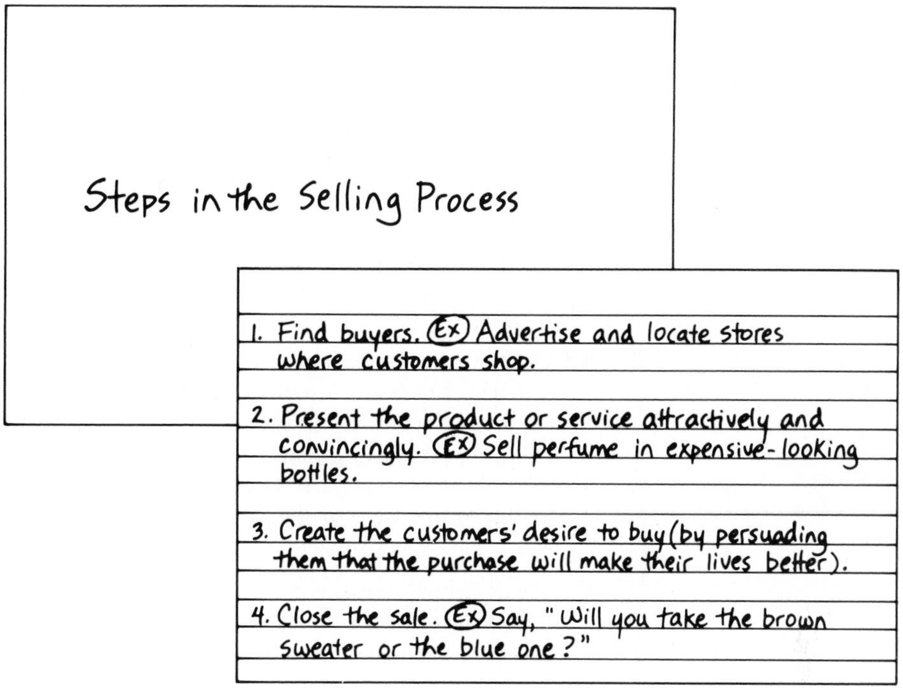
Steps in the Selling Process
1. Find buyers. (Ex) Advertise and locate stores where customers shop.
2. Present the product or service attractively and convincingly. (Ex) Sell perfume in expensive-looking bottles.
3. Create the customers' desire to buy (by persuading them that the purchase will make their lives better).
4. Close the sale. (Ex) Say, "Will you take the brown sweater or the blue one?"

Numbers and Vertical Lines

It is often more appropriate to number details rather than to underline them. For example:

Legalization of Marijuana

Should marijuana be legalized so that it could be commercially manufactured and sold like alcohol and tobacco? Because of the extent of marijuana use, the issue has become a serious one for politicians. Although arrest for possession seldom leads to jail, proponents* of legalization argue that (1) inconsistency of enforcement leads to disrespect for the law. In addition, (2) the problems of enforcement become enormous, diverting police efforts from other kinds of crime, and (3) the government is unable to collect taxes on the drug as it can on alcohol and tobacco. Furthermore, (4) buyers are not protected from overpriced, low-quality marijuana.

If the four details in this passage were underlined, the entire last half of the paragraph would be underlined.

Vertical lines are useful for a variety of purposes, including marking definitions and examples.

*Words underscored in blue are defined in the vocabulary list on pages 310–315.

How to Mark Books

Use the following guidelines when you mark, underline, or highlight your books:

- **Read a section before you mark it.** If you mark as you read, you may mark information that you later decide is not especially important.
- **Do not mark too much.** If almost everything on a page is marked, it is the same as if nothing were marked. As a general rule, don't underline more than 20 percent of the information on a page. For instance, if there are 40 lines of print on the pages of a book, don't underline more than about 8 lines on a page. Avoid excessive underlining by numbering details and by using vetical lines to mark information that you might otherwise underline.
- **Mark information that will help you make notes.** The purpose of marking a book is to make a permanent record that will help you later make notes for learning information.
- **Make major details stand out.** You use major details to make well-organized notes, and it is almost always important to learn them.
- **Mark definitions of terminology.** On many college tests up to 70 percent of questions directly or indirectly test students' knowledge of terminology.
- **Mark examples.** Learn the examples included in your book so you will recognize them if they are used in test questions.

Colloquialisms

The term **colloquial** is defined by *The American Heritage Dictionary* as
Def "characteristic of or appropriate to the spoken language or writing that seeks its effect; informal in diction or style of expression." Colloquialisms are not "incorrect" or "bad" English. They are the kinds of words people, educated and uneducated alike, use when they are speaking together informally. Their deliberate use in writing conveys the impression of
Ex direct and intimate conversation. To achieve this effect, you might use contractions (*don't, wasn't, hasn't*) or clipped words (*taxi, phone*).

Def is used above as an abbreviation for *definition,* and *Ex* is an abbreviation for *Examples.*

In the following example, *Imp't* is used as an abbreviation for *Important* to draw attention to information a reader decided is especially important.

The Family

The family is without doubt the most significant single agent of socializa-
Imp't tion in all societies. One reason for the importance of the family is that

Imp't it has the main responsibility for socializing children in the crucial early years of life. The family is where children establish their first emotional ties, learn language, and begin to internalize cultural norms and values.

Some students write asterisks (*) next to information they decide is especially important and question marks (?) next to material that is unclear to them. Write any symbols or words in your books that help you to learn the information in them.

Many scholars write comments in the margins of books as they study them. For example, if while reading a statement written by Carl Jung, students of psychology recall that Sigmund Freud expressed a similar point of view, they may write "Freud agrees" in the margin. You, too, may interact with the authors of your books by writing whatever comments you want in the margins of the books you own.

Helps for Finding Details

Authors and editors provide five helps for locating details to mark in textbooks: (1) subheadings, (2) words in italics or boldface, (3) numbers, (4) bullets, and (5) statements in introductions.

1. **Subheadings may name details.** Use the subheadings to locate the major details in the following passage:

The Characteristics of Money

Money should be stable in value, divisible, portable, durable, and it should be difficult to counterfeit.

Stability of Value The value of money should not change significantly over the short run. An item valued at $100 today should be worth the same amount tomorrow or next month and approximately the same next year and the year after. Of course, inflation erodes the value of all currencies. The dollar has decreased in value over the last half century.

Divisibility For a currency to work efficiently, its units of measure must permit precise valuation. The units should range from very small to extremely large and be divisible by the smallest unit. Goods and services in the United States can be precisely valued, and we can make exchanges in exactly the right amounts. It is no trick to buy a $1.29 bag of cheese popcorn with two $1 bills and get back 71 cents in coins. Similarly, it is not too difficult to figure out the divisibility of the British pound, which is equal to 20 shillings or 100 new pence.

But it's not always so easy. In the Yap Islands of the South Pacific, great stone wheels were still used as money at the beginning of the twentieth century. In East Africa, cows were money until very recently.[1] To arrive at an exchange that matched whole stones or cows required an infinitely more complicated process than our monetary exchanges. Today, virtually all currencies use a decimal system like ours.

Portability The holders of a currency must be able to move it easily to wherever a transaction takes place. In facilitating exchanges, the advantage of a decimal currency over stone wheels and cows is obvious. In North America, people began using paper money in 1685.[2]

Durability Any currency must be able to survive many transactions without wearing out. When it does not need replacement, people must know that they can exchange it for new currency without its suffering any loss of value. The average $1 bill lasts one and a half years. It is equally a dollar for both its first and its last holder.

Not Easily Counterfeited A currency's users must have confidence that what is in circulation is genuine. The federal government therefore goes to great lengths to make the design of bills difficult to counterfeit. The U.S. Bureau of Engraving and Printing uses paper containing silk threads as well as special inks and dyes to make paper money difficult to counterfeit.

References

1. Adam Smith, *The Money Game* (New York: Random House, 1967), p. 54; Arthur Fromm, *The History of Money* (New York: Archer House, 1957), p. 31.
2. Mark Goodman, "Designing the Dollar," *Money*, November 1986, pp. 112–118.

Notice that the subheadings make it clear that there are five characteristics of money.

2. **Words printed in italics or boldface may name details.** Words printed in boldface name the details that are discussed in the following passage:

The Purposes of Money

Money serves three essential purposes. It is a measure of value, a medium of exchange, and a store of value.

As a **measure of value,** money is a readily accepted means of relating or comparing the worth of different things. Money permits people to identify the relative value of two items—say, a blank videocassette at $4.99 and a videocassette of a recent movie for $39.95. Clearly, the price tag of the two videocassettes indicates that more value is placed on the movie videocassette.

Money is also a **medium of exchange,** anything that people are willing to accept in return for goods or services and that they in turn can exchange for other goods or services. For example, when a consumer buys a new car stereo, the dealership may use the money it receives either to buy more inventory or to pay salaries.

Money is also a **store of value,** a means of holding and collecting wealth. A farmer could not amass wealth by keeping milk that his or her cows produce over the years. Instead, the farmer exchanges the milk, which would spoil in a few weeks, for money, which he or she can hold indefinitely without risk of spoilage.

Notice that the three purposes of money are printed in boldface.

3. **Arabic numerals, such as *1, 2,* and *3,* or number words, such as *first, second,* and *third,* may indicate details.** A combination of numerals and italics is used to indicate details in the following passage:

When to Visit a Physician

Your decision to seek professional assistance for a symptom is generally guided by your previous history of medical problems and the nature of the symptom you are experiencing. In general, you should check with a physician for symptoms that are

1. *Severe.* If the symptom is very severe or intense, medical assistance is advised. Examples include severe pains, major injuries, and other emergencies.
2. *Unusual.* If the symptom is very peculiar and unfamiliar, it is wise to check it out with your physician. Examples include unexplained lumps, changes in a skin blemish or mole, problems with vision, difficulty swallowing, numbness, weakness, unexplained weight loss, and blood in sputum, urine, or bowel movement.
3. *Persistent.* If the symptom lasts longer than expected, seek medical advice. Examples include fever for more than five days, a cough lasting longer than two weeks, a sore that doesn't heal within a month, and hoarseness lasting longer than three weeks.
4. *Recurrent.* If a symptom tends to return again and again, medical evaluation is advised. Examples include recurrent headaches, stomach pains, and backache.

Sometimes a single symptom is not a cause for concern; but when the symptom is accompanied by other symptoms, the combination may suggest a more serious problem.

Numbers such as *first* and *second* are used to help you locate the details in the following passage. Underline the numbers in the passage to emphasize how many characteristics of professions are stated.

Professions

Professions are distinguished from other occupations by several characteristics. First, the skill of professionals is based on systematic, theoretical knowledge, not merely on training in particular techniques. Second, professionals have considerable autonomy over their work. Their clients are presumed to be incompetent to make judgments about the problems with which the profession is concerned; you can give instructions to your hairdresser or tailor but cannot advise a doctor or lawyer on matters of medicine or law. Third, professionals form associations that regulate their profession's internal affairs and represent its interests to outside bodies. Fourth, admission to a profession is carefully controlled by the existing members. Anyone can claim to be a salesperson or a carpenter, but someone who claims to be a surgeon or a professor without having the necessary credentials is an impostor. Becoming a professional involves taking an examination, receiving a license, and acquiring a title, and this process is usually regulated by the professional association concerned. Fifth, professions have a code of ethics that all their members are expected to adhere to.

You should have underlined the words *first, second, third, fourth,* and *fifth.*

4. **Bullets may indicate details.** Bullets are dots or squares that are used to draw attention to items in a list. Square bullets indicate the details in the following passage:

Private Space

Hall suggests that there are four distinct zones of private space:

- *Intimate distance.* This zone extends up to 18 inches from the body. It is reserved for people with whom one may have such intimate physical contact as lying together with bodies touching.
- *Personal distance.* This zone extends from 18 inches to 4 feet. It is reserved for friends and acquaintances. Some physical intimacy is permitted within this zone, such as putting one's arm around another's shoulder or greeting someone with a hug, but there are limits.
- *Social distance.* This zone extends from 4 to 12 feet. It is maintained in relatively formal situations, such as job interviews. There is no actual physical contact within this zone.
- *Public distance.* This zone extends for 12 feet and beyond, and is maintained by people wishing to distinguish themselves from the general public. Speakers addressing an audience, for example, maintain this distance.

Notice that bullets give prominent emphasis to the four zones of private space.

5. **Introductory statements often give information about details.** An introduction may state the number of details in a passage, or it may name the details. The following introduction to "The Purposes of Money" on page 178 states that there are *three* purposes, and it names them:

The Purposes of Money

Money serves three essential purposes. It is a measure of value, a medium of exchange, and a store of value.

It is very common for textbook passages to begin with specific information about the details in them.

EXERCISE 18.1 **"How to Improve Your Memory"**

Use the *subheadings* to guide you in marking the following passage.

How to Improve Your Memory

No matter how good (or bad) your basic memory is, you could probably make much better use of the capacity you do have. As James Weinland (1957) has said, "A person is entitled to say that he has a poor memory only if he forgets many things that deeply interest him and that he has made an effort to remember." Weinland's point is aptly illustrated by the student who complains he can't remember facts in his classes, but who can remember the names of every part in an automobile, the names of all the players in the National Football League, and the cubic displacement and horsepower of every motorcycle sold in the United States.

In this and previous chapters, many factors affecting learning and memory have been mentioned. The list below summarizes these factors and some not previously discussed. You can improve your memory and study efficiency by controlling as many of these factors as possible.

Knowledge of Results Learning proceeds most effectively when feedback or knowledge of results allows you to check to see if you are learning. Feedback also helps you identify material that needs extra practice, and it can be rewarding to know that you have remembered or answered correctly. A prime means of providing feedback for yourself when studying is *recitation.*

Recitation Recitation means repeating to yourself what you have learned. If you are going to remember something, eventually you will have to retrieve it. Recitation forces you to practice retrieving information as you are learning. When you are reading a text, you should stop frequently and try to remember what you have just read by summarizing it aloud. In one experiment the best memory score of all was earned by a group of students who spent 80 percent of their time reciting and only 20 percent reading (Gates, 1958). Maybe students who talk to themselves aren't crazy after all!

Overlearning Numerous studies have shown that memory is greatly improved when study is continued beyond "bare mastery." In other words, after you have learned material well enough to remember it once without error, you should continue studying. Overlearning is your best insurance against "going blank" on a test because of nervousness or anxiety.

Selection The Dutch scholar Erasmus said that a good memory should be like a fisherman's net: It should keep all the big fish and let the little ones escape. If you boil down the paragraphs in most textbooks to one or two important terms or ideas, you will find your memorization chores more manageable and will probably remember more than you would if you tried to retain everything. Practice careful and selective marking in your texts and use marginal notes to further summarize ideas. Most students mark their texts too much instead of too little. If everything is underlined, you haven't been selective.

Spaced Practice Spaced practice is generally superior to massed practice. Four 15-minute study periods will produce more learning than a one-hour study session. Perhaps the best way to try to make use of this principle is to *schedule* your time. If the average student were to keep a totally honest record of his weekly activities, he would probably find that very few hours were spent really studying. To make an effective schedule, designate times during the week before, after, and between classes when you will study particular subjects. Then treat these times just as if they were classes you had to attend.

Organize Assume that you must memorize the following list of words: north, man, red, spring, woman, east, autumn, yellow, summer, boy, blue, west, winter, girl, green, south. This rather difficult list could be reorganized as follows: north, east, south, west, spring, summer, autumn, winter, red, yellow, green, blue, man, woman, boy, girl. This simple reordering made the second list much easier to learn when college students were tested on both lists (Deese and Hulse, 1967). In another experiment, students who made up stories using long lists of words to be memorized learned the lists better than those who didn't (Bower and Clark, 1969). Organizing class notes and outlining chapters can be very helpful when studying. It may even be helpful to outline your outlines, so that the overall organization of ideas becomes clearer and simpler.

Whole Versus Part Learning If you had to memorize a speech, would it be better to try to learn it from beginning to end or in smaller parts like paragraphs? Generally, it is better to practice whole packages of information rather than smaller parts. This is especially true for fairly short, organized information. An exception is that learning parts may be better for extremely long, complicated information. Try to study the largest *meaningful* amount of information possible at one time. It is also important to remember the *serial position effect.* This is the tendency to master material in the order: first, last, then middle. Since information in the middle is the last learned, it should be given special attention.

Sleep Remember that sleeping after study produces the least interference. Since you obviously can't sleep after every study session, or can't study everything just before you sleep, your study schedule (see above) should include ample breaks between subjects. Using your breaks and free time in a schedule is as important as living up to your study periods.

Review If you have spaced your practice and overlearned, review will be like icing on your study cake. Review shortly before an exam cuts down the time during which you must remember details that may be important for the test but not otherwise meaningful to you. When reviewing, hold the amount of new information you try to memorize to a minimum. It may be realistic to take what you have actually learned and add a little more to it at the last minute by cramming, but remember that more than a little new learning will confuse you and interfere with what you already know.

If you consistently use the principles reviewed above, you should get grades at least one step higher without increasing your study time, or you should get the same grades after spending less time. Give this an honest try, and we can almost guarantee these results.

References

Bower, G. H. and M. C. Clark. "Narrative Stories as Mediators for Serial Learning." *Psychonomic Science,* 1969, 14, pp. 181–182.

Deese, J. and S. H. Hulse. *The Psychology of Learning* (3rd ed.). New York: McGraw-Hill, 1967.

Gates, A. I. "Recitation as a Factor in Memorizing." In *The Psychology of Learning* (2nd ed.), edited by J. Deese. New York: McGraw-Hill, 1958.

Weinland, J. D. *How to Improve Your Memory.* New York: Barnes & Noble, 1957.

EXERCISE 18.2 "Adjusting to Death"

Use the *bullets* to guide you in marking the following passage.

Adjusting to Death

People tend to move through five stages as they face death:

- Denial. In this first stage, people resist the idea that they are dying. Even if told that their chances for survival are small, they refuse to admit that they are facing death.
- Anger. After moving beyond the denial stage, dying people are angry—angry at people around them who are in good health, angry at God, angry at medical professionals for being ineffective. They ask the question "Why me?" and are unable to answer it without feeling anger.
- Bargaining. Anger leads to bargaining, in which the dying try to think of ways to postpone death. They may decide to dedicate their lives to religion if God saves them; they may say, "If only I can live to see my son married, I will accept death then." Such bargains are rarely kept, most often because the dying person's illness keeps progressing and invalidates any "agreements."
- Depression. When dying people come to feel that bargaining is of no use, they move to the next stage: depression. They realize that the die is cast, that they are losing their loved ones and their lives really are coming to an end. They are experiencing what Kübler-Ross calls "preparatory grief" for their own death.
- Acceptance. In this last stage, people are past mourning for the loss of their own lives, and they accept impending death. Usually, they are unemotional and uncommunicative; it is as if they have made peace with themselves and are expecting death without rancor.

While not everyone experiences each of these stages in the same way, if at all, Kübler-Ross's theory remains our best description of people's reactions to their approaching death.

EXERCISE 18.3 "Listening"

Use the *numbers* (*1*, *2*, and so on) to guide you in marking the following passage.

Listening

Research performed at Ohio State University indicates that the amount of time we spend on different parts of the communication process is divided: listening, 45 percent; speaking, 30 percent; reading, 16 percent; writing, 9 percent.[1] Most of us spent first grade learning to write, and we have continued to write throughout our academic careers. In second grade, the entire year focused on teaching reading. Every year thereafter has provided constant practice in reading. Perhaps we took a speech course in high school or college. Yet schools rarely offer a course in listening. This skill is taught the least, yet it is used the most according to the Ohio study. It's no wonder most of us spend our time thinking about what we are going to say next instead of truly listening to what another person has to say. People speak at approximately 150 words per minute. Our listening capacity is 450 words per minute. Since the message is usually much slower than our capacity to listen, we have plenty of time to concentrate on all aspects of the message. Why, then, are messages lost between the sender and the receiver?

All too frequently, hearing is confused with listening. To hear is simply to perceive sounds by the ear. To listen, however, is to make a conscious effort to hear something and to blend it with reason and understanding. We may not be able to improve our hearing, but we can improve our listening skills. Communication expert John T. Samaras of the University of Oklahoma points out six signs of poor listening habits:

1. Thinking about something else while waiting for the speaker's next word or sentence.
2. Listening primarily for facts rather than ideas.
3. Tuning out when the talk seems to be getting too difficult.
4. Prejudging, from a person's appearance or manner, that nothing interesting will be said.
5. Paying attention to outside sights and sounds while talking to someone.
6. Interrupting with a question whenever a speaker says something puzzling or unclear.[2]

Several years ago, J. Paul Lyet, chairman and chief executive officer of Sperry Corporation, discovered that when customers talked, few of his employees were really listening. The result—a sizeable amount of lost business. He also found that the problem was not unique to Sperry. It was costing other companies billions of dollars in lost revenues.

Lyet began to stress communication skills—particularly good listening habits—in company training programs. His first aim was to train those employees who have contact with customers. Sperry turned for help to

Dr. Lyman K. Steil, a communication expert who believes that ". . . listening is a human behavior, a set of skills that flows from attitudes and knowledge you can measure, observe, test, and improve."

Listening, speaking, writing, and reading—these are the four basic skills of communication that everyone should learn early in life. According to many studies, we don't learn them well. We need to accept the fact that listening is a skill. It can be taught, and it can be learned. Most of all, it needs to be practiced. Dr. Steil and other communication experts offer some general guidelines for teaching people to be better listeners.

1. *Don't anticipate.* Resist the temptation to finish a speaker's sentences or jump to conclusions when only part of the message has been given. Give the speaker time to find the right words and to finish the message. Too often, the conclusions we jump to are the wrong ones.

2. *Avoid prejudging the speaker.* A poor listener usually decides in advance that the topic is dull and tunes out the message after the first few sentences. A good listener may not be any more impressed with the topic but will still attempt to evaluate the concepts to determine if any can be used. In addition, a poor listener will be distracted by the speaker's delivery or appearance. A good listener focuses on the content and on learning what the speaker knows about the subject. On a one-to-one basis, a critical listener can bring a conversation to a quick end. Good listening means creating a climate of trust, mutual respect, and warmth.

3. *Eliminate distractions.* A good listener creates a quiet, comfortable environment for listening. Closing a door, turning off noisy machinery, moving closer to the speaker, or changing to a quieter location can ensure that both sender and receiver can communicate well.

4. *Ask for clarification; restate important points.* Good listeners make sure they understand the terms and concepts the other person is using. One must not only be aware of the everyday meaning of words but also realize that each person has his or her own unique definitions associated with them. If there is confusion about what the speaker means, the listener can ask questions or restate what has been said until the points are clear.

5. *Be ready to give feedback.* When asked, a listener should give feedback as soon as possible. The response should be specific and framed in "I" statements. Instead of saying, "Your thinking is fuzzy here," the listener must pinpoint what needs to be done or changed. "I feel an important step has been overlooked. I suggest you check with inventory before planning that large an order."

References

1. Thomas Koziol, "Listening . . . A Lost Skill?" *The Hot Buttoneer,* August 1984, p. 1.
2. *American Salesman,* November 1981, p. 17.

EXERCISE 18.4 "Maslow's Hierarchy of Needs"

Use the *introduction, subheadings,* and Figure 18.3 to guide you in marking the following passage.

Maslow's Hierarchy of Needs

Abraham Maslow, a noted psychologist, found that people tend to satisfy their needs in a particular order—a theory he called the "hierarchy of needs."[1] Maslow's theory rests on two assumptions: (1) people have a number of needs that require some measure of satisfaction, and only unsatisfied needs motivate behavior; and (2) the needs of people are arranged in a hierarchy of prepotency, which means that as each lower-level need is satisfied, the need at the next level demands attention.[2] Basically, human beings are motivated to satisfy physiological needs first (food, clothing, shelter), then the need for safety and security, and then social and esteem needs. Finally, they seek to realize their potential, what Maslow called "self-actualization." Maslow's theory is illustrated in Figure 18.3. It is not difficult to see how this theory can be applied to motivation on the job.

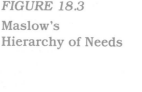

FIGURE 18.3
Maslow's Hierarchy of Needs

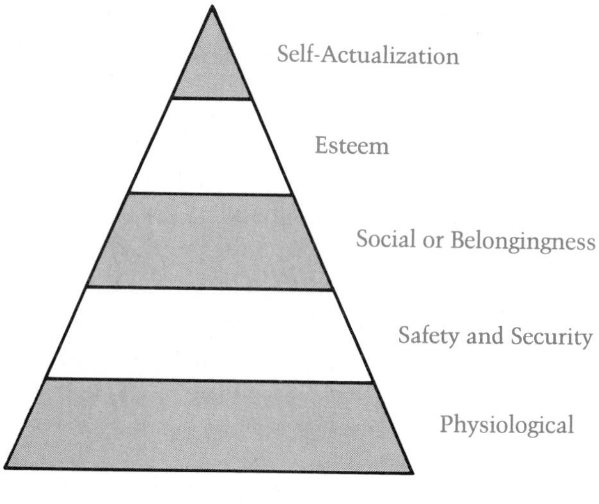

Physiological Needs

The needs for food, clothing, sleep, and shelter, or *physiological needs,* were described by Maslow as survival or lower-order needs. In most work environments, these basic needs rarely dominate because they are reasonably well satisfied. During the Great Depression, however, many people worked solely to ensure their own and their families' survival. In most cases, they were not concerned with the type of work they did or whether they liked it.

Safety and Security Needs

People's desire for some sort of order and predictability in the world is reflected in *safety and security needs.* In general, people tend to look for security in the known and familiar and avoid what they don't know or understand. They like to know that they won't lose their jobs, that they can provide for their families, and that they will have enough money and resources to take care of themselves in sickness or old age. During the recession in the early 1980s, massive layoffs put employees in a state of limbo. Even those not laid off wondered from day to day if they would have a job the next week. In the late 1980s it was the heavy volume of mergers, buy-outs, and business closings due to the movement of production facilities to other countries that created a feeling of insecurity among many workers. Even the oldest and largest of organizations were not immune to the economic volatility that spread across America. This insecurity often affected productivity and strained human relations at home and at work.

Organizations recognize the need for security by offering employees pensions, profit sharing, stock option plans, and insurance plans. Workers are not simply earning a paycheck but protecting themselves against injury and laying aside money for retirement. Several American companies have made a major effort to avoid layoffs. Job security is given a very high priority at such companies as Hallmark Cards Inc., Johnson Wax, Federal Express Corp., and Worthington Industries.

Safety needs usually focus on protection from physical harm. On the job, this means a guarantee of safe working conditions. Unions or employee groups can make sure employers maintain safety standards and reduce the risk of accidents or injuries resulting from environmental hazards. Congress established the Occupational Safety and Health Act (OSHA) to help reduce deaths and injuries on the job.

Safety needs are also satisfied in other ways outside work. Advertisements for additional life or medical insurance, smoke detectors or burglar alarms, or guaranteed savings programs all appeal to people's need for safety and security.

Social or Belongingness Needs

Whereas the first two types of needs deal with aspects of physical survival, *social* or *belongingness needs* deal with emotional and mental well-being. Ron Parks, manager of manufacturing operations and human resources at the Dana Corp. plant in Columbia, South Carolina, can use his computer to contact any of his fifty-one employees. With a few keystrokes he can send a message to the video-display terminals at their work stations. However, he does not rely on this modern technology for all of his communication with the workers. Every Monday morning he goes to the plant with the plant manager to meet with the workers over coffee. These informal meetings not only improve communication, but also meet the social needs of many workers.[3]

Research has shown that fulfillment of people's needs for affection, a sense of belonging, and identification with a group are as important to their health as are food and safety.

Although social needs are felt throughout childhood, they may become more intense during adolescence, when the need to belong to a group becomes more important than family ties or what parents think. As adults, the need for belonging may take the form of joining various organizations—professional associations, church groups, amateur sports teams, or social clubs. Special uniforms or membership privileges reflect the desire to feel part of a group in which individuals share the same interests, values, and goals.

Many people's social needs are also satisfied on the job. People form attachments with coworkers and may join the company sports teams, take part in company picnics or outings, and get together after work. A growing number of business firms are sponsoring softball teams made up of their employees. Employers who are eager to see teamwork develop at the plant or office often pay for all or part of the bill for jerseys, equipment and postgame refreshments. David Abramis, an organizational psychologist at California State University at Long Beach, says, "People who play company-sponsored softball tend to think of work as being more fun."[4] In many cases, friendships developed at work may function like a "second family." This is not surprising when you consider that many employees spend more time with people on the job than they do with their own family members. Many people are more highly motivated when they work as members of a team. Managers have found that when employees have a strong sense of being a part of the team, they are likely to be more productive.

Esteem Needs

Self-esteem is a term that describes how you feel about yourself. Self-esteem influences work behaviors and attitudes in two fundamental ways. First, employees bring to their work settings different levels of self-esteem, which in turn influence how they act, feel, and think while on the job. Second, individuals need to feel good about themselves; thus, much of what workers do and believe serves to enhance, preserve, or restore their self-esteem.[5]

Esteem needs relate to one's self-respect and to the recognition and respect one receives from others. Arthur Witkin, chief psychologist for the Personnel Sciences Center, believes that: "Perhaps the single most important thing is to be aware of a worker's need for self-esteem. Everyone needs to feel good about himself; if he doesn't, he'll not only turn in a poor job performance, he'll keep others from doing their best."[6]

Esteem needs can be satisfied in many ways. You may set your sights on winning the top-salesperson-of-the-year award, work to build a reputation as a highly skilled and reliable employee, or volunteer to chair a committee for the annual charity drive. Often, managers miss opportunities to reinforce the self-esteem of their workers. For most people, a word of appreciation or praise is a strong motivator. One employee stated, "It's such a simple thing, but hearing the boss say I did a great job makes me feel that all the work I put into a project was worth it. I go away wanting to work even harder on the next one."

Self-actualization Needs

The four needs just described motivate people by their *absence,* that is, when people feel a lack of food, security, social relationships, or esteem. *Self-actualization needs,* on the other hand, represent the need for growth and motivate people by their *presence.* Self-actualization is fulfilling one's potential or realizing one's fullest capacities as a human being.

Maslow used *self-actualization* in a very specialized sense to describe a rarely attained state of human achievement. Because of the uniqueness of each person, the form or content of self-actualization is a very individual thing.[7] Most of us will probably not reach self-actualization in Maslow's sense of the term, but we do make steps toward it by seeking to expand ourselves through setting new goals and finding new means of expression. The achievement of one goal stimulates the search for new challenges. It is like being on a fascinating journey where the goal is not the end of the road but the journey itself.

Each person's journey toward self-actualization will be individual and unique. It may be difficult to satisfy this need on the job, since most jobs are limited in scope and have their duties fairly clearly defined. However, this is not to say that people haven't found ways to change their jobs, create new positions for themselves, or set new goals year after year. George Guzewicz took a $15,000 pay cut to leave Xerox Corporation, the company where he had worked for seventeen years, to enter a sales job.[8] (He had never sold a product or service before.) Feeling that his job at Xerox was not challenging enough, he went to work for Lambda Semiconductors. After only a few months in the new position, Mr. Guzewicz was achieving success and feeling a new sense of accomplishment. He was already setting his sights on another position within the company that would offer an even greater challenge.

The self-actualizing person may not only create his or her own job, but may have two or three careers in one lifetime. A retired elementary school teacher learned Braille at age sixty-five and taught blind children for fifteen years. In another case, a printer turned his carpentering skills into a side business and began manufacturing grandfather clocks. He kept at his "hobby" until well into his eighties.

References

1. A. H. Maslow, *Motivation and Personality* (New York: Harper & Row, 1954).
2. H. C. Kazanas, *Effective Work Competencies for Vocational Education* (Columbus, Ohio: National Center for Research in Vocational Education, 1978), p. 12.
3. Stephen A. Stromp, "The Art of Corporate Communicating," *U.S. Air*, January 1989, p. 34.
4. James Cox, "Business Playing Softball," *USA Today*, July 8, 1988, p. B-1.
5. Joel Brockner, *Self-Esteem at Work* (Lexington, Mass.: Lexington Book, 1988), p. xi.
6. "How Bosses Get People to Work Harder," *U.S. News and World Report*, January 29, 1979, p. 63.
7. "Maslow's Term and Themes," *Training*, March 1977, p. 48.
8. "Eight Who Switched to Selling—Thanks to Hard Times," *Sales and Marketing Management*, September 13, 1982.

EXERCISE 18.5 "What Is a Brand?"

Use the words printed in *boldface* to guide you in marking the following passage.

What Is a Brand?

A **brand** is a name, term, symbol, design, or any combination of these that identifies a seller's products and distinguishes them from competitors' products. A **brand name** is the part of a brand that can be spoken. It may include letters, words, numbers, or pronounceable symbols, like the ampersand in *Procter & Gamble.* A **brand mark,** on the other hand, is the part of a brand that is a symbol or distinctive design, like Planters' "Mr. Peanut."

A **trademark** is a brand that is registered with the U.S. Patent and Trademark Office and is thus legally protected from use by anyone except its owner. Among the many registered trademarks are the shape of the Coca-Cola bottle and the CBS eye.

Brands are often classified according to who owns them: manufacturers or stores. A **manufacturer** (or **producer**) **brand,** as the name implies, is a brand name that is owned by a manufacturer. The majority of foods, major appliances, and gasolines, as well as all automobiles, are sold with producer branding. So is much of today's clothing. Names such as Jonathan Logan, Calvin Klein, Bill Blass, and Gloria Vanderbilt are examples of producer brands that appeal to both department stores and consumers. Many consumers prefer producer brands because they are nationally known, offer consistent quality, and are widely available.

A **store** (or **private**) **brand** is one that is owned by an individual wholesaler or retailer. Among the better-known store brands are Kenmore and Craftsman (owned by Sears, Roebuck) and KMC (owned by K mart). Owners of store brands claim that they can offer lower prices, earn greater profits, and improve customer loyalty with their own brands. Companies that manufacture a private brand often find such operations profitable because they can use excess capacity and at the same time avoid most marketing costs. About one-third of all tire, food, and appliance sales are of store-branded items. Sears generates more than one-half of its sales from its own brands.

Consumer confidence is the most important element in the success of a branded product, whether the brand is owned by a producer or a store. Because branding identifies each product completely, consumers can easily repurchase products that provide satisfaction, performance, and quality. And they can just as easily avoid or ignore products that do not. In supermarkets, among the products most likely to keep their shelf space are the brand leaders having the greatest share of sales and deepest consumer commitment.

A **generic product** (sometimes called a **generic brand**) is a product with no brand at all. Its plain package carries only the name of the product—applesauce, peanut butter, potato chips, or whatever—in black type. Usually, generic products are made by the major producers that manufacture name brands. Generic products have been available in supermarkets since 1977. They appeal mainly to customers who are willing to sacrifice consistency in size or quality for a lower price. However, generic products are not necessarily lower in quality.

EXERCISE 18.6 "Emotions"

Use the *introduction* (first sentence) and the *number words* (*first, second,* and so on) to guide you in marking the following passage.

Emotions

Emotions are transitory states, characterized by six features. First, emotions are neither overt behaviors nor specific thoughts; they are experiences. As a result, emotions are often mixed and even contradictory; assigning specific labels to them may be difficult. For example, you might find it difficult to determine all of your feelings about a friend's serious illness. Certainly you feel sadness, but it may be mixed with guilty relief that you remain healthy.

Second, emotional experience has *valence*, which means it is either positive or negative, something you would like either to enhance or eliminate. Thus, changes in emotions can change your motivation. Most people tend to act in ways that bring about happiness, satisfaction, and other positive emotions and to avoid doing things that cause pain, anxiety, disgust, or sadness.

Third, emotions are passions, not actions. Eating, for example, is an action, but hunger is a passion. Actions are initiated by the actor, whereas passions happen to the actor. You eat, but hunger happens to you. Similarly, emotions happen to you. You cannot decide to experience joy or sorrow; instead, you "fall in love" or are "overcome by grief."

The passionate nature of emotions does not mean that you have no control over them, however, because of their fourth feature: emotions arise in part from a cognitive appraisal of a situation. Seeing a lion elicits different emotions depending on whether you think the animal is a tame pet or a wild, hungry beast; your *interpretation* of the situation can alter your emotional reaction to it. Emotions depend not just on situations but on what you *think* about those situations, such as how you interpret their potential for threat or pleasure.

Although you cannot consciously determine your emotions, part of the situation you interpret is your own emotions as they develop. Emotions are, therefore, experiences that are both triggered by the thinking self and experienced by the self as happening to the self. They reveal the individual as both agent and object, as both I and me, both the controller of thoughts and the recipient of passions. The extent to which you are a "victim" of your passions versus a rational designer of your emotions is one of the central dilemmas of human existence, and a subject of literature as much as of psychology.

Fifth, emotions are accompanied by bodily responses. When you are surprised, for example, you probably show a wide-eyed, open-mouthed expression and raise your hands to your face. The facial and bodily movements that accompany emotion are partly reflexive and partly learned. In addition, internal, *visceral* responses—changes in heart rate, for example—also accompany emotion. These visceral responses are reflexive, occurring as automatically as salivation in response to food.

Finally, emotions vary in intensity, from the quiet satisfaction of a person watching a beautiful sunset to the raging fury of a wronged lover. The importance of this feature of emotion is evident in people whose emotional intensity is very low. Nothing seems to get them excited; they appear to take no real pleasure in anything, and they do not get very upset about anything. An extreme lack of emotion may make it difficult or impossible to hold a job or to function normally in other ways. Too much emotional arousal can also cause problems. An overly emotional person may be unable to concentrate or to coordinate thoughts and actions efficiently. Stage fright—which brings sweaty palms, dry mouth, tremors, and other signs of strong physiological arousal—is one example; it can lead to forgotten lines, botched musical numbers, and other performance disasters.

In summary, an emotion is a valenced experience that is felt with some intensity as happening to the self, generated in part by a cognitive appraisal of the situation, and accompanied by both learned and reflexive physical responses.

EXERCISE 18.7 "Advertising Media"

Use the *introduction, subheadings,* and Figure 18.4 to guide you in marking the following passage.

Advertising Media

The **advertising media** are the various forms of communication through which advertising reaches its audience. They include newspapers, magazines, television, radio, direct mail, and outdoor displays. Figure 18.4 shows how businesses allocate their advertising expenditures among the various media. The *print media*—which include newspapers, magazines, direct mail, and billboards—account for more than 50 percent of all advertising expenditures. The *electronic media*—television and radio—account for about 28 percent.

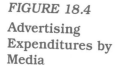

FIGURE 18.4
Advertising Expenditures by Media

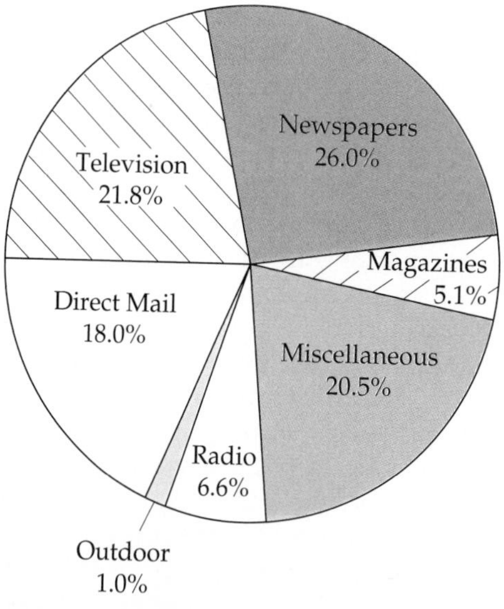

Newspapers Newspaper advertising accounts for about 26 percent of all advertising expenditures. More than half is purchased by retailers.

Newspaper advertising is used so extensively by retailers because it is reasonable in cost. Furthermore, because it provides only local coverage, advertising dollars are not wasted in reaching people who are outside the store's market area. It is also timely. Ads can usually be placed the day before they are to appear, and their effectiveness can be measured easily.

There are some drawbacks, however, to newspaper advertising. It has a short life span; newspapers are generally read through once and then discarded. Color reproduction in newspapers is usually poor; thus most ads must be run in black and white. Finally, marketers cannot target specific markets through newspaper ads, except with regard to geographic area.

Magazines The advertising revenues of magazines have been climbing dramatically since 1976. In 1988 they reached $6.1 billion, or about 5.1 percent of all advertising expenditures.

Advertisers can reach very specific market segments through ads in special-interest magazines. A boat manufacturer has a ready-made consumer audience in subscribers to *Yachting* or *Sail.* Producers of cameras and photographic equipment advertise primarily in *Travel & Leisure* or *Popular Photography.* A number of more general magazines like *Time* and *Cosmopolitan* publish regional editions, which provide advertisers with geographic segmentation as well.

Magazine advertising is more prestigious than newspaper advertising, and it provides high-quality color reproduction. In addition, magazine advertisements have a longer life span than those in other media. Issues of *National Geographic,* for example, may be retained for months or years by subscribers, and the ads they contain are viewed over and over again.

The major disadvantages of magazine advertising are high cost and lack of timeliness. Magazine ads—especially full-color ads—are expensive, although the cost per reader may compare favorably with that of other media. And, because magazine ads must normally be prepared more than a month in advance, they cannot be adjusted to reflect the latest market conditions.

Direct Mail **Direct-mail advertising** is promotional material that is mailed directly to individuals. Direct mail is the most selective medium: Mailing lists are available (or can be compiled) to reach almost any target market, from airplane enthusiasts to zoologists. The effectiveness of direct-mail advertising can be measured easily because recipients either buy or don't buy the product that is advertised.

The success of direct-mail advertising depends on appropriate and current mailing lists. A direct-mail campaign may fail if the mailing list is outdated and the mailing does not reach the right people. In addition, this medium is relatively costly. Nevertheless, direct-mail advertising expenditures in 1988 amounted to more than $21 billion, or about 18 percent of the total.

Outdoor Advertising **Outdoor advertising** consists of short promotional messages on billboards, posters, and signs, and in skywriting. In 1988 outdoor advertisers spent $1.1 billion, or approximately 1 percent of total advertising expenditures, on outdoor advertising.

Sign and billboard advertising allows the marketer to focus on a particular geographic area; it is fairly inexpensive. However, because most of it is directed toward a mobile audience (the advertising on buses and taxis is itself mobile), the message must be limited to a few words. The medium is especially suitable for products that lend themselves to pictorial display.

Television Television is the newest advertising medium, and it ranks second only to newspapers in total revenue. In 1988, 21.8 percent of advertising expenditures, or $25 billion, went to television. Approximately 98 percent of American homes have at least one television set, which is used an average of seven hours each day.[1] The average U.S. household can receive nearly twenty-eight TV channels, including cable and pay stations, according to Nielson Media Research. Fifty-four percent of households receive twenty or more channels, and 39 percent can get between seven and nineteen channels.[2] Television obviously provides a massive market for advertisers.

Television advertising is the primary medium for larger firms whose objective is to reach national or regional markets. A national advertiser may buy *network time,* which guarantees that its message will be broadcast by hundreds of local stations that are affiliated with the network. And both national and local firms may buy *local time* on a single station that covers a particular geographic selling area.

Advertisers may *sponsor* an entire show, alone or with other sponsors. Or they may buy *spot time* for a single 10-, 20-, 30-, or 60-second commercial during or between programs. To an extent, they may select their audience by choosing the day of the week and the time of day when their ads will be shown. Anheuser-Busch advertises Budweiser Beer and Noxell Corporation advertises Noxema shaving cream during the TV football season because the majority of viewers are men, who are likely to use these products.

Unlike magazine advertising, and perhaps like newspaper ads, television advertising has a short life. If a viewer misses a commercial, it is missed forever. Viewers may also become indifferent to commercial messages. Or they may use the commercial time as a break from viewing, thus missing the message altogether. (Remote-control devices make it especially easy to banish at least the sound of commercials from the living room.)

Radio Advertisers spent about $7.8 billion, or 6.6 percent of total expenditures, on radio advertising in 1988, up from $7.2 billion in 1987. Like magazine advertising, radio advertising offers selectivity. Radio stations develop programming for—and are tuned in by—specific groups of listeners. There are almost half a billion radios in the United States (about six per household), which makes radio the most accessible medium.

Radio can be less expensive than other media. Actual rates depend on geographic coverage, the number of commercials contracted for, the time period specified, and whether the station broadcasts on AM, FM, or both. Even small retailers are able to afford radio advertisements.

References

1. *Chicago Sun-Times,* January 25, 1984, pp. 1, 26.
2. *Wall Street Journal,* June 7, 1989, p. B1.

EXERCISE 18.8 "Television"

Use the *subheadings* and *dates* to guide you in marking the following passage.

Television

The history of television goes a lot further back than many people suppose. In fact, in 1884, a German experimenter, Paul Nipkow, developed a rotating disk with small holes arranged in a spiral pattern that, when used with a light source, had unusual properties. Aiming a strong light at the disk so that light passed through the holes produced a very rapid "scanning" effect. That is, pinpoints of light came through the holes in the whirling disk and across from left to right or right to left, depending on whether the disk was whirling clockwise or counterclockwise in a pattern that was somewhat like the movements a human eye makes while scanning across a page. It was realized quite early that the perforated whirling disk could produce electrical impulses that could be sent along a wire so as to transmit pictures. The "Nipkow disk" became the central technology for further experimentation on the transmission of images, both by wire and later by radio waves. This scanning concept is at the heart of television, even today, although it is accomplished by electronic means rather than by a mechanical disk.[1]

Early in the 1920s, such corporations as General Electric and RCA allocated budgets for experiments with television, and other corporations soon followed. The idea seemed far-fetched and futuristic to many in the industry, but television research was authorized in the hope that it would eventually pay off. General Electric employed an inventor, Ernst Alexanderson, to work exclusively on the problem, and within a short time he had developed a workable system based on the Nipkow disk. However, it was not to be the system that the industry finally adopted. What was needed was a completely electronic system.

Developing an Electronic System

Perhaps the most remarkable of the inventors who played a key role in developing the needed electronic technology was a skinny high school boy in an isolated part of the United States. Philo T. Farnsworth was a poor youngster from a large family in Rigby, Idaho, a small farm community. As a child he had started reading about electricity, and in 1922 he astounded his high school science teacher by showing him diagrams for electronic circuits that would make it possible to transmit and receive moving pictures over the air.

Philo had studied reports of television experiments that were based on the Nipkow disk. He correctly reasoned that such a system was primitive and clumsy. He had reached the conclusion that electronic devices were needed to sweep across a scene or picture rapidly in a series of horizontal lines, detect points of light and dark along these lines, and transform those variations into signals that could be broadcast over the air. Parallel electronic devices for reception and viewing were also needed. He had come up with designs of circuits for each apparatus and calculations as to how they could function. Philo's teacher enthusiastically encouraged him to try to perfect and patent the system.

During this same period, just after World War I, a talented Russian, Vladimir K. Zworykin, had come to the United States to work on radio research at Westinghouse. He had been a communication specialist in the army of Tsar Nicholas, where he had worked on early television experiments, before the Russian Revolution. He asked for permission to continue development of television at Westinghouse. Directors of the huge corporation thought it was a long shot, but decided to finance the work. Zworykin was also unimpressed with the mechanical-disk approach and believed that electronic systems were needed for practical television transmission and reception. He set out to work on them with the full facilities of the great Westinghouse laboratories.

Meanwhile, as Zworykin was closing in on the problem, a friend of Philo Farnsworth took him to California and provided him with funding for his experiments. There, on a shoestring budget, Farnsworth transformed his circuits and drawings into a working apparatus, which he built in an apartment where he kept the blinds drawn. (The neighbors thought he was a bootlegger running a still, and he was "raided" by the police.) Then, in 1927, the young man was able to make actual transmissions. He showed his friend how his apparatus could broadcast and receive both fixed images and small scenes from motion pictures.

Having created a working system, Farnsworth took his drawings to federal authorities and applied for the first electronic television patent. His application created an uproar. The great radio corporations, taken completely by surprise, were shocked and outraged that an obscure nobody had invented, built, and asked to patent a system that Westinghouse, RCA, and others had spent fortunes trying to develop and were themselves about to patent. They immediately contested the application.

After a great deal of controversy and legal maneuvering, Farnsworth won. To regain control, RCA haggled with Farnsworth, who held out for a very profitable royalty settlement. Although Farnsworth reached his solution just before Zworykin did, the latter invented some of the most critical components of television technology—the iconoscope (electronic picture tube) and the image orthicon camera, without which television would not have been workable as a mass medium.

The Early Broadcasts

The earliest experimental television receivers used tiny screens, based on cathode ray tubes about 4 inches in diameter. Cameras were crude and required intense lighting. People who appeared on the screen had to wear bizarre purple and green make-up to provide contrast for the picture. Nevertheless, in 1927, a picture of Herbert Hoover, then Secretary of Commerce, appeared on an experimental broadcast.

By 1932 RCA had built a TV station, complete with studio and transmitting facilities, in New York City's Empire State Building. RCA set aside a million dollars to develop and demonstrate the new broadcast medium. In 1936 it began testing the system, broadcasting two programs a week. By that time a few hundred enthusiasts in the New York area had constructed or obtained TV receivers and were able to pick up the transmissions in their homes. Meanwhile, the federal government had developed procedures for awarding licenses to transmitters and had granted a limited number. Thus, by 1940, the medium was set to take off.

Suddenly, the whole world changed. After the Japanese attack on Pearl Harbor in December 1941, the war effort completely monopolized the country's attention. Along with almost every other aspect of American life, the manufacture of the new television receivers was temporarily delayed. All the electronics manufacturers turned to producing equipment for the armed forces, and not until 1945 did these companies return to making products for the civilian market. In the immediate postwar years, however, television stations were quickly established in a number of major cities, and the public was ready to buy sets. TV was finally ready for home use.

Rapid Adoption

By 1946, the FCC had issued twenty-four new licenses for television transmitters. The networks and advertising agencies were eagerly waiting for the new medium to enter American homes. It seemed clear to all concerned that television might become a truly important broadcast medium. There was a great scramble to take part.

The manufacture and sale of home receivers began that same year. As sets became available, Americans rushed to buy them. However, they were quite expensive. In 1947, a set with a picture about 6 by 7 inches cost around $400. That was more than a month's wages for many blue-collar working families, and it did not include the special antenna that had to be installed on the roof. A truly deluxe set, with a fancy wood cabinet and a mirror system for making the picture seem larger, sold for about half as much as a modest car. Obviously, only more affluent families could afford such a luxury, and so a TV set became a new kind of status symbol. Families who had one often invited their envious neighbors in to watch the transmissions (and to see visible evidence of their affluence). Stories circulated of people who put up an antenna to make their neighbors think that they had TV, when all they really had was the antenna—with no set hooked up below. In fact, TV was regarded as such a luxury that if a family that was receiving welfare was found to have a television set, it was regarded as a moral outrage.

One establishment that could afford a set was the local tavern. By 1948, a television set was a central feature in almost every tavern in the country. Sports programs were the favorite, and big crowds would gather to watch the games. It is probably no exaggeration to say that the local tavern was a significant element in demonstrating and popularizing the new medium.

The Big Freeze

By the beginning of 1948, the FCC had issued approximately one hundred licenses. Some cities had two or even three stations, although many still had none. Soon, however, problems developed of the kind that had troubled radio in the early years. The signals of one station sometimes interfered with those of another. This led the FCC to conclude that drastic action was needed to avoid upcoming difficulties. Beginning in 1948 and extending through 1952, the commission ordered a freeze on the issuance of new licenses and construction permits (previously licensed stations were allowed to start up). As a result, TV transmitters could not be built in many American communities until after the freeze was lifted. The FCC wanted to study thoroughly the technical aspects of television and related broadcasting so that it could allocate frequencies to TV, FM radio, and other kinds of transmissions appropriately.

During the freeze, the FCC developed a master plan that still governs TV broadcasting today. The system prevents one television station from interfering with the broadcasts of another, thus avoiding the chaos that characterized early radio broadcasting. When the freeze was lifted in 1952, television spread quickly throughout the United States. Within a remarkably short time, it became so ubiquitous that most American families had a set. Social commentators began to speak of the "television generation" of Americans born after World War II who never knew a world without television. The medium is presumed to have shaped their lives in significant ways.

The Coming of Color

Color television got off to a slow start. Experiments had been performed with color test pictures as early as 1929, and there was much talk about commercial broadcasts in color, even as early as 1940. But there were problems in settling on the best technology. By 1946 two separate color systems had been perfected. CBS had developed a system based on a rotating disk that actually gave very good results. However, it had one major problem: the FCC insisted that the system for color transmission be such that existing black-and-white television sets could still receive a picture (though not in color), and with the CBS system they would not be able to. In 1953 the FCC approved a different system, developed by RCA. Although it produced less refined colors, it did allow existing black-and-white sets to receive programs.

References

1. For a thorough history of television up to the mid-1970s, see Eric Barnouw, *Tube of Plenty: The Evolution of American Television* (New York: Oxford University Press, 1975).

EXERCISE 18.9 "Conversation"

Use the *introduction, subheadings, numbers,* and *italics* to guide you in marking the following passage.

Conversation

People use a variety of communication strategies and types at various stages of their relationships. In this section we will consider the kinds of communication that are most prevalent in starting conversations with strangers, keeping conversations going, and sharing ideas and feelings with close friends and intimates.

Starting Conversations

Many people have great difficulty starting conversations with complete strangers. We don't know what kind of potential relationship we might have with a person until we talk with the person. The first step to establishing a relationship, then, is building up the courage to say something.

In male-female encounters, same-sex encounters, and business encounters, what happens in the first few minutes of an initial conversation will have a profound effect on the nature of the relationship that develops. How do you go about striking up a conversation with strangers? For some people the advice given in this next section will be second nature. For those who find starting conversations difficult, however, the following suggestions for initial interaction with a stranger may be some of the most important information in this chapter.

1. *Formally or informally introduce yourself.* Start a conversation with a person by introducing yourself (or by getting someone else to introduce you). For example, "Hi, my name is Gordon. What's yours?" may sound trite, but it works. Or you might have a friend introduce you by saying, "Doris, I'd like you to meet my friend Bill. Bill, Doris is Susan's sister."
2. *Refer to the physical context.* One of the safest ways of starting a conversation is by referring to some aspect of the physical context. Certainly, one of the oldest and most effective of these is a comment about the weather: "This is awful weather for a game, isn't it?" Other contextual references includes such statements as "They've really decorated this place beautifully," "I wonder how they are able to keep such a beautiful garden in this climate?" and "Doesn't it seem stuffy in here?"
3. *Refer to your thoughts or feelings.* A very direct way to make contact is by commenting on what you are thinking or feeling at the moment: "I really like parties, don't you?" or "I live on this floor too—do these steps bother you as much as they do me?"
4. *Refer to the other person.* "I don't believe I've ever seen you—have you been working here long?" "President and Mrs. Phillips have sure done a lovely job of remodeling this home. Did you ever see it before the renovation?"

None of these statements is particularly threatening, so if the person you want to meet feels the same way about you, chances are he or she will respond pleasantly.

Keeping Conversations Going

Once two people have begun an interaction, they are likely to engage in relatively unthreatening conversations, that is, "small talk." Small talk typifies early stages of relationships and serves to meet many social needs with relatively low amounts of risk and disclosure of self and personal feelings. Moreover, small talk provides a basis on which to decide whether to move a relationship to the next level.

One common type of small talk is to refer to people you both know. Statements such as "Do you know Bill? I hear he has a really great job," "Would you believe that Mary Simmons and Tom Johnson are going together? They never seemed to hit it off too well in the past," and "My sister Eileen is really working hard at losing weight. I saw her the other day and all she talked about was the diet she's on" are all examples of small talk. This kind of small talk, often referred to as *gossip,* occurs during all phases of a relationship but is most common in the early phase because it is considered safe. You can gossip for a long time with another person without really saying anything about yourself or without learning anything about the other person. Gossip can be a pleasant way to pass the time of day with people you know but with whom you have no desire or need for a deeper relationship. It can also provide a safe way to explore the bases for attraction because it allows each person to see whether the other reacts similarly to the views expressed about the object of the gossip. Gossip can, of course, be malicious. More often than not, however, gossip represents a means of interacting amicably with others without becoming personally involved. This is why conversations at parties are comprised largely of gossip.

Another kind of small talk is simple idea exchange. In *idea-exchange communication* people share information that contains facts, opinions, and beliefs and that occasionally reflects values. Idea exchange is a common type of communication between both new acquaintances and old friends. At the office Dan may talk with Walt about sports, Martha may talk with Louise about new cars, and Pete may talk with Jack about landscaping. Or, on a more serious level, Jan may talk with Gloria about the U.S. role in the Middle East and Dave may talk with Bill about abortion. Although the discussions of foreign policy and abortion are "deeper" than conversations about sports or cars, both sets of conversations represent idea exchanges. This type of communication is important to early stages of relationships because you learn what the other person is thinking, reassess your attraction level, and decide whether or not you want the relationship to grow.

EXERCISE 18.10 "The Power of Positive Impressions"

This is the second of five exercises for applying study skills to the sample textbook chapter on pages 286–309 of the appendix. The other exercises are for surveying (Exercise 16.3), making notes (Exercise 19.8), reciting and rehearsing (Exercise 20.4), and test taking (Exercise 21.3).

Marking a Chapter

Mark the information in the sample chapter on pages 286–309 of the appendix that answers the following eleven questions. Each question below is followed by a suggestion to help you in underlining or highlighting.

1. What is the *primacy effect*? (Use the term *primacy effect* printed in boldface on page 288.)
2. Why are the first few minutes of a meeting extremely important? (Use the heading on page 289.)
3. What are some common assumptions, or stereotypes, that persist because of cultural influence? (Use the term *cultural influences* printed in boldface and the bulleted list on page 292.)
4. What is *surface language,* and what kinds of decisions do people make about you solely on the basis of your surface language? (Use the subheading on page 293 and the bulleted list on page 294.)

5. What four factors should influence your choice of clothing for work? (Use the numbered list on page 297 and the subheadings on pages 297–298.)
6. What are some wardrobe suggestions about which many wardrobe engineers and image consultants agree? (Use the numbered list on pages 299–300.)
7. How can facial expression create a positive impression? (Use the subheading on page 300.)
8. How can your carriage create a positive impression? (Use the subheading on page 300.)
9. How can your voice create a positive impression? (Use the subheading on page 301.)
10. How can your handshake create a positive impression? (Use the subheading on page 301 and the numbered list on page 302.)
11. What rules of etiquette are particularly important to working in an organization? (Use the subheading on page 302 and the numbered list on pages 303–304.)

19

Make Notes for Books

The first way to organize information in a textbook is to mark it using methods that are explained in Chapter 18. The second way is to make notes on the information.

Making notes will help you learn in three ways. First, to make notes, you must think about what you read and restate it in your own words. In many instances, you will learn information as you process it in this way. Second, since notes are summaries, you will have much less to learn when you study from notes than when you study directly from textbooks. Third, when you make notes, you don't need to learn information exactly as it is presented in a book—you can rearrange it in formats that make it easier for you to learn.

Examine the examples of notes on pages 205–210 before you read the following discussions.

Notes on Cards

Most students make notes on notebook paper, but some very successful students prefer to study from notes written on index cards. Whether you use notebook paper or cards, make notes using the procedures in "How to Make Textbook Notes" on page 204.

Figure 19.1 on page 204 illustrates how to make notes on 3-by-5-inch index cards.

- Write a descriptive title on the blank side of a card.
- Write details on the back of the card upside down in relation to the title on the front.

When you make notes in this way, the information on the backs of cards is in the proper position for reading when you turn the cards over.

There are four advantages of making notes on 3-by-5-inch cards rather than on notebook paper. First, since cards are small, they require you to summarize and condense information. Second, cards make it easy to integrate class notes and textbook notes, because you can copy information in your class notes onto related textbook notes so that all the information about a topic is in one place for efficient study. Third, cards make it possible to separate information that

FIGURE 19.1
Notes on an Index Card

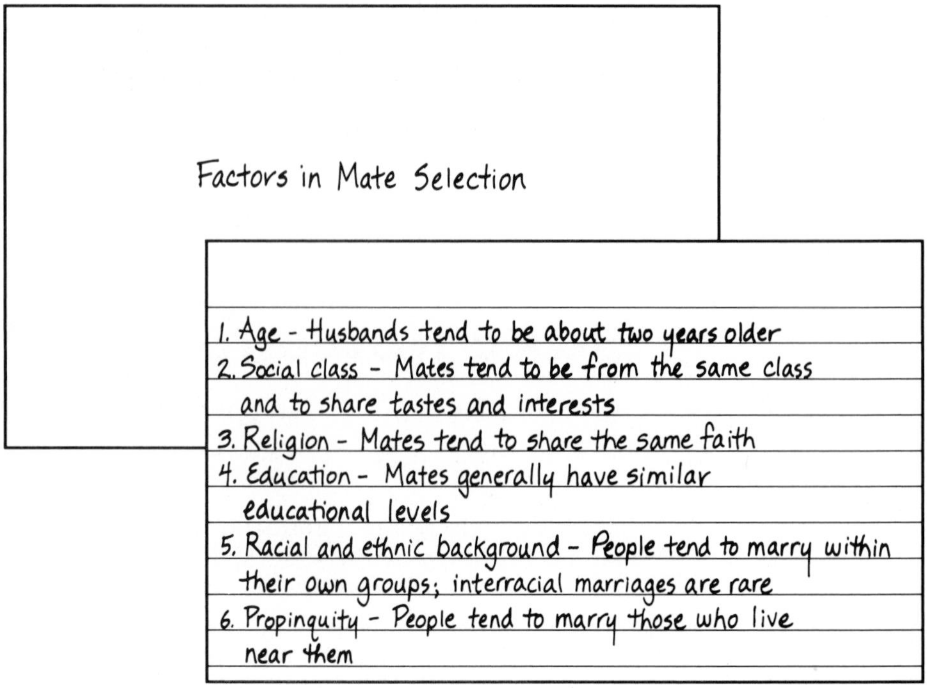
Factors in Mate Selection
1. Age - Husbands tend to be about two years older
2. Social class - Mates tend to be from the same class and to share tastes and interests
3. Religion - Mates tend to share the same faith
4. Education - Mates generally have similar educational levels
5. Racial and ethnic background - People tend to marry within their own groups; interracial marriages are rare
6. Propinquity - People tend to marry those who live near them

you have learned from information that you have not learned. By separating "learned" notes from "unlearned" notes, you can readily direct your attention toward studying information that you have not yet learned. Fourth, cards are convenient to study at times when studying from a notebook is inconvenient. You can study notes on cards while walking from class to class or even while standing on a bus; notes on notebook paper are inconvenient to study at such times.

How to Make Textbook Notes

Use the underlining and other marks you made in your textbook to guide you in making notes on a passage.

- Decide what format you will use for the notes (see pages 205–210).
- Begin the notes with a title that accurately describes the information you want to learn.
- Make the major details stand out in your notes.
- Include some minor details.
- Include examples, because they help in understanding and learning information and because they may appear in test questions.

Major and Minor Details

American Values

Positive values

1. The work ethic — we believe that work is good and necessary and that it will lead to wealth.
2. Pragmatism — we try to find solutions to problems.
3. Thrift and delayed gratification — we believe it is better to save for tomorrow than to spend today.
4. Activism — we work hard to do things better and to make our lives better.

Negative values

1. Wastefulness — we spend money on things we don't need, and we waste our natural resources.
2. Indifference to social needs — we believe the strong are the ones who should survive, and we don't look after the basic needs of all our people.

When you make textbook notes, first consider whether you should prepare them so that major and minor details stand out, as you learned to do when you studied Chapters 12 and 13. The notes above have the following characteristics:

- The title describes the content of the notes, and it is written in the center of the page.
- A line is left blank before each major detail.
- Minor details are indented and listed neatly under major details.

Exercises 19.1 and 19.2 provide practice in making textbook notes that give prominence to major and minor details.

Paragraph Summaries

Reasons for Immigration to America

Economic People in the Old World had difficulty finding employment, and they had little opportunity to acquire land. Many of them didn't have adequate food, clothing, housing, or health care. They believed they would find in America these things that they didn't have in the Old World.

Social Equality Europeans believed they would find greater equality in America. They knew that higher earnings made it possible for poor Americans to dress, eat, and acquire property in ways that were not possible for poor people in the Old World.

American Persuasiveness American businesses used advertising to encourage immigration because they wanted immigrants who would work for low pay. In addition, they wanted to make money by selling passages on ships and by selling land in America.

When you cannot organize information in notes that emphasize major and minor details, it may be appropriate to make notes in paragraph summaries. The paragraph summary notes above have the following characteristics:

- The title describes the content of the notes, and it is written in the center of the page.
- A line is left blank before each paragraph.
- Each paragraph is indented.
- Each paragraph begins with an underlined title, which is the topic of the paragraph.

Exercise 19.3 provides practice in making textbook notes in the paragraph summary format.

Definitions of Terminology

Psychology

hormones	Chemicals formed in and given off by organs of the body that affect growth and behavior
rationalization	The giving of reasonable reasons for unreasonable or unacceptable behavior (Ex) A child with a poor report card claims, "The teacher doesn't like me."
hallucination	The seeing or hearing of something that is not there (Ex) A mentally ill person reports things he heard God say to him
pornography	Writings, pictures, and other materials that are intended to be sexually arousing
syndrome	A group of symptoms that occur together and that are typical of a particular disease or reactive pattern

On many college tests, 70 percent or more of questions directly or indirectly test knowledge of terminology; therefore, it is extremely important for you to learn the terminology that is defined in your textbooks. The definitions-of-terminology notes above have the following characteristics:

- Terms are written on the left side of the page.
- Definitions and examples are written on the right side of the page.
- Blank space is left before each new term.

The definitions are statements about the meanings of the terms, and the examples reveal the basic characteristics of the behavior named by a term.

Exercise 19.4 provides practice in making textbook notes in the definitions-of-terminology format.

Classification Charts

The Psychosexual Stages, According to Freud

	Age	Characteristics
Oral Stage	Birth to 1 year	Gets pleasure from mouth by sucking, eating, biting, and chewing.
Anal Stage	1 year to 3 years	Gets pleasure from holding and letting go of body waste.
Phallic Stage	3 years to 6 years	The child derives pleasure from his or her own primary sex organs.
Latency Period	6 years to about 11 years	Child denies attraction for parent of opposite sex and identifies with parent of the same sex.
Genital Stage	Adolescence	Awakening of sexuality and desire for heterosexual love

Classification charts are useful for organizing information that explains how two or more persons, places, or things are alike or different in two or more ways. The chart above summarizes Sigmund Freud's theory about the psychosexual stages of human development, which is explained in many psychology textbooks. The information is summarized under headings that explain the two ways in which the stages differ from one another: "Age" and "Characteristics." The notes also emphasize the sequence of the stages.

When you have difficulty making good notes, ask this question: "Does this information explain how two or more persons, places, or things are alike or different in two or more ways?" If the answer to this question is yes, make notes in a classification chart.

Exercise 19.5 provides practice in making a classification chart.

Time Lines

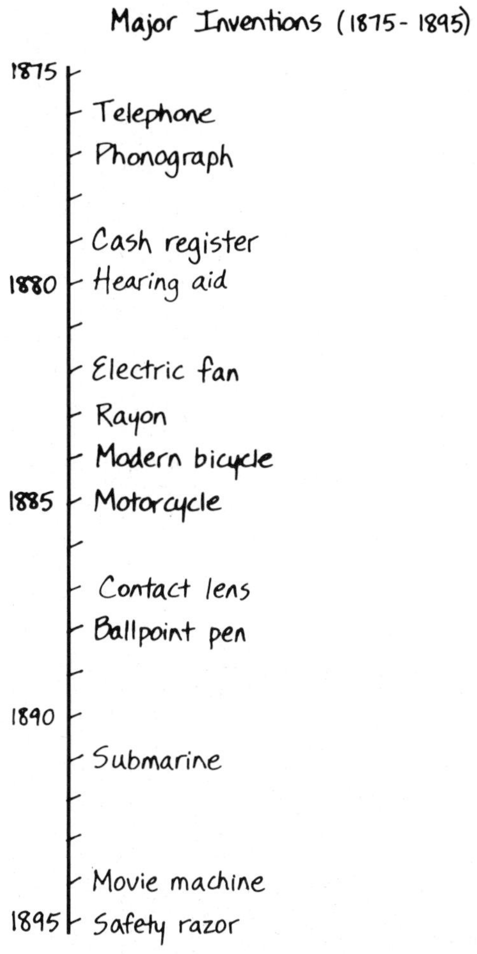

A time line is useful when you want to learn the chronological sequence of events. To prepare a time line, draw a line, and mark it off in equal time intervals. In the example above, a line is marked off in five-year intervals; however, in other time lines the intervals may represent one week, one month, one year, one hundred years, or any other period. The major advantage of time lines is that they make it easy to visualize the passage of time between events.

After you have marked off the intervals on a time line, write events in the places where they belong. In the example above, "Cash register" is written on the line before 1880 because it was invented in 1879, and "Motorcycle" is written next to 1885 because it was invented in 1885.

Exercise 19.6 provides practice in making textbook notes in a time line.

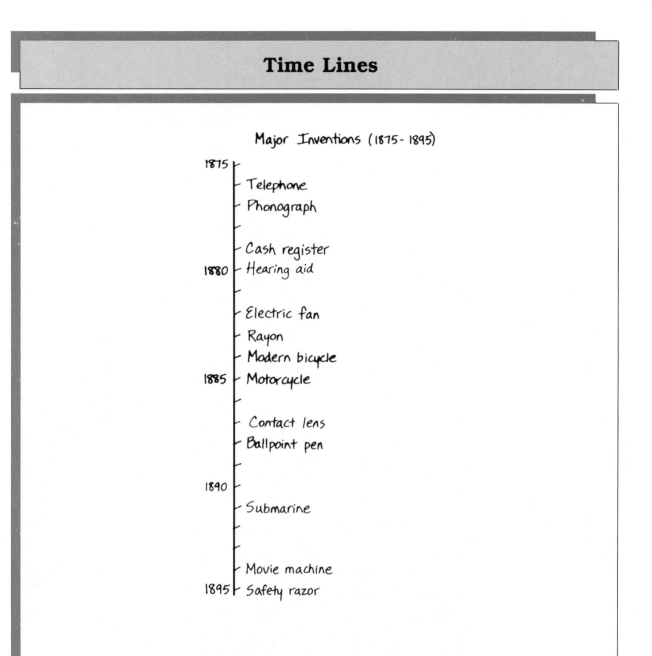

Maps

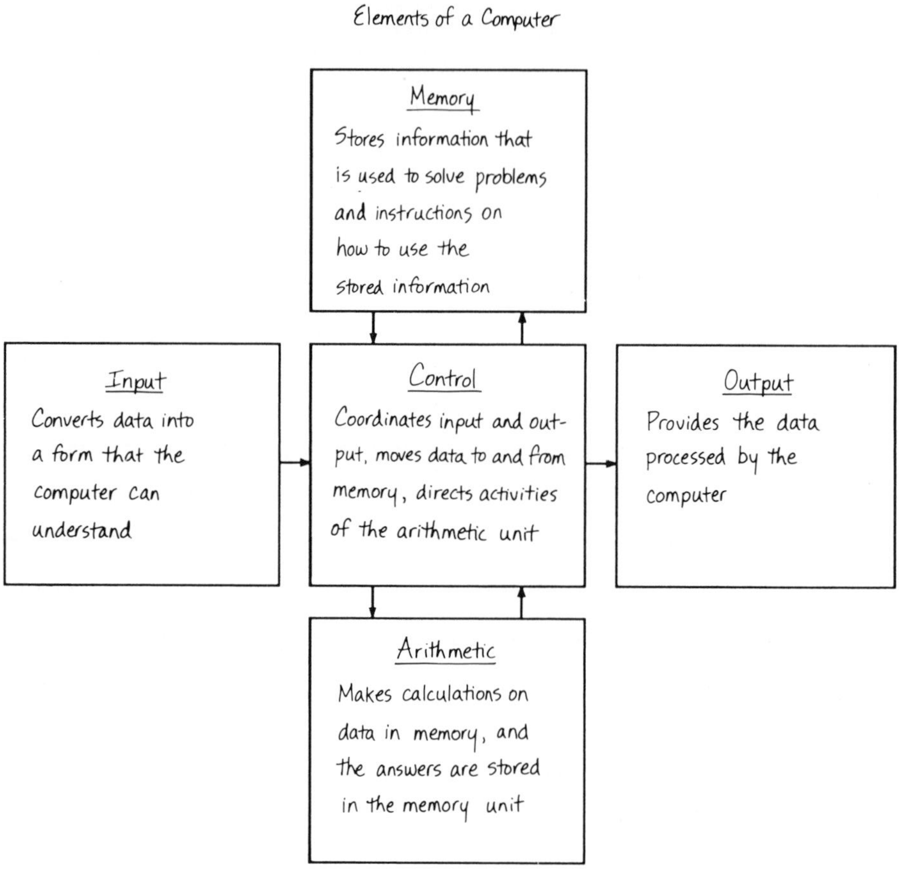
Elements of a Computer
Memory
Stores information that is used to solve problems and instructions on how to use the stored information
Input
Converts data into a form that the computer can understand
Control
Coordinates input and output, moves data to and from memory, directs activities of the arithmetic unit
Output
Provides the data processed by the computer
Arithmetic
Makes calculations on data in memory, and the answers are stored in the memory unit

Maps used in traveling show the relations between places; maps used for notes show the relations between ideas, information, and concepts. In **maps,** information enclosed within squares, circles, or other forms is connected by lines to information enclosed within other forms to indicate how the information is interrelated.

In the map above, descriptions of the elements of a computer are enclosed within rectangles, which are connected by arrows to show how the elements of a computer are interrelated. For example, one arrow between "Input" and "Control" indicates that data flow from input to control, but not from control to input. On the other hand, two arrows between "Memory" and "Control" indicate that data flow back and forth between memory and control.

Exercise 19.7 provides practice in making a map.

EXERCISE 19.1 Index Card

Use the form for an index card, below, to make notes for "Adjusting to Death" on page 183. See pages 204 and 205 for examples of the type of notes you should make.

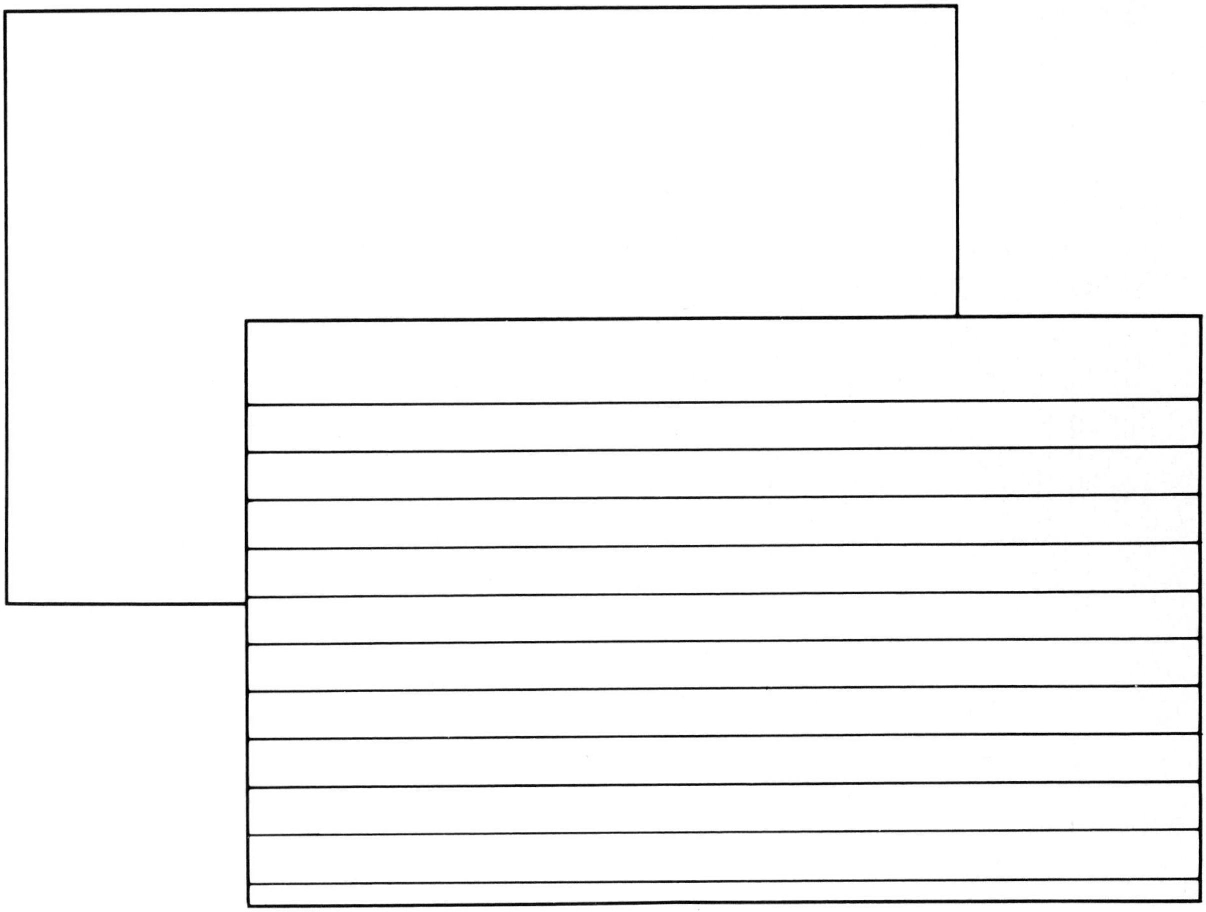

EXERCISE 19.2 Major and Minor Details

Use notebook paper to make major-and-minor-detail notes for "Listening" on pages 184–185. See page 205 for an example of the type of notes you should make.

EXERCISE 19.3 Paragraph Summary

Use notebook paper to make paragraph summary notes for "Maslow's Hierarchy of Needs" on pages 186–189. See page 206 for an example of the type of notes you should make.

EXERCISE 19.4 Definitions of Terminology

Use notebook paper to make definitions-of-terminology notes for "What Is a Brand?" on page 190. See page 207 for an example of the type of notes you should make.

EXERCISE 19.5 Classification Chart

Use notebook paper to make classification chart notes for "Advertising Media" on pages 192–194. See page 208 for an example of the type of notes you should make. Use the following headings from left to right across the top of your chart: "Media," "Expenditure," "Advantages," and "Disadvantages." The headings from top to bottom on the left of your chart should be "Newspapers," "Magazines," "Direct Mail," "Outdoor Advertising," "Television," and "Radio."

EXERCISE 19.6 Time Line

Use notebook paper to make time-line notes for "Television" on pages 195–198. See page 209 for an example of the type of notes you should make. Your notes should include events that occurred during the following years: 1922, 1927, 1929, 1932, 1936, 1940, 1941, 1945, 1946, 1947, 1948, 1952, and 1953.

EXERCISE 19.7 Map

Use the form on page 213 to make a map of the information in "Conversation" on pages 198–200. Write "Conversation" in the box at the top of the page, "How to Start" in the shaded box on the left, "How to Keep Going" in the shaded box on the right, and list the details in the other boxes.

FIGURE 19.2

Form for Exercise 19.7

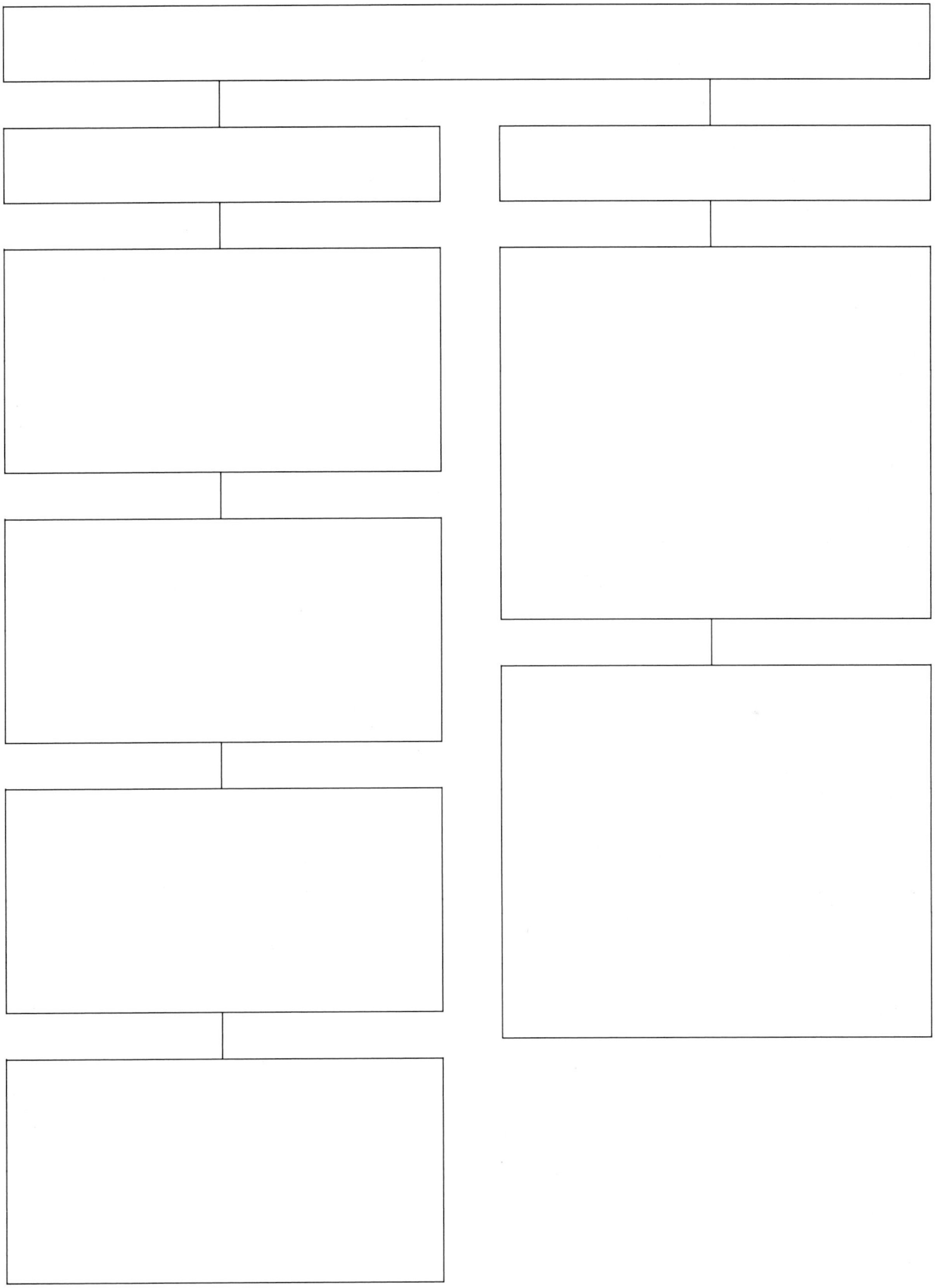

EXERCISE 19.8 "The Power of Positive Impressions"

This is the third of five exercises for applying study skills to the sample textbook chapter on pages 286–309 of the appendix. The other exercises are for surveying (Exercise 16.3), marking books (Exercise 18.10), reciting and rehearsing (Exercise 20.4), and test taking (Exercise 21.3).

Making Notes for a Chapter

Use the marks you made when you did Exercise 18.10 and the guidelines on page 204 to make notes on the information in the sample textbook chapter on pages 286–309 of the appendix. Use the following titles for your notes—they correspond to the questions in Exercise 18.10 on pages 200–201.

1. The *Primacy Effect*
2. The First Few Minutes
3. Assumptions or Stereotypes
4. Decisions Based on Surface Language
5. Influences on Choosing Work Clothing
6. Wardrobe Engineering Suggestions
7. Positive Facial Expression
8. Positive Carriage
9. Positive Voice
10. Positive Handshake
11. Important Rules of Etiquette

20

Remember and Recall Information

If you have ever sat in a test room upset because you could not recall answers that you were certain you knew, you will probably be grateful for this chapter—it explains how to store information so that you can retrieve it when you want it. The suggestions are based on the following concepts about memory that were introduced in Chapter 5:

Important Memory Concepts

- Most information stays in your memory for less than one minute unless you store it there.
- Prepare information for storage by organizing it in a logical manner.
- Store information with a retrieval cue.
- Use recitation and rehearsal to store information.

In this chapter, the terms *storage, recitation, rehearsal,* and *retrieval* have the same meanings as in Chapter 5, and **memory** is used to mean "the total of what one remembers." See "How to Remember and Recall Information" on page 218 for a summary of the instruction in this chapter.

Retrieval Cues

In preparing information for storage, the first step is to write good **retrieval cues,** which are words or images that will later help in retrieving, or recalling, information. In Figure 20.1 on page 216, the descriptive title "Types of Advertising" is a retrieval cue for recalling the information written on the back of the card. The student who prepared the card will read "Types of Advertising" and use the words to help her retrieve from her memory what she has stored there about selective advertising, primary demand advertising, and institutional advertising.

One reason that the outlining and note-taking instruction in *College Study Skills* emphasizes writing descriptive titles is that they are effective retrieval cues. There are additional suggestions for creating retrieval cues on pages 221–224 of this chapter.

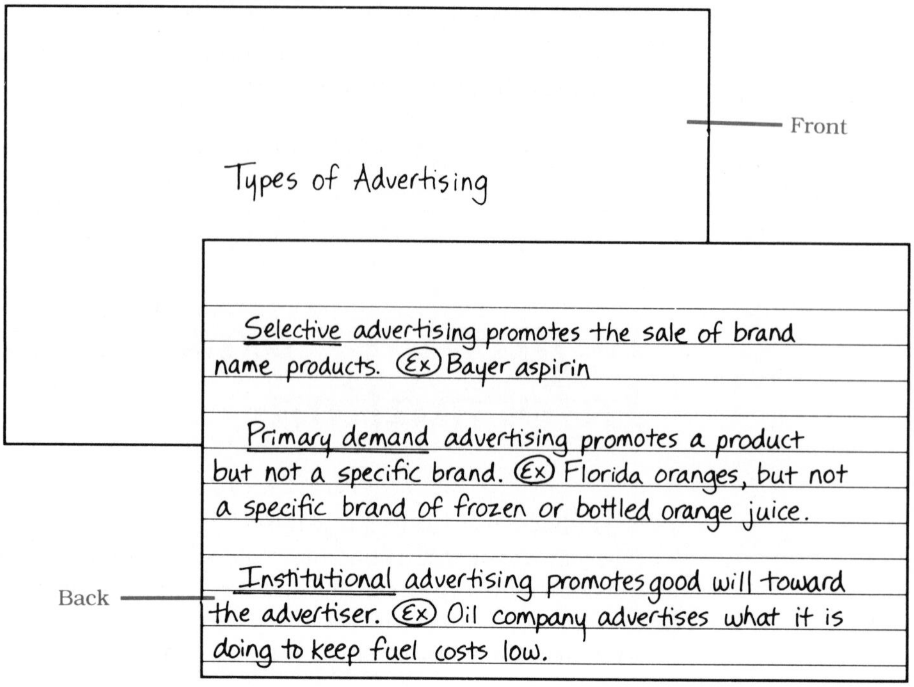

FIGURE 20.1
Notes Used for Reciting

Logical Organization

It has been mentioned several times in *College Study Skills* that information is easier to recite and rehearse if it is logically organized. Figure 20.1 is an example of notes that are logically organized on a 3-by-5-inch card; the major thought, or descriptive title of the notes, is prominently written on the front of the card, and the details are listed neatly on the back. On pages 205–210 there are examples of six other formats for logically organized notes.

Another level of organization is to integrate class notes with textbook notes so that all information about a topic is in one place. If you make textbook notes on 3-by-5-inch cards, prepare class notes for rehearsal by summarizing them on cards. Then, organize the cards by topic so that textbook notes *and* class notes about a single topic are together. Rehearsal is more efficient when all notes about a topic are together rather than in different places.

If you recite and rehearse directly from your class notes, highlight the major headings and key terminology in the notes and use the highlighted words as retrieval cues. For instance, if "Types of Advertising" is a topic in the notes, highlight these words and use them to recall information about the types of advertising in the notes.

Recitation

Recitation is the act of repeating information silently or aloud for the purposes of storing it in memory. Use the procedure on the following page to recite information in notes.

FIGURE 20.2
Recitation of the Information in Figure 20.1

A student read the title on the front of the card in Figure 20.1 and changed it into the following question:

What types of advertising are there?

She then answered her question by reciting the information on the back of the card in the following way:

- Primary demand, selective, and institutional advertising.
- Primary demand advertising sells a product without trying to sell any particular brand-name product . . . for example, sells cotton as a desirable material with many uses, rather than selling specific products, such as Arrow shirts or Cannon towels.
- Selective advertising is used to sell specific brand-name products, such as Comet cleanser and Skippy peanut butter.
- Institutional advertising tries to increase good will toward the advertiser . . . as when Mobil Oil sponsors a movie on public television.

How to Recite

- Read the descriptive title of your notes and use it as a retrieval cue to recollect the information about it in your notes.
- Try to say the information in your notes silently or aloud to yourself without reading your notes.
- Read the information in your notes to make certain that you recited it correctly; if you did not, reread the information and then immediately try to recite it again.

Compare the example of recitation and rehearsal in Figure 20.2 to the notes in Figure 20.1 to notice the differences in the wordings. When you recite and rehearse, do not engage in rote, word-for-word memorization. Rather, learn the general meaning of information using your own words whenever possible. However, keep in mind that when you change wordings you run the risk of changing meanings, and if you change meanings you will learn incorrect information. When you recite and rehearse, take great care *not* to change the meaning of things you learn.

Rehearsal

Use recitation in conjunction with **rehearsal,** or **elaborative rehearsal,** which is the act of analyzing information and relating it to information that is already stored in memory. To **analyze** is to separate something into its parts for the purpose of studying its parts or understanding how they are related. Compare

COVER IN CLASS

How to Remember and Recall Information

Organize the information you want to learn into notes that have the characteristics explained in Chapter 19.

1. Use descriptive titles in your notes as retrieval cues for recalling the information in them.
2. Use good organization of details in your notes to help you store and recall the information in them.
3. Recite the information in your notes.
   - Read the title.
   - Try to say the information in your notes silently or aloud to yourself without reading your notes.
   - Read the information in notes to make certain that you recited it correctly; if you did not, reread the information and then immediately try to recite it again.
4. Rehearse the information in your notes.
   - Analyze it into its parts to study them and to understand how they are related.
   - Relate the information to other information in your memory.
5. Review the information frequently to ensure that you can retrieve it quickly when you need it.
6. Use one or more of the following aids to facilitate recitation and rehearsal.
   - Schedule many short study sessions over a long period rather than a few long sessions over a short period.
   - Join a study group.
   - Recite while walking outside rather than while sitting inside.
   - Rehearse by writing on paper rather than by repeating information silently or aloud to yourself.
   - Record hard-to-learn information on audiocassettes and recite it after you have listened to it enough times to learn it.
   - Use mnemonic acronyms, mnemonic sentences, and visualizations as retrieval cues (see pages 221–224).

the example of rehearsal in Figure 20.2 with the notes in Figure 20.1. Notice how the student used the rehearsal technique to analyze and break down the information in her notes. She was then able to relate the new material to information previously stored in her memory.

- **Analyzing.** In the student's first response in Figure 20.2, she analyzed that the information is divided into three categories—three types of advertising. In the other three responses she further analyzed that each category is explained by a definition and an example.
- **Relating.** In the last three responses in Figure 20.2, the student related the information in her notes to information in her memory by giving examples of products that are different from the examples of products in the notes.

Storage is further enhanced by systematic review.

Review

Review is an essential but often overlooked step in the study process. To **review** is to repeatedly recite and rehearse information to ensure that it can be retrieved quickly when it is needed.

When you study, you will often find that you are unable to remember information that you knew the day before. This loss of information is due to the normal process of forgetting—we tend to forget 30 to 40 percent of what we learn within twenty-four hours after we learn it! For example, after reciting and rehearsing for an hour, a student had learned the information on twenty of eighty cards she had prepared to study for a physics test. However, when she reviewed the twenty "learned" cards the next day, she discovered that she had forgotten information on six of them. What happened to her is what happens to all of us; we tend to forget a substantial portion of what we learn within twenty-four hours after we learn it. This is the reason that review is an essential part of the study process.

1. **To review notes on cards, maintain a deck of "learned" cards and a deck of "unlearned" cards.** Then each time you recite:

- Begin by reviewing the deck of "learned" cards. If you have forgotten information on a card, put it back in the "unlearned" deck.
- Recite and rehearse the "unlearned" cards, attempting to move as many as you can into the "learned" deck.

Continue in this way until you can accurately recall all the information twenty-four hours after you have moved all cards to the "learned" deck.

2. **To review notes on notebook paper, place checks in pencil next to information as you learn it.** Then, each time you recite:

- Begin by reviewing checked information, and erase checks next to information you have forgotten.
- Recite and rehearse the information that is not checked, attempting to place checks next to as much of it as you can.

Continue in this way until you can accurately recall the information twenty-four hours after you have placed pencil checks next to all of it.

Aids to Recitation and Rehearsal

One or more of the following strategies may help you learn more quickly when you recite and rehearse information.

Schedule Study Time Properly

Learning can be improved by scheduling study time in a way that fosters the effective storage of information. The most common error students make in scheduling study time is to plan insufficient time for reciting and rehearsal. As a result, they experience the stress of having to learn too much in too little time, and the stress interferes with their ability to concentrate on studying. You cannot learn efficiently when you are worrying that you have too little time to learn everything you need to learn.

A less obvious error is to schedule sufficient time for rehearsal but to schedule it in too few study sessions over too few days. Learning is more effective when material is learned during short study sessions over as many days as possible. You know, for example, that you are likely to be a better typist if you practice typing one hour a day for thirty days in a row than if you practice six hours a day for five days in a row. The same principle that applies to learning how to type applies to learning information and skills for your college courses.

In scheduling study time, it is also essential to keep in mind that there is *not* a one-to-one relationship between the amount of information to store and the amount of time needed to store it. For instance, if you study the meanings of sixty terms for a psychology test, you may learn thirty of them in an hour and, as a result, schedule one hour to learn the other thirty terms. However, it might take you two or three hours to learn the remaining thirty terms because some of them may have meanings that are especially difficult for you to understand or remember.

Study with Others

Some students learn better when they study with a group of other students. A study group can help you become more involved in a course. It can also be a source of ideas about what to study, and it can provide you with a stimulating setting for reciting, rehearsing, and reviewing. However, study groups can also become places for complaining, gossiping, and joking around, and they are a waste of time unless all members are properly prepared. Study groups are most effective when they are limited to no more than five members and when *all* members have the same academic goals, are prepared and serious about studying and learning, and are available to participate in the group at the same time.

If you organize a study group, discuss and agree on the group's purpose the first time it meets. Then, at the beginning of each meeting, decide what you will study, how long you will study, and when and for how long you will take a break. At the end of each session, summarize what was accomplished, discuss ways the next meeting might be more productive, and plan what you will study the next time the group meets.

Walk While Reciting

When I was a college student, I told a friend that I was having extreme difficulty learning information for a test. She suggested that I might benefit from the advice her drama coach gave her, that she could learn parts in plays more quickly if she studied them while walking rather than while sitting. I did what she recommended and found that I learned information more quickly when I recited it while walking outside rather than while sitting at a desk. When you have difficulty learning material, experiment to find out whether you learn more efficiently while walking than while sitting.

Rehearse by Writing

Writing is used to learn many of the skills that are taught in colleges, such as the skills that you need to solve mathematical problems and to translate a foreign language into English. You can also use writing to learn information of the kind that is usually recited silently or aloud. If you have difficulty learning material by reciting and rehearsing it, try writing it on paper. Some students report that writing provides them with the additional reinforcement they need when they recite.

Use Audiocassettes

Some students find that the most efficient way for them to recite is by listening to notes recorded on audiocassettes. One of my students, for example, had a job that required him to spend much time driving. To take advantage of his time in his car, he recorded his class notes and listened to them as he drove from place to place. He checked his learning by turning off his cassette player, reciting what he heard, and replaying the material to make certain he had recited it correctly.

If you are an auditory learner, audiocassettes can be useful learning tools for you, whether you listen to them in a car, at home, or over headphones as you walk from place to place.

Mnemonic Devices as Retrieval Cues

You may recall from Chapter 5 that two prominent theories about forgetting agree that once information is stored in memory, it stays there. As a result, these theories propose that forgetting is not a matter of losing information from memory but of being unable to retrieve it. When logical organization and descriptive titles are insufficient for retrieving information from memory, you may need to use a mnemonic device as a retrieval cue.

Mnemonic (ni-mon′ik) means "to help the memory." There are many different kinds of **mnemonic devices.** For example, the rhyming jingle "i before e, except after c" is a mnemonic for remembering a spelling principle. The following sentence is a mnemonic for remembering the reciprocal of pi = .318310:

Can	I	remember	the	reciprocal?
3	1	8	3	10

By counting the number of letters in each word of this sentence, one can recall that the reciprocal is .318310.

The following discussions explain three types of mnemonic devices that are widely used as retrieval cues: mnemonic acronyms, mnemonic sentences, and visualizations.

FIGURE 20.3
A Mnemonic Device on an Index Card

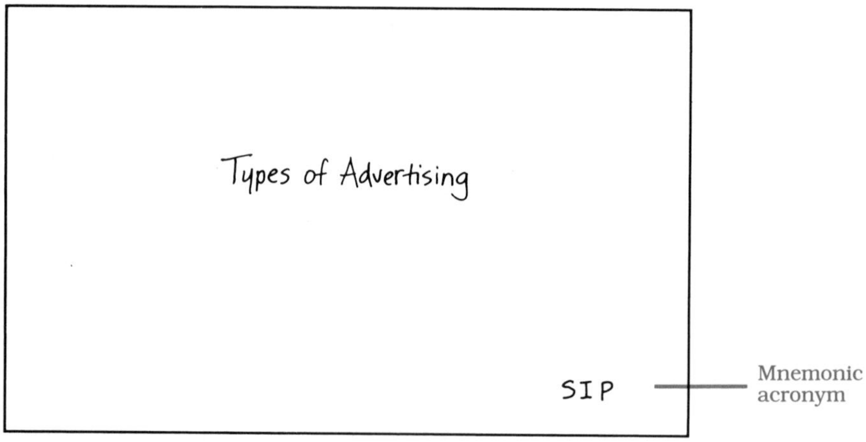

Mnemonic Acronyms

A **mnemonic acronym** is a word made from the first letters of words you want to recall. One of the best-known mnemonic acronyms is HOMES, which is used to recall the names of the Great Lakes: Huron, Ontario, Michigan, Erie, Superior. H recalls Huron, O recalls Ontario, and so on.

In Figure 20.3 above, the acronym SIP is written in the lower right-hand corner of the index card as a reminder of the letters with which the three types of advertising begin: Selective, Institutional, Primary demand.

Acronyms are widely used by students who have a great deal to learn, such as students studying for medical professions. Mnemonics such as the following are passed on among students in much the same way nursery rhymes are passed on among children:

- SKILL is used to recall the excretory organs of the body: Skin, Kidneys, Intestines, Liver, Lungs.
- A PAIL is used for remembering the five types of wounds: Abrasion, Puncture, Avulsion, Incision, Laceration.

Acronyms may also be used to recall phrases. The American Cancer Society recommends using the acronym CAUTION to remember the common warning signs of cancer:

Change in bowel or bladder habits
A sore that does not heal
Unusual bleeding or discharge
Thickening or lump in the breasts or elsewhere
Indigestion or difficulty in swallowing
Obvious change in a wart or mole
Nagging cough or hoarseness

Though these are not certain signs of cancer, the American Cancer Society advises that they indicate the advisability of visiting a physician for an examination and consultation.

When you have difficulty recalling information, try using acronyms as retrieval cues. Your acronyms do not need to be real words—any combination of letters that you recall easily can serve as a mnemonic acronym for you.

Mnemonic Sentences

A **mnemonic sentence** is a sentence made of words that begin with the same letters as the first letters of words you want to recall. They are particularly useful for learning information in a specific sequence. For instance, the acronym HOMES may be used to recall the names of the Great Lakes, but the following sentence may be used to remember the names of the Great Lakes in correct sequence going from West to East.

She Must Have Eaten Onions.

The first letters of the words in this sentence are the same as the first letters of the names of the Great Lakes in correct sequence from West to East: Superior, Michigan, Huron, Erie, Ontario.

Some mnemonic sentences are passed on from student to student in the same way as acronyms. Here are some well-known ones.

My Very Earthy Mother Just Served Us Nine Pizzas.

In this sentence, the underscored letters are the same as the first letters in the names of the planets, starting with the one nearest the sun and proceeding to the one farthest from the sun: Mercury, Venus, Earth, Mars, Jupiter, Saturn, Uranus, Neptune, Pluto.

The first letters of the words in the following sentence are used to recall the order of operations in algebra:

Please Excuse My Dear Aunt Sally.

The order of operations is Parentheses, Exponents, Multiplication, Division, Addition, Subtraction.

In the following example, the underscored letters are used by biology students to recall the categories into which living things are divided:

King Philip Came Over From Greece Singing.

The categories for living things are Kingdom, Phylum, Class, Order, Family, Genus, Species.

Mnemonic sentences are also useful when the first letters of words to be recalled do not spell a word. The following sentence is used to remember the four sections of a symphony orchestra:

Sinners Will Be Punished.

Since it is not possible to make an acronym from the letters *SWBP*, this sentence helps in recalling the orchestra sections: String, Woodwind, Brass, Percussion.

Consider using mnemonic sentences as retrieval cues whenever you want to learn information in a specific sequence or when the first letters of words you want to remember do not spell a word.

Visualizations

A **visualization** is anything that can be visualized, or pictured in the mind, to aid the retrieval of information. Visualizations are usually examples, and this is one reason I suggested in Chapter 18 that you mark examples in your textbooks and in Chapter 19 that you include examples in your textbook notes.

In rehearsing the notes in Figure 20.1 on page 216, the student used visualizations—products she could picture in her mind, such as Comet cleanser and Skippy peanut butter. Another student devised the following visualizations to help himself understand and retrieve the definitions of three types of social mobility for his sociology course:

Types of Social Mobility	Visualizations
Horizontal (from one status to a similar status)	I changed jobs from pumping gas to parking cars.
Vertical (from one status to a higher or lower status)	I changed jobs from parking cars to being a management trainee for an insurance company.
Intergenerational (when the status of family members changes from one generation to another)	My grandfather was a laborer, but my father supervises skilled factory workers.

The student used the images of himself, his father, and his grandfather to help himself understand, remember, and recall the three types of social mobility.

EXERCISE 20.1 Mnemonic Acronyms

This exercise provides practice in writing mnemonic acronyms.

1. There are four major types of wounds:
   - A *laceration* is a tear.
   - An *incision* is a cut.
   - A *crush* is an injury caused by pressure.
   - A *puncture* is a wound caused by piercing.

   Use the first letters of the italicized words to write an acronym for remembering the four types of wounds.

2. On page 183 there is a summary of Elisabeth Kübler-Ross's theory about the five emotional stages through which people pass when they learn they are about to die:
   - Denial
   - Anger
   - Bargaining
   - Depression
   - Acceptance

   Use the first letters of these words to write a nonsense word that can be used to remember the names of the stages in the correct sequence.

3. A microbiology textbook explains three measures that can be taken to reduce the incidence of rabies:

- *Immunize* more dogs and cats.
- Enforce *leash* laws.
- *Educate* the public about the dangers of rabies.

Use the first letters of the italicized words to write a word for remembering the three measures for reducing rabies.

EXERCISE 20.2 Mnemonic Sentences

This exercise provides practice in writing mnemonic sentences.

1. There are four major categories of drugs:
   - *Depressants* slow body functions.
   - *Stimulants* speed up body functions.
   - *Hallucinogens* cause people to see or hear things that are not actually present.
   - *Marijuana* produces various effects.

   Write a mnemonic sentence in which the first letters of the words are the same as the first letters of the names of the four major types of drugs.

2. On pages 186–189 there is an explanation of Abraham Maslow's "hierarchy of needs"—a theory that there are five basic human needs, which people tend to satisfy in the following order:
   - Physiological needs
   - Safety needs
   - Social needs
   - Esteem needs
   - Self-actualization needs

   Write a mnemonic sentence in which the first letters of the words are the same as the first letters of the names of the human needs, arranged in the correct sequence.

3. Following are the six principle components of soil:
   - Air
   - Humus
   - Mineral salts
   - Water
   - Bacteria
   - Rock particles

   Write a mnemonic sentence in which the first letters of the words are the same as the first letters of these ingredients: *A, H, M, W, B,* and *R.*

EXERCISE 20.3 Visualizations

This exercise provides practice in writing visualizations.

1. On page 180 there is a passage that describes four zones of private space. Read the passage and then devise visualizations for remembering the differences between the four zones: intimate distance; personal distance; social distance; and public distance.

2. On page 116 there is a passage that explains three types of advertising. Read the passage and then devise visualizations for remembering the differences between the three advertising categories: selective advertising; primary demand advertising; and institutional advertising.

3. On page 174 there is a passage that explains the steps in the selling process. Read the passage and then devise visualizations for remembering the steps: find buyers; present the product in an attractive and convincing way; create the customer's desire to buy; and close the sale.

EXERCISE 20.4 "The Power of Positive Impressions"

This is the fourth of five exercises for applying study skills to the sample textbook chapter on pages 286–309 of the appendix. The other exercises are for surveying (Exercise 16.3), marking books (Exercise 18.10), making notes (Exercise 19.8), and test taking (Exercise 21.3).

Reciting and Rehearsing

Use the suggestions in this chapter to recite and rehearse the notes you took for Exercise 19.8. Use the following questions as retrieval cues:

1. What is the primacy effect?
2. What is the four-minute barrier?
3. What are some common stereotypes?
4. What decisions are made from surface language?
5. What factors influence choice of work clothing?
6. What are image consultants' wardrobe suggestions?
7. How can facial expression create a positive impression?
8. How can carriage create a positive impression?
9. How can voice create a positive impression?
10. How can a handshake create a positive impression?
11. What are important rules of etiquette for organizations?

PART V

Do Well on Tests

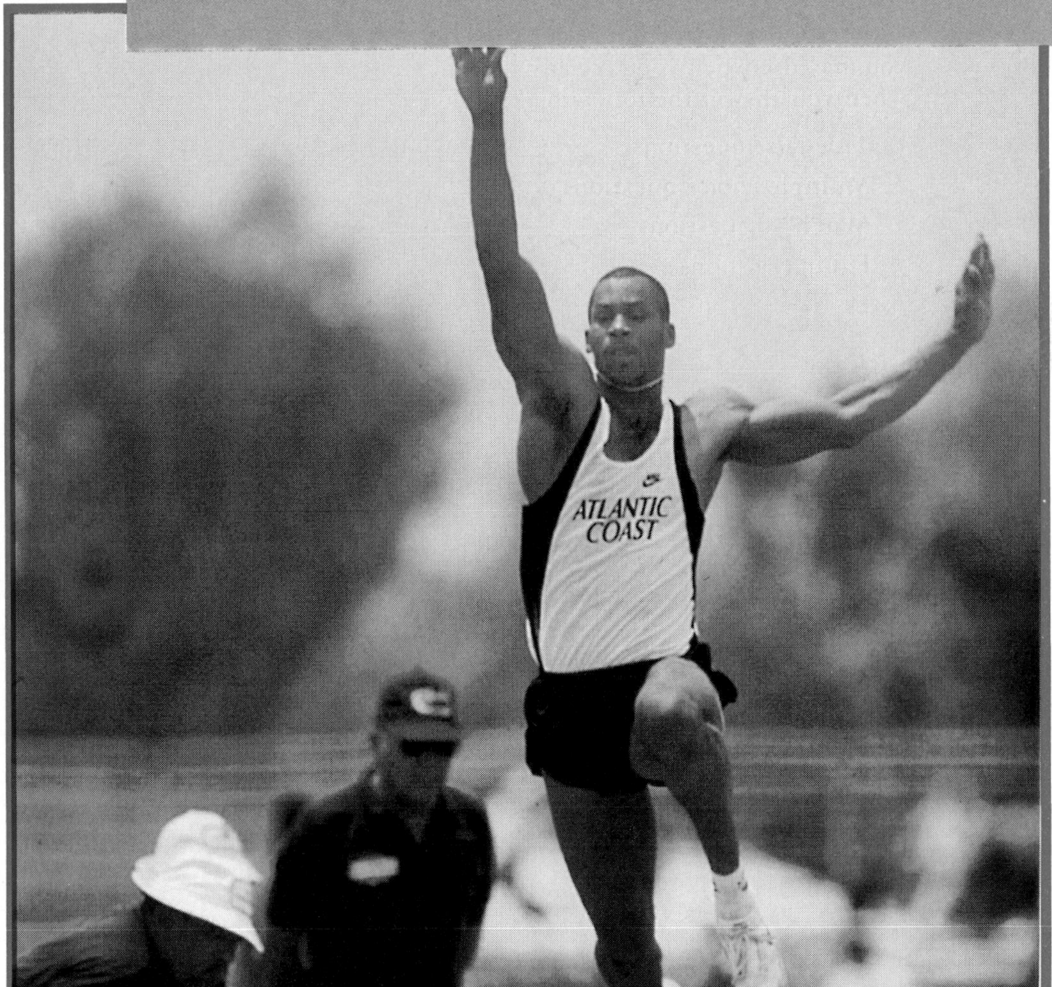

Preview of PART V

Considering the importance test scores have in determining course grades, it is surprising that schools give little attention to teaching students how to do their best when they take tests. But test taking is a skill that can be learned in the same way the skills of reading and writing are learned. The following chapters explain strategies you may use when you take any test and specific techniques to use when you answer the following kinds of questions:

- True-false questions
- Multiple-choice questions
- Matching questions
- Fill-in questions
- Essay questions

Use what you learn when you study the following chapters to earn the highest test grades you can.

21

Strategies for Any Test

Virtually all teachers give a **midterm** and a final exam, and many teachers give two, three, or more additional tests or quizzes during a term. Following are some of the reasons you will take many tests during your college career:

Reasons for Tests

- Test scores are used to help decide students' course grades.
- Tests motivate students to study and learn course content.
- Students' test scores provide teachers with feedback about the effectiveness of their teaching.
- Tests provide students with feedback about how well they are doing in their courses.

Chapters 14–20 explain what to do *before* you take tests; this chapter suggests what you should do *while* you take them. "How to Take a Test" on page 230 summarizes methods that apply to all tests. Specific strategies for answering true-false, multiple-choice, matching, fill-in, and essay questions are explained in Chapters 22–27.

Reduce Your Test Anxiety

Test anxiety is the uneasiness or apprehension students experience because they must take a test. Check the statements in the following checklist that describe you:

Test Anxiety Checklist

- ☐ I worry about failing tests.
- ☐ I do not sleep well the night before a test.
- ☐ I sometimes try to figure out how I can avoid taking a test.
- ☐ Before or during a test I often perspire excessively, have an upset stomach, feel my heart beating rapidly, or experience shortness of breath.
- ☐ I have difficulty concentrating when I take tests.

How to Take a Test

- Reduce anxiety by reminding yourself that you studied thoroughly before the test and you know how to use good test-taking strategies.
- Survey the test to learn what types of questions you must answer, whether questions are printed on both sides of each page, and where you must write your answers.
- Read the directions carefully and follow them exactly.
- Listen attentively to everything the teacher says before and during the test.
- Plan your test-taking time so you will answer all the questions you know in case time runs out.
- Answer the easiest questions first.
- Answer all the questions unless you are instructed not to.
- Check your answers, but be careful not to change correct answers to incorrect answers.
- Don't let other students see your answers. (You may be accused of cheating.)
- When a test is returned, study your incorrect answers to learn how you might do better on the next test the teacher gives.

- ☐ While taking tests I am often unable to recall information that I learned.
- ☐ I make foolish mistakes when I answer test questions.
- ☐ I become upset when I don't know the answer to a test question.
- ☐ I become very nervous if time runs out before I am able to answer all the questions on a test.
- ☐ While taking tests, I worry that other students will finish before me or do better than me.

All students experience some test anxiety; however, if you checked five or more items in this list, you suffer from a greater amount of test anxiety than most students do.

Since anxiety results from fear, you can usually avoid test anxiety by preparing thoroughly for tests, using the methods that are explained in Chapters 14–20. If you are well prepared for a test, you will not have much to fear. It is also important to arrive at tests well rested and without rushing. You will not do your best on a test if you are tired or if you have created unnecessary anxiety for yourself by rushing into the test room at the last minute.

In addition, knowing and using good test-taking procedures will help you to reduce test anxiety. Anxiety directs thoughts *inward,* to think about discomfort; but good test-taking methods direct thoughts *outward,* to think about answering test questions correctly. If you use the methods that are explained

FIGURE 21.1
An Essay Test

Test: Mass Communication

Answer any two of the following four questions. Each answer has a value of 50 points. You have 50 minutes to write your answers.

1. What part should the media play in changing the public's attitudes and opinions?
2. Compare the importance of movies as a mass medium in the 1940s to their importance today.
3. What issues and problems would each of the following disciplines emphasize in studying mass communication: psychology, sociology, and linguistics?
4. What questions and issues are of concern when studying broadcasting from a content point of view?

in this chapter and in Chapters 22–27 when you take tests, you will be so busy in the worthwhile pursuit of answering questions correctly that your mind will probably not turn to futile thoughts of fear of taking tests.

If you become excited during a test, keep in mind that it is normal to be excited and that excitement can help you do your best, in the same way it helps athletes do their best during athletic competition. You may also find that the following exercise helps you to relax when you are anxious:

Relaxation Exercise

- Without actually smiling, relax your face and feel yourself smiling on the inside.
- Take a very deep breath—a breath so deep that you imagine it reaches to the soles of your feet.
- Then, still smiling inside, let your breath out very slowly.

If you cannot conquer test anxiety by using these methods, seek professional help. Many colleges have counselors who provide assistance to students who experience acute and disabling test anxiety.

Survey Tests

Before you answer any questions on a test, survey it to learn what types of questions you must answer, whether questions are printed on one or both sides of each page, and where you must write your answers.

Then read the test directions; they may be different from what you expect. For example, students usually expect that they are to answer all questions on tests; however, the directions for the essay test in Figure 21.1 instruct students to answer only two of the four questions. Students who answer all four questions make a serious mistake because they will not receive credit for their answers to the third and fourth questions (and their answer to the third or fourth question might be better than their answer to the first or second question).

It is absolutely essential to listen attentively to everything that teachers say on test days. Before tests they often explain directions that give students difficulty, and during tests they sometimes warn students about typographical errors on tests.

Also, when there are only a few students left in a test room, instructors sometimes answer questions or make comments that help the remaining students give a correct answer to a difficult question. If you leave a test room before the end of a test period, you may miss information other students received and used to answer a question correctly.

Plan Test-taking Time

Since there is often too little time to answer all test questions, you must plan how to use the available time. Allocate your test-taking time by finding the answers to the following questions:

- How many questions must I answer?
- How many points is each question worth?
- How much time do I have to answer the questions?

For example, a student took a psychology test with the following directions: "You have fifty minutes to answer twenty-five multiple-choice questions (2 points each) and five short-answer questions (10 points each)." He computed that the multiple-choice questions had a value of 50 points ($2 \times 25 = 50$), and the short-answer questions had a value of 50 points ($10 \times 5 = 50$). Therefore, he allotted twenty-five minutes for answering the multiple-choice questions and twenty-five minutes for answering the short-answer questions (about one minute for each multiple-choice question and about five minutes for each short-answer question).

Answer the Easiest Questions First

After you have planned how to use your test-taking time, determine which questions are easiest to answer and answer these questions first. There are at least three benefits to answering the easiest questions before answering the more difficult ones:

- *You will answer all the questions you can answer correctly,* in case time runs out before you answer all the questions. When test-taking time is limited, do not waste it trying to answer questions that you will almost certainly answer incorrectly.
- *You might think of answers* to some of the difficult questions. While you are answering other questions, you will often remember answers to questions that you could not answer the first time you read them.

- *You might find answers* to some of the difficult questions. True-false and multiple-choice questions are sometimes interrelated, so that one question suggests the correct answer to another question. As you take tests, look for information in questions that can help you select correct answers to other questions that you could not answer the first time you read them.

When you answer true-false or multiple-choice questions, read each question twice and answer it or move on to the next question. When you have read each question twice and answered as many as you can, reread the first unanswered question twice again and answer it or move on to the next unanswered question. Work through the test in this way as many times as necessary to select an answer to each question.

Check the time every ten minutes to make certain that you are answering questions at the rate that will help you get the highest possible score. During the last minute or two of the test period, mark some answer for each question. For instance, you might mark all unanswered true-false questions true, and you might mark *c* for all unanswered multiple-choice questions.

Write Clearly

When you take tests, remember that your teachers have to read your answers. Be considerate of them—write using the best handwriting you possibly can while working under the pressure of time limitations. Also, write clearly when you answer true-false and multiple-choice questions. Do not write a *T* that could be mistaken for an *F,* an *a* that looks like a *d,* or a *c* that resembles an *e.* All teachers are familiar with these ploys, and they are annoyed by students who use them.

Usually Answer All Questions

Give an answer to every question on a test unless you are specifically told not to answer all questions, as on an essay test (see Figure 21.1 on page 000). When you do not know an answer to a true-false or a multiple-choice question, guess the answer—you might guess correctly.

When you guess the answer to a true-false question, you have a 50 percent chance of guessing the correct answer. There is a 50 percent chance the answer is true and a 50 percent chance the answer is false. When you guess the answer to a multiple-choice question with four answers (*a, b, c,* and *d*), you have a 25 percent chance of guessing the correct answer. There is a 25 percent chance the answer is *a,* a 25 percent chance the answer is *b,* and so on.

Check Your Answers

Always carefully check your answers before you give a test to a teacher. If, after careful consideration, you are certain you answered questions incorrectly, write the correct answers, but cross out the original answers in a way that leaves them visible. After the teacher has graded your test, analyze whether you tend to change incorrect answers to correct answers *or* change correct answers to incorrect answers. If you find that you have a tendency to change correct answers to incorrect ones, you will want to use extreme care in changing test answers in the future.

Ignore Other Test Takers

Do you ever worry that students who finish a test before you may receive higher grades than you? If so, there is no need to have this concern. Some of the people who finish tests quickly do receive high test grades, but others complete tests quickly because they do not know the answers to many questions. Many of the students who receive high test grades use every minute of test-taking time to make certain that their answers are correct. Therefore, when you take a test, ignore other students and concentrate on answering questions correctly.

Also, if a classmate should ever ask you to share answers to test questions, don't do so. If another student is poorly prepared for a test, do not let this be your problem. If you let another student read your test answers, you may be accused of cheating; those who allow others to read their answers are as guilty of cheating as those who read them! Cheating in college is a serious offense that could result in disciplinary action or dismissal. Therefore, during tests, sit so other students cannot see your answers (and so you cannot see their answers).

Learn from Incorrect Responses

Test taking is a skill, and skills are improved by making mistakes and learning not to make them. For instance, if you are a good automobile driver, you have learned not to make mistakes you made while you were learning to drive. Similarly, you may become an expert test-taker by learning not to make mistakes that you now make when you take tests.

When tests are returned to you, analyze them to understand why you answered questions incorrectly. You may decide that you did not plan test-taking time carefully enough or that you did not review class notes as much as you should have. You may also find it helpful to discuss your incorrect test answers with classmates and teachers. Use what you learn from your analyses and discussions to do better when you take future tests.

EXERCISE 21.1 Planning Test-taking Time

Practice planning test-taking time by answering the following questions.

1. You have fifty minutes to solve ten mathematical problems, which have a value of 10 points each. How many minutes should you spend solving each problem?

____

2. You have one hour and forty minutes to answer four essay questions. One answer has a value of 40 points and three answers have a value of 20 points each. How many minutes should you plan to spend answering the 40-point question?

   ____

   How many minutes should you plan to spend answering each of the 20-point questions?

   ____

3. You have sixty minutes to answer twenty-five multiple-choice questions and ten short-answer questions. The multiple-choice questions have a value of 2 points each, and the short-answer questions have a value of 5 points each. How many minutes should you plan to spend answering the twenty-five multiple-choice questions?

   ____

   How many minutes should you plan to spend answering each short-answer question?

   ____

EXERCISE 21.2 Test-taking Methods Checklist

Use the following checklist to evaluate your test-taking strategies. Write checks in pencil so you can erase them and reuse the checklist after each test you take.

- ☐ I prepared for the test using the methods that are explained in Chapters 14–20 of *College Study Skills.*
- ☐ Before I answered any questions, I surveyed the test to learn what types of questions I would answer, whether questions were printed on both sides of pages, and where to write answers.
- ☐ I read the test directions and followed them exactly.
- ☐ I listened attentively to everything the teacher said before and during the test.
- ☐ I planned my test-taking time carefully so I was able to answer all the questions for which I knew answers.
- ☐ I checked the time every ten minutes to make certain that I would answer questions at the rate that would help me get the highest possible score.
- ☐ I answered the easiest questions first.
- ☐ I picked up extra points by correctly guessing the answers to some questions.
- ☐ I double-checked my answers after I wrote them.

- ☐ I was careful not to let any classmate see my answers during the test.
- ☐ When the test was returned, I studied my incorrect answers to learn how I might do better on the next test.

If there is a statement you did not check, use it as a hint to how you might do better the next time you take a test for the course.

EXERCISE 21.3 "The Power of Positive Impressions"

This is the fifth of five exercises for applying study skills to the sample textbook chapter on pages 286–309 of the appendix. The other exercises are for surveying (Exercise 16.3), marking books (Exercise 18.10), making notes (Exercise 19.8), and reciting and rehearsing (Exercise 20.4).

Test Taking

You may take a true-false, multiple-choice, or short-answer test your instructor distributes, or you may answer some of the following questions.

15-Point Questions

Check the boxes in front of the *two* questions in the following list that your instructor requests you to answer. Each correct answer has a value of 15 points.

☐ 1. What is the primacy effect?

☐ 2. Give examples of stereotypes that are sometimes used to form impressions of others during a first meeting.

☐ 3. What is surface language?

☐ 4. What is wardrobe engineering?

35-Point Questions

Check the boxes in front of the *two* questions in the following list that your instructor requests you to answer. Each correct answer has a value of 35 points.

☐ 5. List six work wardrobe suggestions about which wardrobe engineers and image consultants agree.

☐ 6. Explain how one's facial expression, carriage, and voice can be used to create a positive impression.

☐ 7. Identify the characteristics of a handshake that create a positive impression.

☐ 8. What six rules of etiquette are of special importance in organizations?

22

True-False Questions

True-false questions are statements that test takers must decide are either true or false. They are well suited for testing whether students have learned facts such as the following.

☐ T ☐ F The United States entered World War II in 1941.

The United States either entered World War II in 1941 or it did not. It did; the statement is true.

True-false questions are easy for teachers to write and grade, and students can answer them in a very short time. As a result, true-false questions appear frequently in tests for psychology, history, business, and other college courses for which instructors want to determine whether students have learned factual information.

Assume Statements Are True

When you answer true-false questions on college tests, mark *true* those statements that you know are true and mark *false* those that you know are false. When you are uncertain whether a statement is true or false, assume it is true. The reason for assuming that statements are true is that there is a definite *tendency* for true-false tests to include more true statements than false ones. As a result, when you guess the answer to a true-false question, you are more likely to guess the correct answer if you guess it is true.

However, keep in mind that a true-false statement is false if any part of it is false. For example,

☐ T ☐ F George Washington, Benjamin Franklin, and Abraham Lincoln were presidents of the United States.

This statement is false because Benjamin Franklin was not a president of the United States.

"How to Answer True-False Questions" on page 238 summarizes the suggestions in the following discussion.

How to Answer True-False Questions

Answer all questions that you know are true or false. When you are uncertain whether a question is true or false, use the following hints to help in locating statements that are likely to be false:

- Questions that contain extreme modifiers such as *always, all, only,* and *never* tend to be false.
- Questions that state a reason tend to be false (and they often contain the words *reason, because,* or *since*).

When you are uncertain whether a statement is true or false, guess that it is true.

Extreme Modifiers

Extreme modifiers are words such as *always, all, only,* and *never;* they tend to appear in false statements. On the other hand, statements that include **qualifiers** such as *some, frequently, many,* and *sometimes* tend to be true. Compare the following statements.

□ T □ F **All** businesses adopt and use new technology.

□ T □ F **Many** businesses adopt and use new technology.

The first statement is false, but the second statement is true. All businesses do not adopt and use new technology, but many of them do.

Compare the following false and true statements, paying attention to the words printed in boldface.

False Statements	True Statements
1. Parents **always** love their children.	1. Parents **usually** love their children.
2. **All** children love chocolate.	2. **Many** children love chocolate.
3. The **only** reason people work is to earn money.	3. A **major** reason people work is to earn money.
4. Men are **never** nurses.	4. Men are **seldom** nurses.
5. **Nobody** reads dictionaries for pleasure.	5. **Few** people read dictionaries for pleasure.

The false statements in the left column contain extreme modifiers, such as *always* and *all,* which do not allow for exceptions. Following are more examples of extreme modifiers.

Extreme Modifiers Often in False Statements

all	none	best	absolutely
always	never	worst	absolutely not
only	nobody	everybody	certainly
invariably	no one	everyone	certainly not

The true statements often contain qualifiers, such as *usually* and *many,* which allow for exceptions. Following are more examples of qualifiers.

Qualifiers Often in True Statements

usually	frequently	often	sometimes
some	seldom	many	much
probably	a majority	apt to	most
might	a few	may	unlikely

Some students have difficulty deciding which words are extreme modifiers. If you have this problem, keep in mind that an extreme modifier is simply a qualifier that identifies the greatest degree and does not allow for exceptions, such as *always.* In contrast, *usually, frequently,* and *often* are not extreme modifiers—they are qualifiers that allow for exceptions.

Though true-false statements that contain extreme modifiers tend to be false, they can, of course, be true. For instance,

☐ T ☐ F Identical twins are **always** the same sex.

This statement is true; if twins are not the same sex, they are not identical.

Reasons

True-false questions that state reasons tend to be false, either because they state an incorrect reason or because they do not state all the reasons. For instance,

☐ T ☐ F The **reason** the government protects consumers is that consumer lobbyists fought for this protection.

This statement is false because it states an incomplete reason. The government protects consumers as a result of the actions of *many* groups and individuals who were not or are not necessarily lobbyists. Though we tend to think of the consumer movement as a new force in our society, it has been very strong since the 1880s, and it was not started by lobbyists.

The following true-false questions illustrate that the statement of a reason does not have to contain the word *reason.*

☐ T ☐ F The government protects consumers **because** lobbyists fought for this protection.

☐ T ☐ F **Since** consumer lobbyists fought to protect consumers, the government now protects them.

The words *because* and *since* indicate that these true-false questions state reasons.

True-false questions that state reasons can, of course, be true. For instance,

☐ T ☐ F Stores make much use of newspaper advertising **because** it is low in cost and has a high impact on consumers.

This statement is true—it gives two of the reasons stores use newspaper advertising.

Exercises 22.1–22.5 provide practice in learning how to select correct answers to true-false questions; the answers to the questions in the exercises are correct according to the sources upon which they are based. Use what you learn by doing the exercises to answer more true-false questions correctly on college tests.

Negatives and Double Negatives

When you answer test questions, be alert for negative words, such as *not*, and negative prefixes, such as *un-*. Compare the following questions, paying special attention to the word *not*, which is printed in boldface in the second version of the question.

☐ T ☐ F Alcohol is a depressant.

☐ T ☐ F Alcohol is **not** a depressant.

The first statement is true, but the word *not* in the second statement makes it false.

Also, compare the following questions, paying special attention to the negative prefix *un-*, which is printed in boldface in the first version of the question.

☐ T ☐ F Most **un**saturated fats are of vegetable origin.

☐ T ☐ F Most saturated fats are of vegetable origin.

The prefix *un-* in the first statement makes it true, but the second statement is false.

Negatives

Not and *cannot* are the most common negative words. Following are the most common negative prefixes. Learn any that are new to you.

Prefix	Example
un-	**Un**truthful means **not** truthful.
non-	**Non**alcoholic means **not** alcoholic.
in-	**In**direct means **not** direct.
im-	**Im**perfect means **not** perfect.
il-	**Il**legal means **not** legal.
ir-	**Ir**responsible means **not** responsible.
dis-	**Dis**agreeable means **not** agreeable.

Double Negatives

Test writers also sometimes include double negatives in questions. **Double negatives** are statements that include two negatives, usually *not* and a negative prefix. A double negative is printed in boldface in the following sentence.

She is **not un**intelligent.

To interpret a statement of this type, cross out both negatives.

She is ~~not~~ ~~un~~intelligent.

Then read the statement as though it contains no negatives.

She is intelligent.

"She is not unintelligent" means "she is intelligent."

The most common double negatives are printed in boldface in the following list on the left.

Double Negative	Interpretation
not untruthful	truthful
not nonalcoholic	alcoholic
not indirect	direct
not imperfect	perfect
not illegal	legal
not irresponsible	responsible
not disagreeable	agreeable

Exercises 22.6 and 22.7 provide practice in interpreting statements that include negatives and double negatives.

 NAME ________________________________ DATE ____________

EXERCISE 22.1 True-False Questions

The following statements are true, except for those that have an extreme modifier or that state a reason. Check **T** for true statements and **F** for false statements. When you check **F**, underline the word in the statement that indicates it is false.

1. □ T □ F Young people tend to consider as necessities many products that adults categorize as luxuries.

2. □ T □ F Criminologists are concerned only with the reasons people commit crimes and not with what happens to people after they are imprisoned.

3. □ T □ F We do not know for certain what causes lightning.

4. □ T □ F Men seem to fall in love more quickly and easily than women.

5. □ T □ F Laws do nothing to diminish discrimination because it is not possible to legislate morality.

6. □ T □ F All people are psychologically mature at age eighteen.

7. □ T □ F The right hemisphere of the brain is believed to be the center for nonverbal reasoning.

8. □ T □ F The reason for underlining textbooks is that, if they are underlined, students do not need to make notes on the information in them.

9. □ T □ F The halo effect refers to the tendency always to rate individuals positively.

10. □ T □ F Joggers can maintain the same physical fitness as runners by jogging the same distances that runners run.

11. □ T □ F Since markup pricing complicates the process of deciding what prices to charge for products, retailers do not use it often.

12. □ T □ F In the past, population growth was sometimes controlled by killing newborn babies.

EXERCISE 22.2 True-False Questions

The following statements are true, except for those that have an extreme modifier or that state a reason. Check **T** for true statements and **F** for false statements. When you check **F,** underline the word in the statement that indicates it is false.

1. ☐ T ☐ F International trade is not vital to our economy because we are the world's leading economic and military power.

2. ☐ T ☐ F In American society, people tend to marry others who are much like themselves with regard to age, social class, education, and so on.

3. ☐ T ☐ F Prejudice is based only on fear, ignorance, and cultural conditioning.

4. ☐ T ☐ F During the Civil War, more northern soldiers died from diseases or accidents than from combat.

5. ☐ T ☐ F Psychologists have shown that all six-year-olds can perform the thinking skills needed to learn to read.

6. ☐ T ☐ F College graduates usually earn more money than high school graduates.

7. ☐ T ☐ F People who divorce and remarry are more likely to divorce than people who marry for the first time.

8. ☐ T ☐ F The reason tropical Africa has a very good agricultural economy is that it has a very long growing season.

9. ☐ T ☐ F The decision to commit suicide is never made suddenly or impulsively.

10. ☐ T ☐ F Gambling is usually more profitable to organized crime than either prostitution or drugs.

11. ☐ T ☐ F The Old Testament does not report an incident in which a woman was put to death for sleeping with a man other than her husband.

12. ☐ T ☐ F It makes sense to choose a college major in the same field as one's intended career, because most graduates are employed in the general field of their college major.

EXERCISE 22.3 True-False Questions

The following statements are true, except for those that have an extreme modifier or that state a reason. Check **T** for true statements and **F** for false statements. When you check **F**, underline the word in the statement that indicates it is false.

1. ☐ T ☐ F The United States has one of the most severe systems for punishing criminals in the civilized world.

2. ☐ T ☐ F Highly talented people always have highly positive self-concepts.

3. ☐ T ☐ F Of the slaves who were taken from Africa, approximately 6 percent were brought to the United States.

4. ☐ T ☐ F The population is increasing rapidly in less developed countries of the world because of the high birthrates in those regions.

5. ☐ T ☐ F People are more likely to be murdered in their homes by somebody they know than on the streets by a stranger.

6. ☐ T ☐ F Women seem to fall out of love more quickly and with less difficulty than men.

7. ☐ T ☐ F Colorblindness is a vision problem of men, but never of women.

8. ☐ T ☐ F Average weekly movie attendance in the United States dropped from 90,000,000 in the 1940s to 22,500,000 in the 1980s.

9. ☐ T ☐ F There are almost as many independent nations in Africa as there are states in the United States.

10. ☐ T ☐ F Churchmen formed the only substantial block of white Southerners who criticized slavery during the years before the Civil War.

11. ☐ T ☐ F Since women have less education than men, they earn less money than men.

12. ☐ T ☐ F Sleep was not scientifically investigated until recently because there was no interest in this subject until after World War II.

EXERCISE 22.4 True-False Questions

The following statements are true, except for those that have an extreme modifier or that state a reason. Check **T** for true statements and **F** for false statements. When you check **F,** underline the word in the statement that indicates it is false.

1. ☐ T ☐ F The reason Napoleon sold Louisiana to the United States was that he feared we would take it by force.

2. ☐ T ☐ F It is healthy for us to express our anger.

3. ☐ T ☐ F Most human behavior is learned.

4. ☐ T ☐ F Stock certificates must be issued by all corporations.

5. ☐ T ☐ F People judge others on traits they are born with, such as height, skin color, hairiness, and nose shape.

6. ☐ T ☐ F Psychologists agree that our value systems are always formed by the time we are six years old.

7. ☐ T ☐ F Drug pushers usually become members of criminal organizations because they themselves are addicted and need a source of drugs.

8. ☐ T ☐ F Today, retail stores are staffed largely by part-time sales workers.

9. ☐ T ☐ F The lack of black police officers is due to the fact that there is discrimination against well-qualified black applicants for positions in the police force.

10. ☐ T ☐ F Most jobs contain some dreary activities.

11. ☐ T ☐ F Employers provide orientation for new employees only.

12. ☐ T ☐ F There are at least 7,000 people in the United States over one hundred years old.

EXERCISE 22.5 True-False Questions

The following statements are true, except for those that have an extreme modifier or that state a reason. Check **T** for true statements and **F** for false statements. When you check **F,** underline the word in the statement that indicates it is false.

1. ☐ T ☐ F People of similar intellectual levels tend to marry one another.

2. ☐ T ☐ F Despite great temptation, President Lincoln never used political deception or trickery.

3. ☐ T ☐ F When "senseless" violence occurs, it is always illegal and usually brought about by the victim.

4. ☐ T ☐ F A powerful narcotic was at one time an ingredient in Coca-Cola.

5. ☐ T ☐ F American women were not guaranteed the right to vote until 1920.

6. ☐ T ☐ F Convertible bonds are considered to be more conservative investments than nonconvertible bonds because they may be exchanged for common stock.

7. ☐ T ☐ F Many couples maintain an active sexual relationship into their sixties and seventies.

8. ☐ T ☐ F States with the death penalty actually have higher rates of murder than states without it.

9. ☐ T ☐ F The tone of your voice often creates a strong positive or negative impression.

10. ☐ T ☐ F When employees are fired it is usually because they lack the technical skills to do their jobs.

11. ☐ T ☐ F Children with hearing and vision difficulties should be taught only by specially trained teachers.

12. ☐ T ☐ F Since all property will increase in value, the purchase of real estate is a good hedge against inflation.

EXERCISE 22.6 Negatives

In the following pairs of questions, one statement contains a negative word or prefix and the other one does not. Underline the negatives, and check **T** for true statements and **F** for false statements.

1. ☐ T ☐ F Most people really do not want to work.
   ☐ T ☐ F Most people really do want to work.

2. ☐ T ☐ F Job security is unimportant to most workers.
   ☐ T ☐ F Job security is important to most workers.

3. ☐ T ☐ F Psychologists agree on the definition of intelligence.
   ☐ T ☐ F Psychologists disagree on the definition of intelligence.

4. ☐ T ☐ F Lack of ability to do work is the reason given most often for firing workers.
   ☐ T ☐ F Lack of ability to do work is not the reason given most often for firing workers.

5. ☐ T ☐ F Lateness or absence from work is a frequent reason given for firing workers.
   ☐ T ☐ F Lateness or absence from work is an infrequent reason given for firing workers.

6. ☐ T ☐ F When you want to help friends who have a problem, it is well to be impatient with them.
   ☐ T ☐ F When you want to help friends who have a problem, it is well to be patient with them.

7. ☐ T ☐ F When you want to learn about an occupation by reading published materials, it is relevant when the material was published.
   ☐ T ☐ F When you want to learn about an occupation by reading published materials, it is irrelevant when the material was published.

8. ☐ T ☐ F American society has no social classes.
   ☐ T ☐ F American society has social classes.

EXERCISE 22.7 Double Negatives

Cross out the double negatives in the following statements, and check **T** for true statements and **F** for false statements.

Part 1

1. ☐ T ☐ F Fine crystal drinking glasses are not unbreakable.
2. ☐ T ☐ F A lie is not an untrue statement.
3. ☐ T ☐ F People can write if they are not illiterate.
4. ☐ T ☐ F The totally blind are not unable to see.
5. ☐ T ☐ F Milk is not a nonalcoholic beverage.
6. ☐ T ☐ F A straight line is not an indirect path between two points.
7. ☐ T ☐ F We trust those whom we know we cannot distrust.
8. ☐ T ☐ F If a painting by a dead artist is destroyed by fire, it is not irreplaceable.

Part 2

1. ☐ T ☐ F A surprise is something that is not unexpected.
2. ☐ T ☐ F One million dollars is not an insubstantial sum of money.
3. ☐ T ☐ F Under federal law, it is not illegal to pay women less than men for doing the same or similar work.
4. ☐ T ☐ F Friends should not be inconsiderate of our feelings.
5. ☐ T ☐ F It is not dishonest to tell the truth.
6. ☐ T ☐ F Unfinished work is work that is not uncompleted.
7. ☐ T ☐ F Identical objects are not dissimilar.
8. ☐ T ☐ F It is not unwise to be alert for double negatives in test questions.

23

Multiple-Choice Questions

Multiple-choice questions are incomplete statements followed by possible ways to complete them, or they are questions followed by possible answers. The incomplete statement or question that begins a multiple-choice question is called the **stem,** and the choices for answers are written so that one is the correct answer and the others are **distractors.**

1. United States senators serve
   - ☐ a. two-year terms.
   - ☐ b. four-year terms.
   - ☐ c. six-year terms.
   - ☐ d. eight-year terms.

In this example, the stem is "United States senators serve." The question is written with the intention that students who know the correct answer will select *c* (six-year terms), whereas other students will be distracted and select one of the distractors—*a, b,* or *d.*

Popularity of Multiple-Choice Questions

There are at least three reasons multiple-choice questions are popular among college teachers.

- They can be used to test all aspects of students' knowledge and their ability to reason using information they have learned.
- When answers are recorded on answer sheets, multiple-choice answers are easy to grade.
- Students with poor writing ability are not penalized when they answer multiple-choice questions (as they may be when they are required to give written answers to questions).

For these reasons, you will probably take many multiple-choice tests during your college career.

How to Answer Multiple-Choice Questions

1. Answer all questions for which you know the correct answer.
2. Look for clues to correct answers.
   - "All of the above"
   - One of two similar-looking answers
   - The most inclusive answer
3. Look for clues to *in*correct answers.
   - An extreme modifier (such as *always*)
   - An unfamiliar term
   - A joke or insult
   - The highest and lowest number in a set

Eliminate the Distractors

Multiple-choice questions are prepared by first writing a stem and the correct answer. For instance,

2. A speech that has as its purpose to inform how to plan a successful party must use
   ☐ a. exposition.
   ☐ b.
   ☐ c.
   ☐ d.

After putting this much on paper, the question writer then fills in the distractors and decides where to locate the correct answer. As a result, the test taker's job is to analyze multiple-choice questions to eliminate distractors and in this way to locate the correct answer that was "hidden" by the question writer.

One way to eliminate distractors is to analyze a multiple-choice question as though it is a series of true-false questions. For instance,

☐ T ☐ F United States senators serve two-year terms.

☐ T ☐ F United States senators serve four-year terms.

☐ T ☐ F United States senators serve six-year terms.

☐ T ☐ F United States senators serve eight-year terms.

Most multiple-choice questions are actually a series of true-false statements, only one of which is true. When you answer a multiple-choice question, analyze it to eliminate distractors and to select as the correct answer the choice that makes the stem a true statement.

When you have difficulty eliminating the distractors in a multiple-choice question, analyze it for the clues to correct answers and incorrect answers. "How to Answer Multiple-Choice Questions" on page 250 summarizes suggestions that are explained in detail in the following discussions.

"All of the Above"

When "all of the above" is a choice in a multiple-choice question, it tends to be the correct answer. Check the correct answer to the following question.

3. Teenage love involves
   - ☐ a. sexual attraction.
   - ☐ b. crushes.
   - ☐ c. a search for identity.
   - ☐ d. all of the above

You should have checked *d;* it is the correct answer.

The question could, of course, have been written so that "all of the above" is not the correct answer. Check the correct answer to the following question.

4. Teenage love involves
   - ☐ a. crushes.
   - ☐ b. expensive dates.
   - ☐ c. guilt and shame.
   - ☐ d. all of the above

According to the source upon which this question is based, the correct answer is *a;* however, keep in mind that in college tests "all of the above" is the correct answer much more frequently than it should be.

Also, when you know that two answers are correct and another choice is "all of the above," you must select "all of the above" as the correct answer. For instance,

5. Silver is used to make
   - ☐ a. knives and forks.
   - ☐ b. jewelry.
   - ☐ c. film for photography.
   - ☐ d. all of the above

If you know that silver is used to make knives, forks, and jewelry, you must select "all of the above" as the correct answer even if you do not know that it is also used to make film for photography. If you select *a,* you do not include jewelry; if you select *b,* you do not include knives and forks. You must select *d* to include knives, forks, and jewelry in your answer.

Two Similar-looking Answers

When two answers are similar looking, the correct answer is often one of the two similar-looking answers. Check the correct answer to the following question.

6. In the brain, language functions are associated mainly with the
   - ☐ a. left hemisphere.
   - ☐ b. right hemisphere.
   - ☐ c. cerebellum.
   - ☐ d. corpus callosum.

You should have eliminated answers *c* and *d* and made your choice between the two similar-looking answers—*a* and *b*. The correct answer is *a*.

Question writers sometimes write multiple-choice questions to eliminate the clue to two similar-looking answers. For instance,

7. Loss of all sensation in your hand would most likely result from damage to
   - ☐ a. afferent spinal nerves.
   - ☐ b. efferent spinal nerves.
   - ☐ c. afferent cranial nerves.
   - ☐ d. efferent cranial nerves.

When questions are written in this way, you cannot use two similar-looking answers as a clue to the correct answer, which in this case is *a*.

Most Inclusive Answer

When one answer to a multiple-choice question is more inclusive than other answers, it is likely to be the correct answer. Check the most inclusive answer to the following question.

8. Output devices on computers produce
   - ☐ a. a permanent copy.
   - ☐ b. a soft copy.
   - ☐ c. both *a* and *b*
   - ☐ d. none of the above

You should have checked *c*, which includes the possibilities stated in answers *a* and *b*; answer *c* is the most inclusive answer, and it is also the correct answer.

It can be a challenge to identify the most inclusive answer. Check the most inclusive answer to the following question.

9. Weight is likely to vary most among a group of
   - ☐ a. men who are football linebackers.
   - ☐ b. women who are ballet dancers.
   - ☐ c. people who are jockeys.
   - ☐ d. people who are college students.

Football linebackers tend to include only heavy people; women ballet dancers and jockeys tend to include only light people. College students, though, include people who are heavy, light, and medium in weight. Answer *d* is the most inclusive, and it is the correct answer.

Extreme Modifiers

In Chapter 22 you learned that extreme modifiers tend to be included in true-false questions that are false; in multiple-choice questions, extreme modifiers tend to appear in distractors. Underline the extreme modifiers in the following question and check the correct answer.

10. Mentally healthy people
    - ☐ a. never change their goals.
    - ☐ b. are always happy when alone.
    - ☐ c. are sometimes anxious or afraid.
    - ☐ d. never examine their mistakes.

You should have underlined *always* and *never,* and you should have checked *c.*

Unfamiliar Terms

Unfamiliar terms or phrases are often included in distractors. Underline the unfamiliar terms in the following question and check the correct answer.

11. Mass hysteria results when large numbers of people
    - ☐ a. believe something that is not true.
    - ☐ b. fear an invasion of iconoclasts.
    - ☐ c. have concomitant exigencies.
    - ☐ d. share incontrovertible perceptions.

You should have underlined *iconoclasts, concomitant exigencies,* and *incontrovertible perceptions;* and you should have checked *a.*

The only time it is wise to pick answers with unfamiliar terms is when you are certain that all the other answers are incorrect. For instance,

12. Jeans are always
    - ☐ a. dark blue.
    - ☐ b. well worn.
    - ☐ c. too tight.
    - ☐ d. bifurcated.

You know that jeans are not always dark blue, well worn, or too tight; therefore, you are forced to conclude that they are *bifurcated,* even though you probably don't know the meaning of the word. To bifurcate is to divide into two parts or branches; the legs of jeans are in two parts—one for each leg. Skirts, in contrast, are not bifurcated.

Jokes or Insults

Answers that are jokes or insults are usually distractors. Check the answer in the following question that is *not* ridiculous or insulting.

13. A common reason students give for leaving college is that they
    - ☐ a. aren't smart enough to do college work.
    - ☐ b. find that they dislike other college students.
    - ☐ c. are treated badly by their instructors.
    - ☐ d. decide that something else interests them more.

Answers *a*, *b*, and *c* are either ridiculous or insulting; you should have eliminated them as distractors and checked *d*, which is the correct answer.

Extreme Numbers

When answers are a series of numbers that go from high to low, the extreme numbers (the highest and lowest ones) tend to be incorrect. Answer the following question by eliminating the extreme numbers as distractors.

14. According to the U.S. Department of Agriculture, how many servings of vegetables should we eat each day?
    - ☐ a. one to three
    - ☐ b. two to four
    - ☐ c. three to five
    - ☐ d. four to six

You should have eliminated the extreme numbers in answers *a* and *d* and made your choice between *b* and *c*. The correct answer is *c*. According to the U.S. Department of Agriculture, we should eat three to five servings of vegetables and two to four servings of fruit each day.

EXERCISE 23.1 Multiple-Choice Questions

Use the clues to correct and incorrect answers summarized on page 250 to select the correct answers to the following questions.

1. Learning how to play the piano while singing occurs in the
   - ☐ a. motor domain.
   - ☐ b. cognitive domain.
   - ☐ c. affective domain.
   - ☐ d. motor and cognitive domains.

2. After the Civil War, Reconstruction legislatures in the South were successful in
   - ☐ a. making prison reforms.
   - ☐ b. integrating public schools.
   - ☐ c. improving facilities for the handicapped.
   - ☐ d. achieving all of the foregoing.

3. On June 21, the sun is found directly over the
   - ☐ a. Tropic of Cancer.
   - ☐ b. Tropic of Capricorn.
   - ☐ c. Equator.
   - ☐ d. North Pole.

4. The normal adult temperature of 98.6°F is equivalent to
   - ☐ a. 18°C.
   - ☐ b. 27°C.
   - ☐ c. 37°C.
   - ☐ d. 42°C.

5. Those who believe in the work ethic believe that
   - ☐ a. all people will do good work.
   - ☐ b. hard work is always rewarded.
   - ☐ c. work is good and important.
   - ☐ d. only workers should receive money.

6. The biosphere consists of
   - ☐ a. air above the earth.
   - ☐ b. the earth's surface.
   - ☐ c. bodies of water on earth.
   - ☐ d. air, earth surface, and water bodies.

7. The median is a measure that is similar to
   - ☐ a. the average.
   - ☐ b. a histogram.
   - ☐ c. the skewness.
   - ☐ d. a coefficient.

8. Educators refer to individuals of very low intelligence as
   - ☐ a. idiots.
   - ☐ b. morons.
   - ☐ c. imbeciles.
   - ☐ d. totally dependent.

9. Studies of workers' attitudes have found that
   - ☐ a. most workers feel they should have better jobs.
   - ☐ b. many workers would rather have better jobs than more pay.
   - ☐ c. workers are motivated by conflicting drives.
   - ☐ d. all of the above

10. Children begin to understand some of the concepts associated with religious beliefs when they are
    - ☐ a. toddlers.
    - ☐ b. preschoolers.
    - ☐ c. school aged.
    - ☐ d. teenagers.

EXERCISE 23.2 Multiple-Choice Questions

Use the clues to correct and incorrect answers summarized on page 250 to select the correct answers to the following questions.

1. Most Jewish immigrants to the United States came from
   - ☐ a. Eastern Europe.
   - ☐ b. Western Europe.
   - ☐ c. Israel.
   - ☐ d. Africa and Asia.

2. Partners in a marriage are likely to be similar in
   - ☐ a. height and weight.
   - ☐ b. hair and skin color.
   - ☐ c. general health.
   - ☐ d. size, coloring, and health.

3. People work because they
   - ☐ a. need to feel productive.
   - ☐ b. must pay for necessities.
   - ☐ c. want to achieve dignity.
   - ☐ d. all of the above

4. Brazil was colonized by
   - ☐ a. Indians.
   - ☐ b. North Americans.
   - ☐ c. a heterogeneous group of Europeans.
   - ☐ d. a homogeneous group of Europeans.

5. A zero-growth family is one that has
   - ☐ a. no children.
   - ☐ b. one child.
   - ☐ c. two children.
   - ☐ d. three children.

6. Members of one's family of orientation are
   - ☐ a. blood relatives.
   - ☐ b. affinal relatives.
   - ☐ c. tertiary relatives.
   - ☐ d. misogynistic relatives.

7. The difficulty of reading material can be estimated by studying the lengths of
   - ☐ a. words.
   - ☐ b. sentences.
   - ☐ c. both *a* and *b*
   - ☐ d. none of the above

8. Which of the following statements about ability is true?
   - ☐ a. People differ in their abilities.
   - ☐ b. All people are equal in abilities.
   - ☐ c. There is only one basic type of ability.
   - ☐ d. Ability never changes over one's lifetime.

9. More doctors are males than females, probably because
   - ☐ a. women don't want prestigious jobs.
   - ☐ b. of established occupational expectations.
   - ☐ c. males make better doctors.
   - ☐ d. most women crack under pressure.

10. A common physical symptom of depression is
    - ☐ a. constipation.
    - ☐ b. decreased pulse.
    - ☐ c. decreased blood pressure.
    - ☐ d. all of the above

EXERCISE 23.3 Multiple-Choice Questions

Use the clues to correct and incorrect answers summarized on page 250 to select the correct answers to the following questions.

1. About how much time should one spend doing aerobic activity to attain top conditioning?
   - ☐ a. 1 hour 6–7 days a week
   - ☐ b. ½ hour 3–5 days a week
   - ☐ c. ¼ hour 3–5 days a week
   - ☐ d. ½ hour 6–7 days a week

2. Harmony between one's beliefs and behavior is called
   - ☐ a. cognitive consonance.
   - ☐ b. cognitive dissonance.
   - ☐ c. personality agreement.
   - ☐ d. belief-system integration.

3. Our sexual attitudes develop
   - ☐ a. solely from what we learn from our parents.
   - ☐ b. from positive and negative sexual experiences.
   - ☐ c. from satisfying sexual experiences.
   - ☐ d. from unfortunate sexual experiences.

4. The burning of fossil fuel is causing a build-up of carbon dioxide that may eventually
   - ☐ a. affect the global radiation balance.
   - ☐ b. create a warming trend on earth.
   - ☐ c. irreversibly alter world ecosystems.
   - ☐ d. all of the above

5. In the 1840s the great potato famine in Ireland resulted from
   - ☐ a. wet weather.
   - ☐ b. dry weather.
   - ☐ c. population growth.
   - ☐ d. potato disease.

6. Which of the following age groups most commonly experiences frightening dreams?
   - ☐ a. two-year-olds
   - ☐ b. three-year-olds
   - ☐ c. six-year-olds
   - ☐ d. adolescents

7. The abbreviation SEM refers to a type of
   - ☐ a. serological technique.
   - ☐ b. anaerobic bacteria.
   - ☐ c. microscope.
   - ☐ d. avian embryo.

8. In New England prior to 1780, there were
   - ☐ a. no banks.
   - ☐ b. no schools.
   - ☐ c. no hospitals.
   - ☐ d. both *a* and *c*

9. If a five-year-old says, "I flied to New York," this indicates that the child
   - ☐ a. has ignorant parents.
   - ☐ b. has inferior intelligence.
   - ☐ c. knows language rules but not their exceptions.
   - ☐ d. prefers using incorrect grammatical forms.

10. Cancer cells
    - ☐ a. lack contact inhibition.
    - ☐ b. are "immortal."
    - ☐ c. will not readily rejoin cells of the organ from which they originate.
    - ☐ d. all of the above

EXERCISE 23.4 Multiple-Choice Questions

Use the clues to correct and incorrect answers summarized on page 250 to select the correct answers to the following questions.

1. If a woman's worry over her cat's safety prevents her from leaving home more than twice a week, she is
   - ☐ a. obsessive-compulsive.
   - ☐ b. a dipsomaniac.
   - ☐ c. somewhat abnormal.
   - ☐ d. a fruitcake.

2. The first book published in the New World was printed in
   - ☐ a. Peru in 1473.
   - ☐ b. New York in 1486.
   - ☐ c. Mexico in 1539.
   - ☐ d. Massachusetts in 1626.

3. The return to a less mature behavior pattern is called
   - ☐ a. repression.
   - ☐ b. regression.
   - ☐ c. reaction formation.
   - ☐ d. none of the above

4. A nurse's first concern upon discovering a fire is to
   - ☐ a. close doors and windows.
   - ☐ b. put out the fire.
   - ☐ c. safeguard patients.
   - ☐ d. set off the fire alarm.

5. Engaging in aerobic exercise at least three times a week may produce
   - ☐ a. positive body perception.
   - ☐ b. more endorphins in the brain.
   - ☐ c. cardiovascular conditioning.
   - ☐ d. all of the above

6. Mary jogs every day because it makes her feel good about herself. She is motivated by
   - ☐ a. an intrinsic reward.
   - ☐ b. an extrinsic reward.
   - ☐ c. a psychological need.
   - ☐ d. peer-group pressure.

7. Children begin to understand that death is final when they are about
   - ☐ a. 5–6 years old.
   - ☐ b. 8–9 years old.
   - ☐ c. 11–13 years old.
   - ☐ d. 15–16 years old.

8. The central processing unit of a computer
   - ☐ a. controls computer operations.
   - ☐ b. performs arithmetic operations.
   - ☐ c. contains memory for the program and data.
   - ☐ d. all of the above

9. The major problem with selling beverages in throwaway cans is that these containers
   - ☐ a. create costly garbage-disposal problems.
   - ☐ b. are expensive to make and dispose of.
   - ☐ c. use a great deal of expensive metal.
   - ☐ d. require much expensive energy to produce.

10. Most psychologists agree that
    - ☐ a. institutionalized children never succeed in life.
    - ☐ b. fatherless boys always become homosexuals.
    - ☐ c. unloved infants often have personality problems.
    - ☐ d. abused children always abuse their own children.

24

Examples in Questions

Questions on college tests may often be stated in ways that are impossible for you to anticipate. The surprise of reading questions worded in ways that you do not expect may unnerve you and cause you to select incorrect answers to questions that you would otherwise answer correctly.

Examples in Stems

If you learn in a psychology course that *frustration* is that which prevents a person from reaching a goal, you could probably correctly answer questions about the definition of *frustration.* However, you may have difficulty correctly answering questions that require you to analyze an *example* of frustration, such as the one in the stem of the following question.

1. John earns a good salary at a job he doesn't like. He has a chance to get a job doing something he would like to do, but the pay is so low that it won't give him the money he needs for his family. So he's still working at his old job. John's frustration is
   - ☐ a. his feelings of unhappiness and discontent.
   - ☐ b. the present job that he doesn't like.
   - ☐ c. the job that he would like to have.
   - ☐ d. the low pay for the job he'd like to have.

To answer this question, you must compare the example in the stem to the definition of *frustration* (that which prevents a person from reaching a goal). You must ask yourself, "What is John's goal?" and "What is preventing him from reaching it?" John's goal is to have a job he would like, but he is prevented from reaching his goal because the job he would like pays too little money. The correct answer to the question is *d.*

Examples in Answers

A multiple-choice question may have examples in answers rather than in the stem. See question 2 on the next page.

2. Which of the following statements does *not* contain a frustration?
   - ☐ a. Al wants to be a doctor, but he can't get into medical school.
   - ☐ b. Ann wants to go to work, but she has children to care for.
   - ☐ c. Bob wants to be a fireman, but he isn't tall enough.
   - ☐ d. Mary wants to be a dancer, but she also wants to be a singer.

To answer this question, you must compare examples in the answers to the definition of *frustration* (that which prevents a person from reaching a goal). You must ask questions such as the following to eliminate the distractors.

- For *a,* ask "Does this state what is preventing Al from reaching his goal of being a doctor?" Yes, he cannot get into medical school.
- For *b,* ask, "Does this state what is preventing Ann from reaching her goal of going to work?" Yes, she has children to care for.
- For *c,* ask, "Does this state what is preventing Bob from reaching his goal of being a fireman?" Yes, he is not tall enough.
- For *d,* ask, "Does this state what is preventing Mary from reaching her goal of being a singer or dancer?" No, singers may be dancers and dancers may be singers.

The correct answer is *d;* it does *not* state a frustration.

The following exercises provide practice in answering multiple-choice questions that have examples in stems or answers. By doing the exercises, you should become more confident that you will select correct answers to these types of questions when they appear on tests you take for your college courses.

EXERCISE 24.1 Examples in Questions

Answer the questions about the passages by eliminating distractors and checking the boxes in front of correct answers.

A **euphemism** is an acceptable or inoffensive word or phrase used to describe something that is distasteful, unpleasant, or intimate. "I'm going to wash my hands" is sometimes a euphemism for "I'm going to use the toilet." "Not too good-looking" is a euphemism when it's used to describe an extremely ugly object or person.

1. Which of the following is *not* a euphemism for describing an elderly person?
   - ☐ a. She's a senior citizen.
   - ☐ b. She's in her golden years.
   - ☐ c. She has the benefit of experience.
   - ☐ d. She's older than God.

2. Which of the following is *not* a euphemism for describing a person who has died?
   - ☐ a. He kicked the bucket.
   - ☐ b. He passed away.
   - ☐ c. He went to his reward.
   - ☐ d. He is enjoying eternal rest.

The **one-plus-one rule** is a useful but seldom-taught spelling rule. It applies when (1) joining two words, (2) joining a prefix and a base word, and (3) joining a base word and a suffix. The basic idea is that when elements begin and end with the same consonant at the place where they are joined, both consonants are kept. Thus, *jack* plus *knife* is *jac**kk**nife; mis-* plus *spell* is *mi**ss**pell;* and *brown* plus *-ness* is *brow**nn**ess.*

3. Which of the following correctly spelled words does *not* follow the one-plus-one rule?
   - ☐ a. glowworm
   - ☐ b. soulless
   - ☐ c. eighteen
   - ☐ d. dissimilar

4. According to the one-plus-one rule, which of the following words is spelled correctly?
   - ☐ a. unecessary
   - ☐ b. newstand
   - ☐ c. transshipment
   - ☐ d. bathouse

EXERCISE 24.2 Examples in Questions

Answer the questions about the passages by eliminating distractors and checking the boxes in front of correct answers.

Palindromes are words, phrases, or sentences that spell the same backward and forward: for instance, *radar, civic,* and *nun.* The most famous palindromic sentence is probably "A man, a plan, a canal—Panama," which is spelled *amanaplanacanalpanama* forward and backward.

1. Which of the following is *not* a palindrome?
   - ☐ a. noon
   - ☐ b. repaper
   - ☐ c. pump
   - ☐ d. level

2. Which of the following is *not* a palindrome?
   - ☐ a. a Toyota
   - ☐ b. Don't give in.
   - ☐ c. Dennis sinned.
   - ☐ d. Madam, I'm Adam.

The **average** is found by adding numbers together and dividing the sum by the total number of numbers. To find the average of 5, 7, and 9, add the numbers (21) and divide by the number of numbers (3); the average is 7. The **median** is the middle number in a set—it has the same number of numbers above and below it. The median for the following numbers is 7: 2, 2, 7, 8, 9.

3. What is the median for the following set of numbers: 2, 4, 6, 5, 8, 2, 1?
   - ☐ a. 2
   - ☐ b. 4
   - ☐ c. 5
   - ☐ d. 6

4. What are the average and median for the following set of numbers: 4, 6, 8, 8, 9?
   - ☐ a. 6
   - ☐ b. 9
   - ☐ c. 7 and 8, respectively
   - ☐ d. 6 and 8, respectively

EXERCISE 24.3 Examples in Questions

Answer the questions about the passages by eliminating distractors and checking the boxes in front of correct answers.

Phonemes are the sounds that are heard when words are spoken. For example, the word *can* has three phonemes (*k*, *a*, and *n*). Many words have more letters than phonemes. For instance, *wreck* has five letters but only three phonemes (*r*, *e*, and *k*).

1. Which of the following is *not* a phoneme?
   - ☐ a. n
   - ☐ b. r
   - ☐ c. c
   - ☐ d. k

2. How many phonemes are there in the word *laugh?*
   - ☐ a. two
   - ☐ b. three
   - ☐ c. four
   - ☐ d. five

In a court action the **plaintiff** is the one who claims a wrong has been done, and the **defendant** is the one who is accused of having done the wrong. For instance, if your landlord takes you to court because you do not pay rent, you are the defendant and your landlord is the plaintiff.

3. When Harry's luggage was lost, he took an airline company to court, but the company said Harry lost the luggage. The airline company was the
   - ☐ a. aggressor.
   - ☐ b. prosecutor.
   - ☐ c. defendant.
   - ☐ d. plaintiff.

4. Ted and Alice are married, but Ted runs around with Freda, and Alice goes out with Tony. Alice is taking Ted to court to divorce him. Who is the plaintiff?
   - ☐ a. Freda
   - ☐ b. Tony
   - ☐ c. Ted
   - ☐ d. Alice

EXERCISE 24.4 Examples in Questions

Answer the questions about the passages by eliminating distractors and checking the boxes in front of correct answers.

Open questions are ones that call for rather long answers. For instance, "What are some of your favorite ways to spend leisure time?" is an open question. **Closed questions** are ones that can be answered in a word or two. For instance, "How old are you?" is a closed question.

1. Which of the following is an open question?
   - ☐ a. Do you have a job?
   - ☐ b. How can you become a better conversationalist?
   - ☐ c. Where did you eat lunch on Friday?
   - ☐ d. What grade did you get for your chemistry course?

2. Which of the following is a closed question?
   - ☐ a. What can you do to earn higher grades?
   - ☐ b. What can your teachers do to help you learn?
   - ☐ c. How can you answer more test questions correctly?
   - ☐ d. Do you think it's worthwhile to study test-taking skills?

Parents engage in **sex-typing** when they encourage their children to behave in ways that have been traditionally considered appropriate for males and females. For instance, when parents encourage a son to wrestle but discourage a daughter from wrestling, they are sex-typing.

3. Parents are sex-typing when they encourage a
   - ☐ a. girl to ride a bike.
   - ☐ b. boy to care for a cat.
   - ☐ c. girl to clean house.
   - ☐ d. boy to learn to cook.

4. Which of the following is *not* an example of sex-typing?
   - ☐ a. Telling a boy not to cry
   - ☐ b. Teaching a boy to fight back
   - ☐ c. Telling a girl to be sweet
   - ☐ d. Teaching a girl to fight back

25

Matching Questions

Matching questions present two lists of items and require test takers to associate items in one list with items in the other list. In properly written questions, all items in each list are similar. For example, the following matching question for a music appreciation course requires students to match operas with their composers.

Music Appreciation

_______	1. *Dido and Aeneas*	a. Puccini
_______	2. *Don Giovanni*	b. Mozart
_______	3. *Tosca*	c. Monteverdi
_______	4. *Tristan and Isolde*	d. Purcell
_______	5. *Orfeo*	e. Wagner
_______	6. *Rigoletto*	f. Donizetti
_______	7. *Carmen*	g. Verdi
_______	8. *Lucrezia Borgia*	h. Bizet

It is extremely difficult to guess correct answers to properly written matching questions, such as this one. If you guess at the composers of the operas, you are not likely to guess more than one correct answer.

Answering Matching Questions

When you answer a matching question, scan both lists to understand the types of items you are to match, and then use one list as the starting place for making all the matches. Take care to match only those items that you are absolutely certain are matches because each time you make a mistake, you will be led

How to Answer Matching Questions

- Examine both lists to understand the types of items you are to match.
- Use one list as the starting place for making all the matches.
- If one list has longer statements, use it as the starting place for making matches.
- Cross out items as you match them.
- Match first only those items that you are certain are matches.
- If possible, use logical clues to match items about which you are uncertain.

to make another error. For instance, if you match *3* with *b* when you should match *3* with *f*, you will match *3* with an incorrect letter *and* you will make another mistake when you match *f* with an incorrect number.

Procedures for answering matching questions are summarized in "How to Answer Matching Questions" above.

Lists with Longer Statements

If one list in a matching question has longer statements, use the list of longer statements as the starting place for making matches. For example,

Introduction to Business

______	1. advertising media	a. telling customers that an advertised special is sold out but offering them a more expensive substitute
______	2. sales promotion	b. nonpaid information about the company or its products in the mass media
______	3. bait-and-switch	c. the element of promotional strategy other than personal selling, advertising, and publicity
______	4. promotional mix	d. radio, TV, newspapers, magazine, and direct mail
______	5. publicity	e. combination of advertising, personal selling, sales promotion, and publicity
______	6. frequency	f. average number of times an advertising message reaches a person or household

There are only eleven words in the first column of this matching question, but there are sixty-eight words in the second column. Therefore, if you use the column with the longer statements as the starting place for making matches, you will not have to read through all of the long items each time you attempt to make a match.

Logical Clues

When matching questions are improperly prepared, you may be able to use logical clues to figure out answers to them, as in the following improperly prepared matching question for a psychology course.

Psychology

_______	1. located in the ear	a. James B. Watson
_______	2. behaviorist	b. ideographic study
_______	3. childhood crisis	c. frequency distribution
_______	4. tally of scores	d. to trust others
_______	5. study of an individual	e. organ of Corti

Since this question is improperly written, you should be able to use logical clues to guess some correct answers to it. For example, you will not match *1* with *a* because you know that *James B. Watson* is not *located in the ear.* Guess the answers.

EXERCISE 25.1 Starting with Longer Answers

Use the list with the longer statements as the starting place to make matches. Match first only those items that you are certain are matches and cross out items as you match them.

_____ 1. lecture

_____ 2. syllabus

_____ 3. curriculum

_____ 4. mnemonic

_____ 5. acronym

_____ 6. dean

_____ 7. bibliography

_____ 8. registrar

_____ 9. tutor

_____ 10. bursar

_____ 11. appendix

_____ 12. transcript

a. a word made from the initial letters of other words

b. the part of a book that contains any supplementary materials or information

c. a list of the books, articles, or other sources of information that are referred to by a writer

d. the title of a person at a college who is responsible for money transactions

e. a member of the administration of a college who is in charge of specified aspects of the school's functioning

f. a talk during which an instructor communicates information to students

g. a device used to aid memory

h. the title of a person at a college who is responsible for registering students in courses and for maintaining their academic records or transcripts

i. a summary or outline distributed by an instructor that states the main topics to be discussed in a course

j. the official record of courses taken, grades received, and grade point averages

k. a person who gives individual instruction to students

l. the courses required to earn a particular degree

EXERCISE 25.2 Using Logical Clues

Use logical clues to locate the correct answers to the following poorly written matching questions. Match first only those items that you are certain are matches and cross out items as you match them.

_____ 1. indentured servant

_____ 2. largest city on the eve of the American Revolution

_____ 3. He established the American factory system.

_____ 4. She advocated better care for the insane.

_____ 5. state where Prohibition was strongest

_____ 6. number of Southern slaves in 1860

_____ 7. painters of American life

_____ 8. the Fourteenth Amendment

_____ 9. contribution of black musicians

_____ 10. needed for frontier farming

_____ 11. describes U.S. policy toward Indians

_____ 12. average yearly income in 1890

_____ 13. percent of population living in cities in 1910

_____ 14. popular nineteenth-century entertainment

_____ 15. year the Great Depression started

a. Maine

b. made blacks citizens

c. thirty-eight

d. barbed wire

e. temporary laborer

f. Currier and Ives

g. 1929

h. $486

i. Samuel Slater

j. 4,000,000

k. Dorothea Dix

l. two-faced

m. melodrama

n. jazz

o. Philadelphia

EXERCISE 25.3 Guessing Answers

In order to understand how difficult it is to guess the answers to well-written questions, try to match the items in the right column to the names in the left column. If you are unfamiliar with the facts being tested, you should make no more than one correct match by guessing at the answers. Use all but one of the items in the right column, and use an item one time only.

______	1. Democritus	a. Law of Triads
______	2. Van Helmont	b. naming of cathode rays
______	3. Proust	c. conceived of the atom
______	4. Berzelius	d. discovered sulfanilamide
______	5. Döbereiner	e. discovered DDT
______	6. Zeidler	f. Law of Definite Composition
______	7. Gelmo	g. discovered element 106
______	8. Urey	h. first atomic pile
______	9. Goldstein	i. modern symbols for elements
______	10. Fermi	j. discovered deuterium
		k. foundations of chemical physiology

26

Fill-in Questions

Fill-in questions are statements with deleted portions that test takers must supply. For instance,

> Approximately __________ percent of American land is devoted to the raising of crops.

It is usually impossible to guess the correct answers to fill-in questions that appear on college tests. If you do not know how much American land is devoted to raising crops, you are not likely to guess the answer (17 percent).

Strategies for answering fill-in questions are summarized in "How to Answer Fill-in Questions" on page 272.

Decide the Type of Answer

The basic strategy for answering a fill-in question is to decide what type of answer is required. What type is needed for this question?

> After reading __________, President Theodore Roosevelt ordered an investigation of the meat-packing industry.

You should have decided that the answer for this question is the name of a book, magazine, newspaper, or other written material. However, it is probably impossible that you would have guessed the answer is a book entitled *The Jungle*.

When it is unclear what type of answer is required, ask the instructor for clarification. For instance,

> Alexander Hamilton was born in __________.

Since it is unclear what type of answer is needed for this question, you might ask a teacher, "Do you want me to give the place where he was born or the year in which he was born?" Prepare your question carefully. Don't, for example, point to a question and ask a teacher, "What do you mean?" Request clarification by asking questions that help your teacher understand why you are confused. (Alexander Hamilton was born on the island of St. Kitts in the West Indies; the year was 1755.)

How to Answer Fill-in Questions

Use these three strategies when you answer fill-in questions:

- Decide what type of answer is required.
- When a question contains two blanks with a space between them, give a two-word answer.
- When a blank is preceded by the word *an,* give an answer that begins with a vowel (*a, e, i, o,* or *u*).

Two Blanks

When a fill-in question contains two blanks with a space between them, a two-word answer is required. For instance,

> *Always* and *never* are examples of ____________ ____________.

If you studied Chapters 22 and 23, you should know that the correct answer to this question is *extreme modifiers.*

The "An" Clue

The word *an* before a blank is a clue that the answer is a word that begins with a vowel sound, such as those represented by the letters *a, e, i, o,* and *u.* For instance,

> Compliments satisfy an ________________ need.

Those who have studied the basic human needs know that they are of five basic types: physiological, safety, social, esteem, and self-realization. The word *an* before the blank suggests that the correct answer is the human need that begins with a vowel; the correct answer is *esteem.* However, most instructors eliminate this clue by writing *a(an), a(n),* or *a/an* instead of *an* before blanks.

EXERCISE 26.1 Fill-in Questions

Guess the answers to the following questions to understand that it is practically impossible to guess the correct answers to fill-in questions.

1. The sixth letter of the Greek alphabet is ________________.

2. Mukilteo is located in the state of ________________.

3. Tirana is the capital of ________________.

4. There are ________________ inches in a rod.

5. The two parts of a ratchet are a wheel and a(n) ________________.

The basic strategy for answering a fill-in question is to decide what type of answer is required and to give that type of answer. Use the words in the following list to write the types of answers required by the following nine fill-in questions: Walt Whitman; morpheme; fifteen; 1962; 4,160; first; cyclone; sadist; Hinduism.

6. The Nile River is approximately ________________ miles long.

7. Until as recently as ________________, slavery existed somewhere in the world.

8. It was ________________ ________________ who said, "In the faces of men and women I see God."

9. A(n) ________________ killed 300,000 people in Bangladesh on November 13, 1970.

10. A person who derives pleasure from causing others to suffer physical or mental pain is a(n) ________________.

11. A(n) ________________ is the smallest unit of language that has meaning.

12. One belief of ________________ is that life in all forms is an aspect of the divine.

13. If a federal court gives a criminal a life sentence, the earliest possible parole date is after ________________ years of the sentence have been served.

14. United States presidents enjoy the highest public support during the ________________ year of their terms.

EXERCISE 26.2 Fill-in Questions

The following fill-in questions are based on information in Chapters 21–25 of *College Study Skills.*

1. Test anxiety is uneasiness or ______________ students experience because they need to take a test.
2. When you guess the answer to a multiple-choice question with four answers (*a, b, c,* and *d*), you have a ______________ chance of guessing the correct answer.
3. Cheating in college is a serious offense that could result in disciplinary action or ______________.
4. When you are uncertain whether a true-false question is true or false, assume it is ______________.
5. A true-false question that contains a(n) ______________ ______________ such as *always* or *never* tends to be false.
6. True-false questions that state reasons often contain the word *reason, because,* or ______________.
7. True-false questions tend to be ______________ when they state a reason.
8. Double negatives are statements that include two negatives, usually *not* and a(n) ______________ ______________.
9. The incomplete statement or question that begins a multiple-choice question is called the ______________.
10. Jokes and insults tend to be ______________ answers in multiple-choice questions.
11. High and low numbers tend to be ______________ answers in multiple-choice questions.
12. If one list in a matching question has short statements and the other list has long statements, use the list of ______________ statements as the starting place for making matches.

27

Essay Questions

Essay questions require written responses that are usually a paragraph or more in length.

Students are often instructed *not* to answer all questions on essay tests. For example, the directions for the essay test in Figure 27.1 on page 276 state that students are to answer only three of the five questions. They will be penalized if they answer more than three questions, because only one of the 50-point answers and two of the 25-point answers will be graded. A good answer to the fifth question on the test is illustrated in Figure 27.2 on page 277.

Students usually write answers to essay questions in **bluebooks,** which are small booklets that contain lined paper. At one time the covers of these booklets were always blue, but today covers of bluebooks may be blue, yellow, pink, or some other color.

Variations of the essay test include take-home and open-book tests. A **take-home test** can be test questions that students actually answer at home or test questions that they study at home but answer in class. The questions on take-home tests are usually more difficult than the questions on tests students see for the first time in class. Also, teachers tend to grade answers to take-home tests very strictly.

An **open-book test** is a test during which students may refer to textbooks, and sometimes to notes, as they answer questions. The term *open-book* is misleading because it suggests that students can copy answers to questions from books; however, open-book tests seldom include questions for which answers can be copied. Whatever benefit students gain by referring to books is directly related to how thoroughly they have studied. Prepare for an open-book test just as you would for any other type of test.

The steps for writing good answers to essay questions are summarized in "How to Answer Essay Questions" on page 278.

Understand Direction Words

The first step in answering an essay question is to interpret correctly the meanings of direction words. **Direction words** are italicized in the following questions.

> *Describe* the five principal types of societies.
> *Explain* the benefits of aerobic exercise.

FIGURE 27.1
An Essay Test

Sociology Test

Write your answers to the following questions in the booklet that you have been given. Answer any one of the 50-point questions and any two of the 25-point questions. You have 60 minutes to write your answers.

Answer One (50 points)

1. Describe the five principal types of societies.
2. Compare the functionalist and ecological approaches to understanding cultural variation.

Answer Two (25 points each)

3. Discuss the effects of isolation during childhood on human development.
4. Contrast Freud's, Cooley's, and Mead's theories of how the self emerges.
5. Explain what norms are.

Before you take an essay test, learn the meanings of the following direction words. Pay special attention to the often misinterpreted meanings of *compare, criticize, analyze* and *justify.*

Direction Words

- *Discuss.* Write as much as you can. "Discuss test-taking skills."
- *Describe.* Write about the subject so it can be visualized. "Describe a nutritious diet."
- *Diagram.* Draw a picture and label its parts. "Diagram the parts of the human ear."
- *Illustrate.* Give a long written example. "Illustrate the use of the SQ3R study formula."
- *Enumerate* or *list.* Make a numbered list. "Enumerate (or list) good and bad listening habits."
- *Outline.* Make a numbered or well-organized list. "Outline basic test-taking strategies."
- *Summarize.* Briefly state. "Summarize the accomplishments of President Truman."
- *Define.* Give the meaning. "Define *psychopath.*"
- *Relate.* Discuss the connection between topics. "Relate television viewing to reading habits."
- *Trace.* Discuss in a logical or chronological sequence. "Trace the path by which blood flows through the human body."
- *Explain.* Discuss reasons. "Explain why the United States entered World War II."
- *Compare.* Discuss similarities and differences. "Compare democracy and socialism."
- *Contrast.* Discuss differences. "Contrast Catholicism with Protestantism."

FIGURE 27.2

An Answer to the Fifth Question in Figure 27.1

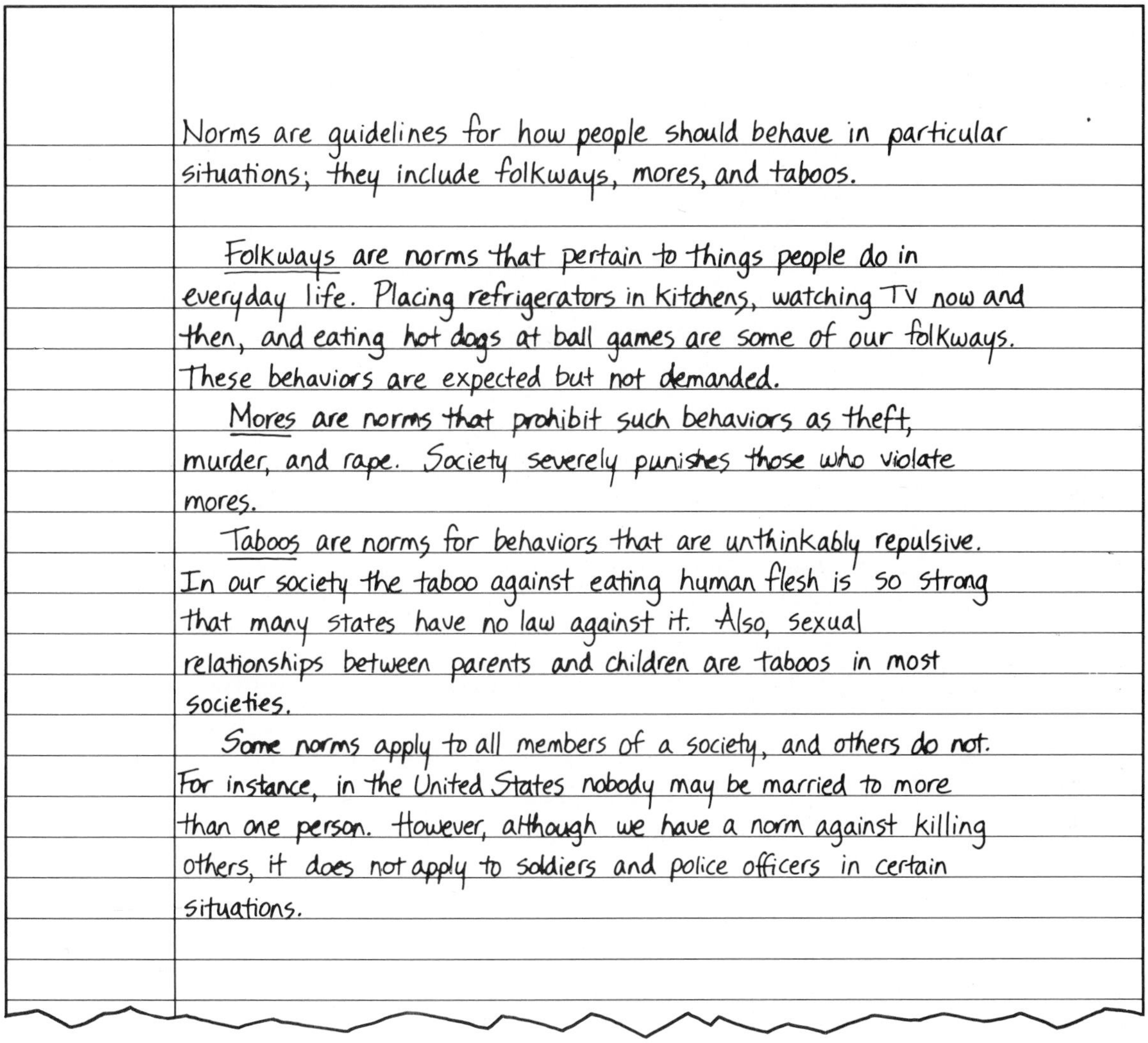

Norms are guidelines for how people should behave in particular situations; they include folkways, mores, and taboos.

Folkways are norms that pertain to things people do in everyday life. Placing refrigerators in kitchens, watching TV now and then, and eating hot dogs at ball games are some of our folkways. These behaviors are expected but not demanded.

Mores are norms that prohibit such behaviors as theft, murder, and rape. Society severely punishes those who violate mores.

Taboos are norms for behaviors that are unthinkably repulsive. In our society the taboo against eating human flesh is so strong that many states have no law against it. Also, sexual relationships between parents and children are taboos in most societies.

Some norms apply to all members of a society, and others do not. For instance, in the United States nobody may be married to more than one person. However, although we have a norm against killing others, it does not apply to soldiers and police officers in certain situations.

- *Criticize* or *evaluate.* Discuss good and bad points of the subject and conclude whether it is primarily good or bad. "Criticize (or evaluate) the death sentence."
- *Argue.* Give reasons for or against a statement. "Argue whether it is morally right or wrong to condemn criminals to death."
- *Analyze.* Discuss the parts of something and show how the parts are related. "Analyze the marketing strategies of Coca-Cola® and Pepsi-Cola®."
- *Justify* or *defend.* Discuss good and bad points and conclude that it is good. "Justify (or defend) U.S. expenditures on military defense."

How to Answer Essay Questions

Use these six procedures when you answer essay questions.

1. Give the type of answer the direction words call for.
2. Answer all parts of questions.
3. Write well-organized answers.
   - Plan the major points.
   - Write an introduction that summarizes the answer.
   - Make the major points stand out.
   - Write a conclusion that reveals your mastery of subject matter or that makes an interesting suggestion.
4. Write complete answers.
   - Include all the information that is relevant to the answer.
   - Write as though you are explaining the subject to a person who is uninformed about it (such as a friend or relative) rather than to a teacher.
5. Write answers that are easy for you to proofread and easy for your teachers to read.
   - Write or print neatly.
   - Use an erasable ball-point pen, so you can correct errors.
   - Write only on right-hand pages of bluebooks, so you can write additions and changes on left-hand pages.
   - Indent each paragraph.
   - Leave one-inch margins on all four sides of answers.
6. Proofread your answers before you give them to your instructor.

Answer All Parts of Questions

Failure to answer all the parts of essay questions is a major reason students sometimes get lower grades on essay tests than they should. Compare the following questions.

> Relate cigarette smoking to heart disease.
> Relate cigarette smoking to heart disease and cancer.

The first question has one part, but the second question has two parts. Answers to the second question must explain how cigarette smoking is related to (1) heart disease and (2) cancer. Answers that respond to only one part of the question will not receive full credit.

Sometimes essay questions are not clearly written. When you cannot understand an essay question, ask the teacher who wrote it for clarification. It is appropriate for you to assume that your teachers want you to understand their test questions.

Write Well-organized Answers

After you have interpreted the direction words and identified all parts of an essay question, write a well-organized answer by planning the major points, by writing a good introduction, and by making major points stand out clearly.

1. **Plan the major points.** Sometimes the major points you should include in your answers are directly stated in essay questions. For instance,

> Define the following terms: folkways, mores, and taboos.

The three major points to include in the answer are stated in the question; they are definitions of the three terms listed at the end of the question. However, the question is worded in the following way in the essay test illustrated in Figure 27.1 on page 276.

> Explain what norms are.

To answer this question, students must recall that folkways, mores, and taboos are three types of norms.

2. **Write an introduction that summarizes the answer.** A good introduction to an essay question is a clear summary of the answer. If an answer has several parts, the introduction should state the parts in the way illustrated in the first paragraph of the essay answer in Figure 27.2 on page 277.

When a question requires an answer with one major point, summarize the major point of your answer clearly in the introduction. For example,

Question	**Introduction to Answer**
Explain whether you believe that advertising benefits consumers.	In my opinion, advertising does not benefit consumers.

Other students may have written, "I believe that advertising benefits consumers." Whichever point of view is taken, it should be clearly stated in the introduction.

3. **Make major points stand out.** Notice in Figure 27.2 on page 277 that major points stand out because they appear in first sentences of paragraphs and because key terms are underlined for additional emphasis. If major points in your essay stand out clearly, it will be easier for your teachers to grade your answers. If you write answers that are easy to read, teachers may show their appreciation by giving your answers higher grades than they give for answers that are difficult for them to read.

4. **Write a conclusion that reveals your mastery of subject matter or that makes an interesting suggestion.** The conclusion of the essay in Figure 27.2 on page 277 demonstrates that the writer knows more about norms than is needed to give a complete answer to the question. If you write an answer in which you explain why you believe advertising does not benefit consumers, you might conclude it with suggestions about ways in which advertising could better serve the public.

FIGURE 27.3

Comparison of a Short and a Long Answer to a Question

Use point value as a guide in deciding the length and completeness of answers. Compare these examples of a 10-point and a 50-point answer to the following question.

QUESTION

What are the four speech-making strategies and how do they differ?

10-point response

There are four basic speech-making strategies. Impromptu speeches are presented on the "spur of the moment"; the speaker has no time to organize or rehearse. Extemporaneous speeches are organized in outline form but are not written word for word. Manuscript speeches are written in advance and then read from a written or typed copy. Memorized speeches are written in advance and then learned word for word, to be presented without a written copy. These four strategies allow speakers to suit their presentations to their speaking situations.

50-point response

Situations for speech making vary and speakers, as a result, choose among four different speech-making strategies to present their ideas most effectively.

Impromptu speeches are given on the "spur of the moment"; the speaker has no chance to organize or rehearse. These highly informal speeches are often unfocused (because they are unplanned) and ineffective (because they were not rehearsed), but they are the usual kinds of speeches given at organization meetings and in class discussions.

Extemporaneous speeches are given from prepared outlines, but they are not completely written. Rather, speakers decide what to discuss and what details or examples to use, and then they choose words as they speak. Extemporaneous speeches have the advantage of being organized, but at the same time they are flexible, allowing speakers to modify what they say to suit the needs of their audiences. For this reason, they are often the most effective speeches at informal meetings.

Manuscript speeches are written in complete form and then read, much like a newscast. Because they are prepared in advance, manuscript speeches are well organized and carefully worded. If they are also well rehearsed, manuscript speeches are effective in formal speaking situations because they present an exact, well-worded version of the speaker's ideas.

Memorized speeches are written in complete form and then committed to memory. Because they are carefully prepared, they often present solid content, but few speakers can memorize a lengthy speech and deliver it well. In addition, memorized speeches are not flexible and only work in highly formal circumstances, like awards ceremonies and formal banquets.

Because of the differences among these four speech-making strategies—in organization, presentation, and flexibility—they provide speakers with a number of ways to share ideas with audiences.

Write Complete Answers

As a general rule, teachers give the highest grades to those answers that include the most relevant information. It is almost always better to include too many facts and details than to include too few. Whenever you are uncertain whether to include a relevant piece of information or example, include it.

You must, of course, use the point value for an answer as a guide in deciding the length and completeness of your answer. Figure 27.3 on page 280 contains a 10-point and a 50-point answer to an essay question on a fifty-minute essay test. Compare the one-paragraph 10-point answer to the six-paragraph 50-point answer.

If you tend to write answers to essay questions that are too short, write them thinking that they will be read by a friend or relative rather than by a teacher. The thought that your answers will be read by a person who is uninformed about the subject might help you to write more complete answers and to explain your thoughts more clearly.

An essay test may be printed on sheets of paper with spaces on the paper for writing answers. When a space is not large enough for a complete answer, continue the answer on the back of the page. For instance, if there is not enough space to write a complete answer to a third question, write as much as you can in the space provided and then write *over* in parentheses. On the other side of the page, write *3* and complete the answer.

Write Easy-to-Read Answers

Some teachers give lower grades to sloppy papers written in hard-to-read handwriting. Therefore, write neatly so that your answers are easy for your teachers to read and grade.

- Use an erasable ball-point pen so you can erase mistakes and correct them.
- Write answers only on right-hand pages of bluebooks so that when you proofread you can write additions and changes on the blank left-hand pages.
- Indent each new paragraph, and leave margins that are at least one inch wide at the top, bottom, left, and right of your answers.

Writing neatly will also help you in proofreading your answers.

Proofread Your Answers

You cannot do your best writing when you answer essay questions under the pressure of time limitations; therefore, plan for time to proofread answers after you write them.

When you proofread, correct errors in spelling, punctuation, and grammar, and add additional relevant information if you can. Any improvements you make when you proofread will benefit you when your answers are graded.

What to Do If Time Runs Out

It is essential to plan test-taking time carefully when answering essay questions (see page 232). However, no matter how carefully you plan, you will not always have enough time to write complete answers to all questions on an essay test. If you do not write an answer, a teacher will assume that you do not know the answer; and if you write a very short answer, a teacher will assume it is the best answer you can write.

One solution to this problem is to write an outline for the answer you would write if you had sufficient time, show it to the teacher, and request additional time to write the complete answer. Another solution is to simply tell a teacher that you did not have enough time to write an answer. A reasonable teacher will offer a solution to this problem.

EXERCISE 27.1 Direction Words

Learn the meanings of the direction words on pages 276–277 and write them on the lines beneath the following questions.

1. **Discuss** three types of social mobility.

   ____

2. **Describe** clothing you enjoy wearing because it is good looking and comfortable.

   ____

3. **Explain** why you have chosen the curriculum in which you are enrolled.

   ____

4. **Compare** your college teachers to your high school teachers.

   ____

5. **Contrast** your college teachers with your high school teachers.

   ____

6. **Criticize,** or **evaluate,** this statement: "All college teachers should correct spelling and grammatical errors in papers they receive from students."

   ____

   ____

   ____

7. **Justify,** or **defend,** guessing at correct answers to true-false and multiple-choice questions.

   ____

   ____

8. **Argue** whether or not the United States should adopt a health plan similar to the one in Canada.

____

____

9. **Diagram** the room in which you are sitting.

____

10. **Illustrate** how you have used study suggestions explained in *College Study Skills.*

____

11. **Enumerate** the guidelines for underlining textbooks.

____

12. **Outline** the characteristics of multiple-choice questions that are sometimes hints to incorrect and correct answers.

____

13. **Summarize** the basic strategies for answering true-false, multiple-choice, and fill-in questions.

____

14. **Define** the following: *appendix, glossary, references.*

____

15. **Relate** the use of effective study skills to good grades on college tests.

____

____

16. **Trace** the path of the last trip you took.

____

____

17. **Analyze** the appeal of last year's three highest-grossing movies.

____

____

EXERCISE 27.2 Answering All Parts of Questions

To receive full credit, an answer to an essay question must respond to all parts of the question. Number the parts of the following questions in the way that is illustrated in the first question.

1. ① Compare narration and exposition and ② give examples of them.

2. Discuss three methods for making ethical decisions, enumerate the problems associated with each method, and evaluate which method is the most difficult to use.

3. Discuss the differences between modern and traditional dating, identify differences you consider to be most important, and hypothesize how dating might be different twenty years from now.

4. How did the following men challenge the accepted religious views during the Age of Enlightenment: Toland, Bayle, Hume, and Voltaire?

5. Is the women's liberation movement a continuation of the women's rights movement, or are they two different movements? Defend your answer.

EXERCISE 27.3 Answering Essay Questions

Write well-organized and complete answers to the following questions, as your instructor requests. Remember to write neatly and to proofread your answers.

1. Summarize the steps in the study process.
2. Summarize the basic strategies for taking any test and the specific strategies for answering true-false, multiple-choice, matching, and fill-in questions.
3. Discuss the methods that may be used to write well-organized and complete answers to essay questions.

Appendix

Textbook Chapter for Practice

This appendix contains a textbook chapter entitled "The Power of Positive Impressions." The underlying assumption of the chapter is that people we come into contact with while we are working form opinions about us using such superficial cues as they way we dress and the way we shake hands; the chapter offers suggestions about what we can do to create a favorable impression of ourselves with people who do not know us.

Use the chapter to practice surveying, underlining or highlighting, making notes, reciting and rehearsing, and test taking.

- Exercise 16.3 on pages 155–156 provides practice in surveying the chapter.
- Exercise 18.10 on pages 200–201 provides practice in marking the chapter.
- Exercise 19.8 on page 214 provides practice in making notes from the chapter.
- Exercise 20.4 on page 226 provides practice in reciting and rehearsing information in your notes.

If your instructor assigns these exercises, he or she will probably request you to answer test questions about the chapter, such as those in Exercise 21.3 on page 236.

As you study the following chapter, evaluate whether it contains any suggestions that you want to try out the next time you meet a new person on the job or elsewhere.

Source of textbook material: Reece, Barry L. and Rhonda Brandt, EFFECTIVE HUMAN RELATIONS IN ORGANIZATIONS, Fifth Edition. Copyright © 1993 by Houghton Mifflin Company. Used with permission.

Chapter 11

The Power of Positive Impressions

Chapter Preview

After studying this chapter, you will be able to

1. Explain the importance of positive impressions.
2. Discuss the factors that contribute to a favorable first impression.
3. Distinguish between assumptions and facts.
4. Define *image* and describe the factors that form the image you project to others.
5. List the four factors that influence your choice of clothing for work.
6. Understand how manners contribute to improved interpersonal relations in the workplace.

SEVERAL YEARS AGO, James Gray, Jr., author of *The Winning Image,* created a college course that was designed to help people refine and enhance their personal image. The course was offered at the American University in Washington, DC, and attracted people who wanted to learn more about the art and science of image projection. To emphasize the importance of this subject, Gray noted that "image is the way others see you, and it often determines how they treat you."[1]

Gray has joined the ranks of a growing number of image consultants who work with individuals and organizations. Today, the *Directory of Personal Image Consultants* includes almost 300 names. An image consultant is someone who helps ensure that all elements of the visible person—speech, dress, body language, and manners—match the inner talents and aspirations of that person. Each year several million dollars are spent on image consulting in the United States.[2]

Lynn Pfaelzer is typical of the new wave of image consultants. This former educator instructs men and women on how to develop what she describes as "visual communication skills." She has discovered that many people do not feel confident about the image they project and want advice.[3] People feel more secure when they look their best and are dressed appropriately for their job. ■

As organizations experience increased competition for clients, patients, and customers, awareness of the importance of public contact increases.[4] They are giving new attention to the old adage "First impressions are lasting impressions." Research indicates that initial impressions do indeed tend to linger. Therefore, a positive first impression can set the stage for a long-term relationship.

Of course, it is not just those *first* contacts with clients, patients, customers, and others that are important. Positive impressions should be the objective of *every* contact. A major goal of this chapter is to discuss the important factors that help us make positive impressions. Another important goal is to examine the factors that shape the image we project to others.

MAKING A GOOD IMPRESSION

There are many personal and professional benefits to be gained from a study of the concepts in this chapter. You will acquire new insights regarding ways to communicate positive impressions during job interviews, business contacts, and social contacts made away from work. You will also learn how to shape an image that will help you achieve your fullest potential in the career of your choice. Most important, the material in this chapter will very likely increase your self-awareness. As we noted in Chapter 1, self-awareness is an important first step toward building more effective relationships with others.

This is not a chapter about ways to make positive impressions with superficial contacts and quick-fix techniques. We do not discuss the "power look" or the "power lunch." The material in this chapter will not help you become a more entertaining conversationalist or win new customers by pretending to be interested in their hobbies or families. Stephen Covey, author of *The 7 Habits of Highly Effective People,* says that the ability to build effective, long-term relationships is based on character strength, not quick-fix techniques:

> You can pick up quick, easy techniques that may work in short-term situations. But secondary traits alone have no permanent worth in long-term relationships. Eventually, if there isn't deep integrity and fundamental character strength, the challenges of life will cause true motives to surface and human relationship failure will replace short-term success.[5]

Covey says that outward attitude and behavior changes do very little good in the long run unless they are based on solid principles governing human effectiveness. These principles include service (making a contribution), integrity and honesty (which serve as a foundation of trust), human dignity (every person has worth), and fairness.[6]

Most of the time it is not possible to fake a sincere greeting or a caring attitude. If you really do not care about the customer's problem, the customer will probably sense your indifference. Your true feelings will be difficult to hide. Ralph Waldo Emerson was right on target when he said, "What you are shouts so loudly in my ears I cannot hear what you say."

The Primacy Effect

The tendency to form impressions quickly at the time of an initial meeting illustrates what social psychologists call a **primacy effect** in the way people perceive one another. The general principle is that first impressions establish the mental framework within which a person is viewed, and later evidence is either ignored or reinterpreted to coincide with this framework.[7]

Martha Kelly met a middle-aged man at an outdoor cookout. He was wearing cutoff blue jeans and an old pair of worn-out sneakers. He had had several drinks and tended to interrupt people and monopolize any conversation. Throughout the afternoon, people avoided him whenever possible. About two weeks later, Martha stopped at a drugstore to get a prescription filled. To her surprise, the pharmacist was the same man she had met at the cookout, only now he was dressed in a neatly tailored white jacket, blue shirt, and pin-striped tie. Although he projected a very professional image in dealing with his customers, Martha left the store and went to another pharmacy to get her prescription filled. The positive impression communicated on this day was not strong enough to overcome her first, negative impression.

The First Few Minutes

When two people meet, their potential for building a relationship can be affected by many factors. Within a few moments, one person or the other may feel threatened, offended, or bored. Leonard and Natalie Zunin, coauthors of *Contact—The First Four Minutes,* describe what they call the **four-minute barrier**.[8] In this short period of time, human relationships are established, reconfirmed (in the case of two former acquaintances meeting), or denied. It is during the first few minutes of interaction with others that people's attention spans are at their greatest and powers of retention at their highest.

Why four minutes? According to the Zunins, this is the average time, determined by careful observation, during which two people in a social situation make up their minds to continue the encounter or to separate. The Zunins say the four-minute concept applies to both casual meetings and ongoing contacts, such as husbands and wives meeting at the end of a day.

The way you are treated depends largely on the way you present yourself—the way you look, the way you speak, the way you behave.[9] Although human contact is a challenge, you can learn to control the first impressions you make on others. The key is to become fully aware of the impression you communicate to other people.

Thinking / Learning Starters

To test the practical application of the Zunin's theory in a real-life setting, examine it in the context of your past experiences. Review the following questions and then answer each with yes or no.

1. **Have you ever gone for a job interview and known instinctively within minutes that you would or would not be hired?**
2. **Have you ever met a salesperson who immediately communicated to you the impression that he or she could be trusted and was interested in your welfare?**
3. **Have you ever entered a restaurant, hotel, or retail store and experienced an immediate feeling of being welcome after the employee spoke only a few words?**

First Impressions in a Work Setting In a work setting, the four-minute period in which a relationship is established or denied is often reduced to seconds. The U.S. Postal Service is concerned about perceptions created during this brief period of time. In selected regions of the nation, postal workers have completed the Dale Carnegie human relations course.[10] The following examples serve to illustrate the effect that immediate first impressions can have in a variety of work situations:

Item: Paula rushed into a restaurant for a quick lunch—she had to get back to her office for a 1:30 P.M. appointment. The restaurant was not crowded, so she knew she would not have to wait for a table. At the entrance of the main dining area was a sign reading, "Please Wait to Be Seated." A few feet away, the hostess was discussing a popular movie with one of the waitresses. The hostess made eye contact with Paula but continued to visit with the waitress. About twenty more seconds passed, and Paula began to feel anxiety build inside her. She tried to get the hostess's attention, but the hostess did not respond. After another ten seconds had passed, Paula walked out of the restaurant.

Item: Terry had completed his business in Des Moines, Iowa, and decided to rent a car for a trip to Omaha, Nebraska. He dialed the number of a popular rental car agency and was greeted by "May I help you?" spoken in a very indifferent tone of voice. Terry said that he wanted to rent a compact car and drive it to Omaha. The agency employee replied irritably, "You can't rent a compact car for out-of-town trips. These cars can only be used for local travel. You'll have to rent a full-sized car." Terry felt as though the employee did not want his business and was criticizing him for not knowing the company's rental policy. He told the employee he would call another rental agency. The entire conversation lasted only thirty-seven seconds.

No matter what career you are pursuing, it is important that you be able to build rapport with a variety of people. A good handshake, eye contact and a pleasant smile can help you make a good first impression. (Photo by Jim Hoffman. Reprinted with permission from Women in Business, *the national magazine of The American Business Association.)*

Total Person Insight

"If people aren't quickly attracted to you or don't like what they see and hear in those first two to four minutes, chances are they won't pay attention to all those words you believe are demonstrating your knowledge and authority. They will find your client guilty, seek another doctor, buy another product, vote for your opponent or hire someone else."

JANET G. ELSEA

President, Communication Skills, Inc.

Item: Sandy and Mike entered the showroom of a Mercedes-Benz dealer. They noticed two salespeople seated at desks near the entrance. One salesperson was wearing a well-tailored blue blazer, gray slacks, and a white shirt with a blue tie highlighted by subtle stripes. The other salesperson was wearing Levi Dockers sport slacks (khaki color), a blue knit pullover shirt (short sleeve), and casual shoes. The salesperson wearing the casual clothing walked over to Sandy and Mike and asked, "May I be of assistance?" Mike said, "We're just looking today." The salesperson returned to his desk. As they left the showroom Sandy said, "I can't believe someone selling a $40,000 automobile would wear such casual clothing." "I agree," Mike said.

In each of these examples, the negative first impression was created in less than sixty seconds. The anxiety level of the restaurant customer increased because she was forced to wait while two employees talked about a personal matter. The rental car employee antagonized a potential customer by using an offensive tone of voice. And the car salesperson apparently was not aware that potential customers were making judgments about him based solely on appearance. Unfortunately, these employees were probably not fully aware of the impression they communicated to customers.

Assumptions Versus Facts The impression you form of another person during the initial contact is made up of both assumptions and facts. Most people tend to rely more heavily on **assumptions** during an initial meeting. As the Zunins state, people live in an assumptive world.

> When you meet a stranger, and sometimes with friends, much of the information you get is based on assumption. You form positive or negative feelings or impressions but you must realize that only superficial facts can be gathered in four minutes.

> Depending on assumptions is a one-way ticket to big surprises and perhaps disappointments.[11]

Cultural influences, especially during the early years of your life, lead you to form impressions of some people even before you meet them. People often stereotype entire groups. Here are a few of the common stereotypes that still persist in our society:

- "Old people are set in their ways."
- "Italians are highly emotional."
- "Football players are dumb."
- "Chess players are intellectual giants."
- "Executive women are aggressive."

These are just a few of the assumptions that some people perceive as facts. With the passing of time some assumptions tend to lose support as factual information surfaces. Fewer people today support the idea that all married couples should have children than was the case a generation ago, and women are no longer viewed as unacceptable candidates for executive positions. Nevertheless, people rarely reach the point in life where they are completely free of assumptions. In fact, the briefer the encounter with a new acquaintance, the greater is the chance that misinformation will enter into your perception of the other person.

THE IMAGE YOU PROJECT

Image is a term used to describe how other people feel about you. In every business or social setting, your behaviors communicate a mental picture that others observe and remember. This picture determines how they react to you. Your image depends on more than exterior qualities such as dress and grooming. In the words of James Gray, author of *The Winning Image,* "Image is more than just a veneer."[12] He observes:

> Image is a tool for communicating and for revealing your inherent qualities, your competence, abilities and leadership. It is a reflection of qualities that others associate with you, a reflection that bears long-lasting influence in your bid for success. Image is not a tool for manipulation. Nor is it a false front. It cannot substitute for substance.[13]

In many respects, the image you project is very much like a picture puzzle, as illustrated in Figure 11.1. It is formed by a variety of factors, including dress and grooming, communication style, technical knowledge, past performance record, manners, and self-confidence. And each of these factors is under your control.

FIGURE 11.1

Factors That Form Your Image

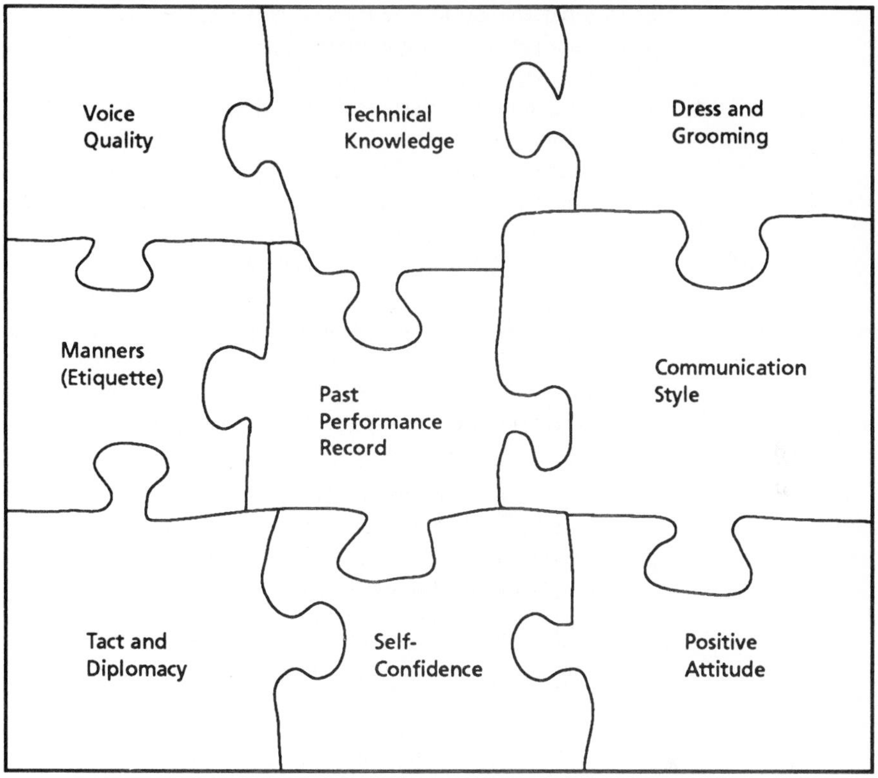

Because many studies indicate that the image you project can be as important to job success as your skills, you are wise to be concerned about your image. Put another way, your ability to get a job and advance to positions of greater responsibility will often depend on the impression you communicate to others.

A growing number of organizations have discovered that there is a direct link between the image projected by employees and the profitability of the company. Financial institutions, public utilities, airlines, retail stores, restaurants, hospitals, and manufacturers face the problem of not only gaining but also retaining the patronage of clients and customers. Consequently, building long-term partnerships with customers has been given a high priority. The image of the company is very important, and that image is shaped in large part by the courtesy and competence of its employees.[14]

Surface Language

As noted earlier, we form opinions about other people based on both facts and assumptions. Unfortunately, assumptions often carry a great deal of weight. Many of the assumptions you develop regarding other people are based upon what the Zunins describe as "surface language." **Surface language** is defined as a pattern of immediate impressions conveyed by appearance. The clothing you wear, your hair style, the fragrances you use, and the jewelry you display all combine to make a statement about you to others.

According to many writers familiar with image formation, clothing is particularly important. John Molloy, author of *Dress for Success* and *The Woman's Dress for Success Book,* was one of the first to acknowledge publicly the link between image and wardrobe. According to his research, what you wear immediately establishes your credibility and likability.[15]

One of the strongest statements made about the importance of clothing in image formation comes from William Thourlby, author of *You Are What You Wear—The Key to Business Success.* He says that when you step into a room, people who have never met you before begin making decisions about you solely on the basis of your appearance. These decisions relate to

- Your trustworthiness
- Your level of sophistication
- Your social heritage
- Your moral character
- Your level of success[16]

Thourlby points out that clothing and appearance are among the most important criteria we use to judge people. In addition, he notes that people judge your appearance long before they judge your talents. You should therefore take your wardrobe seriously. Coco Chanel, a clothing designer, once observed, "Dress shabbily, they notice the dress. Dress impeccably, they notice the person."[17]

Thinking / Learning Starter

Do you recall a teacher, coworker, or supervisor whose surface language impressed you—either positively or negatively? What specific elements (dress, communication style, etc.) were evident in this person's surface language? What type of image do you think he or she was trying to project?

Selecting Your Career Apparel

Large numbers of people employed in the business community wear uniforms. Some employees, such as National Car Rental sales representatives, wear a uniform that is especially designed for their particular job. The mechanics at your neighborhood garage probably wear a special uniform. Today more and more people are getting into uniforms to go to work. According to psychologists, people who serve the public — especially those who are part of a group — often work best in uniform.[18] Wearing the same uniform seems to create a sort of bond among coworkers. Thus, a uniform can make at least a small contribution to building esprit de corps at your local McDonald's restaurant or Holiday Inn hotel.

Dress was the focus of a management decision at the GenCorp Automotive plant at Shelbyville, Indiana. The work force there is divided into twenty-five teams of twelve to fifteen production workers. To build company spirit, a decision was made to adopt the same "uniform" for all employees. Everyone, including managers, wears navy blue skirts or trousers and light blue shirts.[19]

The uniforms worn by United Postal Service employees, airline reservation clerks, and the employees at your local restaurant might be classified as special-design **career apparel**. Some work uniforms are designed by top talents in the fashion industry. In addition to special-design uniforms, there is another type of career apparel, somewhat less predictable, worn by large numbers of people in our labor force. Here are some examples:

- A woman lawyer representing a prestigious firm would be appropriately dressed in a gray or blue skirted suit. A dress with a suit jacket would also be acceptable. She should avoid cute, frilly clothing that might reduce her credibility.

A uniform worn by employees will often contribute to a spirit of teamwork. These uniforms are typical of those worn by food service employees. (Jennifer Waddell 1992)

- A male bank loan officer would be appropriately dressed in a tailored gray or blue suit, white shirt, and tie. This same person dressed in a colorful blazer, sport shirt, and plaid slacks would be seen as too casual in most bank settings.
- A female receptionist at a prominent accounting firm would be appropriately dressed in a skirt and blouse. This same person would be inappropriately dressed if she showed up for work wearing designer jeans, a sweater, and sandals.
- A mechanic employed by an auto dealership that sells new cars would be appropriately dressed in matching gray, tan, or light blue shirt and pants. The mechanic would be inappropriately dressed in jeans and a T-shirt.

Many organizations seek advice about career apparel from image consultants. Since its first year of publication in 1978, *The Directory of Image Consultants* has grown from 37 listings to 250.

Selecting the correct clothing for a career can be difficult—for both men and women. The rules are usually unwritten and quite suitable. One psychologist who took an in-depth look at the subject made this observation:

> This whole business of dress and grooming is actually playing upon unconscious expectations and assumptions about the significance of clothing. For example, the man who's wearing a dark, three-piece suit projects to others that he's a conservative, predictable individual, while the man with frayed cuffs, or unshined shoes, is just naturally going to come off as careless and sloppy.[20]

"Shopping has become such a nuisance that we've been buying everything through mail order catalogues."
©1988 Mike Twohy; Management Solutions

Wearing the appropriate apparel is an important part of the image you project in your work setting. These Chrysler Corporation employees provide some examples. (Courtesy of Chrysler Corporation)

The key idea presented here is **unconscious expectations**. Everyone has certain opinions about what is appropriate in terms of dress. Throughout life we become acquainted with bank loan officers, nurses, police officers, and others employed in a wide range of occupations. We form mental images of the apparel common to each of these occupations. When we encounter someone whose appearance does not conform to our past experiences, we feel uncomfortable.

There is, however, a move away from rigid dress codes under way. The trend in many industries is toward more comfort and individuality. But appropriate career apparel can still give you a head start in obtaining a job or advancing to a new position in the company. In general, four factors influence your choice of clothing for work: (1) the products or services offered by your employer, (2) the type of person served, (3) the desired image projected by your organization, and (4) the region in which you work.

Products and Services Offered Store A sells casual clothing such as blue jeans, corduroy slacks, multicolored shirts, and sweatshirts. Store B sells expensive suits, dress shirts, ties, and other accessories. You would not expect the employees working at Store A to wear suits to work. Casual clothing, similar to that sold by the store, would be very acceptable. But the employees working at Store B should dress up to meet the expectations of the clientele served. The customer who purchases an expensive suit will expect the salesperson to be dressed in a conservative manner.

Type of Person Served What are the expectations of your firm's customers and clients? This is always a key question when you are selecting career apparel. Consider the real estate firm that employs two sales teams: One team sells houses in urban areas, and the other sells rural property, primarily farms. The urban home buyer expects to do business with someone who is conservatively dressed. The farmer does not expect the real estate salesperson to wear a suit when showing property in a four-wheel-drive vehicle.

Desired Image Projected by the Organization Lowe's Companies, Inc., a chain of 300 retail home-center stores, wanted to project the image of an "up-scale" discount retailer. To achieve this goal, employees were encouraged to wear apparel that complemented the store image. In many cases, the corporate culture dictates dress standards. Employees at International Business Machines Corp., for example, dress more conservatively than those working for a high-tech company in Silicon Valley.[21]

Region Dress in the South and Southwest tends to be more casual than in the Northeast. Climate is another factor that influences the clothing people wear at work. In Texas, for example, the warm climate calls for short sleeves and open collars in some work settings.

Thinking / Learning Starter

Assume that you are planning to purchase (1) a life insurance policy, (2) a Rolex wrist watch, and (3) eyeglasses. What types of career apparel would you expect persons selling these products to wear? What grooming standards would you recommend?

Wardrobe Engineering

The term **wardrobe engineering** was first used by John Molloy to describe how clothing and accessories can be used to create a certain image. This concept was later refined by William Thourlby, Jacqueline Thompson, Emily Cho, Susan Bixler, and other noted image consultants. In recent years, hundreds of books and articles on dress and grooming have been written. Although these authors are not in complete agreement on every aspect of dress, they do agree on a few basic points regarding wardrobe.

Reprinted by permission: Tribune Media Services.

1. When meeting someone for the first time, you make an impression even before you open your mouth. People judge your appearance before they know your talents! Keep in mind that nonverbal communication is the first and greatest source of impressions in direct, face-to-face interactions (a job interview for example) and that choice of clothing is a major part of the nonverbal message you send to a new acquaintance.

2. Establish personal dress and grooming standards appropriate for the organization where you wish to work. Before you apply for a job, try to find out what the workers there are wearing. If in doubt, dress conservatively. If you find out the dress code is more relaxed, you can adjust to it later. When you actually begin work, identify successful people in the organization and emulate their manner of dress.

3. Dress for the job you want, not the job you have.[22] If you are currently a secretary and want to become an office manager, do not continue to dress as a secretary. Employees can communicate with their clothing that they are satisfied with their position. Emily Cho, author of *Looking Terrific,* says that the right wardrobe can transform a person from being part of the corporate scenery to being in the forefront.

4. Avoid wearing the newest dress fad in a business or professional setting. In most cases, the world of work is more conservative than college, the arts, or the world of sports. If you are a fashion setter, you might be viewed as unstable or insincere. To be taken seriously, avoid clothing that is faddish or too flashy.

Women generally have more latitude than men in selecting appropriate attire, but they should still exercise some caution in choosing their wardrobe. In some cases, women are entering positions formerly dominated by men. They need to be taken seriously, and the wardrobe they select can contribute to this end.

5. The quality of your wardrobe will influence the image you project. Money spent on career apparel should be viewed as an investment, with each item carefully selected to look and fit well. A poor-quality suit or dress may save dollars initially but my not fit well and may wear out quickly.

6. Selection of a wardrobe should be an individual matter. Diane Harris, a North Carolina–based image consultant who knows the rules about career dress for men and women, says, "Effective packaging is an individual matter based on the person's circumstances, age, weight, height, coloring, and objectives."[23] Even though you should consider the dress and grooming standards of others in your field, blind conformity or duplication is not advisable.

Getting a job, keeping a job, and getting a promotion depend to some degree on your wardrobe. Therefore, research your wardrobe as carefully as you would research a prospective employer. Although the practice of judging people solely by what they wear should not be encouraged, you must recognize that discrimination on the basis of appearance is a fact of life. Make sure that your appearance helps you create a positive first impression.

Your Facial Expression

After your overall appearance, your face is the most visible part of you. Facial expressions are the cue most people rely on in initial interactions. They are the "teleprompter" by which others read your mood and personality.[24]

Studies conducted in nonverbal communication show that facial expressions strongly influence people's reactions to each other. The expression on your face can quickly trigger a positive or negative reaction from those you meet. How you rate in the "good-looks" department may not be nearly as important as your ability to communicate positive impressions with a pleasant smile.

If you want to identify the inner feelings of another person, watch the individual's facial expressions closely. A frown may tell you "something is wrong." A smile generally communicates "things are OK." Everyone has encountered a "look of surprise" or a "look that could kill." These facial expressions usually reflect inner emotions more accurately than words.

In many work settings, a cheerful smile is an important key to creating a positive first impression. A deadpan stare (or frown) can communicate a negative first impression to others. If you find it hard to smile, take time to consider the reasons. Are you constantly thinking negative thoughts and simply find nothing to smile about? Are you afraid others may misinterpret your intentions? Are you fearful that a pleasant smile will encourage communication with people with whom you would rather not spend time?

Your Entrance and Carriage

Susan Bixler, author of *The Professional Image,* says the way you enter someone's office or a business meeting can influence the image you project. She notes that "your entrance and the way you carry yourself will set the stage for everything that comes afterward."[25] A nervous or apologetic entrance may ruin your chances of getting a job, closing a sale, or getting the raise you have earned. If you feel apprehensive, try not to let it show in your body language. Hold your head up, avoid slumping forward, and try to project self-assurance. To get off to the right start and make a favorable impression, follow these words of advice from Bixler: "The person who has confidence in himself or herself indicates this by a strong stride, a friendly smile, good posture, and a genuine sense of energy. This is a very effective way to set the stage for a productive meeting. When you ask for respect visually, you get it."[26] Bixler says the key to making a successful entrance is simply believing—and projecting—that you have a reason to be there and have something important to present or discuss.

Your Voice

Several years ago, a Cleveland-based company, North American Systems, Inc., developed and marketed Mr. Coffee, which makes coffee quickly and conveniently. Some credited the quick acceptance of this product to an effective advertising campaign featuring baseball Hall of Famer Joe Di Maggio. He came across to the consumer as an honest, sincere person. When Joe Di Maggio said Mr. Coffee worked and made good coffee, people believed him.

The tone of your voice, the rate of speed at which you speak (tempo), and the volume of your speech contribute greatly to the meaning attached to your verbal messages. In the case of telephone calls, voice quality is critical because the other person cannot see your facial expressions, hand gestures, and other body movements. You cannot trade in your current voice for a new one, but you can make your voice more pleasing to other people and project a positive tone.

Although there is no ideal voice for all business contacts, your voice should reflect at least these four qualities: confidence, enthusiasm, optimism, and sincerity. Above all, try to avoid a speech pattern that is dull and colorless. Joanne Lamm, founder of Professional Speech Associates, says the worst kind of voice has no projection, no color, and no feeling.[27]

Assess your own speaking voice, and determine if small changes will increase the effectiveness of your verbal communication with others. Try recording your voice to find out how you sound to others. To evaluate the quality of your voice, tape your conversation with another person. Play back the tape, and rate yourself according to the five qualities just listed.

Your Handshake

When two people first meet, a handshake is usually the only physical contact between them. The handshake can communicate warmth, genuine concern for the other person, and strength. It can also communicate aloofness, indifference, and weakness. The message you send the other party via your handshake depends on a combination of the following factors.

Total Person Insight

"In a society as ridden as ours with expensive status symbols, where every purchase is considered a social statement, there is no easier or cheaper way to distinguish oneself than by the practice of gentle manners."

JUDITH MARTIN

Author, *Miss Manners' Guide for the Turn-of-the-Millennium*

1. *Degree of firmness.* Generally speaking, a firm handshake communicates a caring attitude, whereas a weak grip communicates indifference.
2. *Degree of dryness of hands.* A moist palm is unpleasant to feel and can communicate the impression that you are nervous. A clammy hand is likely to repel most people.
3. *Duration of grip.* There are no specific guidelines for the ideal duration of a grip. Nevertheless, by extending the handshake, you can often communicate a greater degree of interest in and concern for the other person.
4. *Depth of interlock.* A full, deep grip is more apt to convey friendship and strength to the other person.
5. *Eye contact during handshake.* Visual communication can increase the positive impact of your handshake. Maintaining eye contact throughout the handshaking process is important when two people greet each other.[28]

Most individuals have shaken hands with hundreds of people but have little idea whether they are creating positive or negative impressions. It is a good idea to obtain this information from those coworkers or friends who are willing to provide you with candid feedback. Like all other human relations skills, the handshake can be improved with practice.

Your Manners

More than a decade ago, Judith Martin started writing a column called "Miss Manners." To her surprise, the column has become extremely popular throughout the United States. Today, more than 250 newspapers carry the column. A growing number of people are seeking expert advice on such topics as how to deal with a coworker who cannot resist talking about confidential matters or how to respond to a customer service representative who tells customers offensive stories. Martin sees good manners as a key to improved interpersonal relations. She notes that in a civilized community, there have to be some restraints: "If we follow every impulse, we'd be killing one another."[29] Renewed interest in manners has also been stimulated by the writings of Letitia Baldridge, author of *Letitia Baldrige's Complete Guide to Executive Manners* and *Letitia Baldrige's The New Manners for the 90s.* Baldrige and others say that good manners increase efficiency, contribute to improved employee morale, and improve the company image.

A study of manners (sometimes called etiquette) reveals a number of ways to improve first impressions. Jonathan Swift recognized the importance of good manners when he said, "Good manners is the art of making people comfortable. Whoever makes the fewest people uncomfortable has the best manners." Making people feel comfortable is at the heart of good human relations. Good manners is a universal passport to positive relationships and respect.

One of the best ways to develop rapport with another person is to avoid behavior that might be offensive to that individual. Although it is not possible to do a complete review of this topic, some of the rules of etiquette that are particularly important in an organizational setting are covered here.

1. *When you establish new relationships, avoid calling people by their first names too soon.* Jacqueline Thompson, author of *Image Impact,* says assuming that all work-related associates prefer to be addressed informally by their first names is a serious breach of etiquette.[30] Use titles of respect—Miss, Mrs., Ms., Mr., or Dr.—until the relationship is well established. Too much familiarity can breed irritation. When the other party says, "Call me Susan," or "Call me Roy," it is all right to begin using the person's first name. Informality should develop by invitation, not by presumption.

2. *Avoid obscenities and offensive comments or stories.* In recent years, standards for acceptable and unacceptable language have changed considerably. Obscenity is more permissible in everyday conversation than it was in the past. But it is still considered inappropriate to use foul language in front of a customer, a client, or, in many cases, a coworker. According to Bob Greene, syndicated columnist, an obscenity communicates a negative message to most people.

> What it probably all comes down to is an implied lack of respect for the people who hear you talk. If you use profanity among friends, that is a choice you make. But if you broadcast it to people in general, you're telling them that you don't care what their feelings might be.[31]

Never assume that another person's value system is the same as your own. Foul language and off-color stories can do irreparable damage to interpersonal relations.

3. *Watch your table manners.* Business is frequently conducted at breakfast, lunch, or dinner these days, so be aware of your table manners. When you invite a customer to lunch, do not discuss business before the meal is ordered unless the client initiates the subject. Begin eating only when most of the people around you have their plates. If you have not been served, however, encourage others to go ahead. Assume responsibility for making sure the conversation moves from topic to topic and person to person. No one likes to

be left out. Ann Humphries, president of Eticon, Etiquette Consultants for Business, says that knowledge of table manners gives employees the confidence they need to do their jobs well.[32]

4. *Avoid making business or professional visits unless you have an appointment.* Walking into someone's office without an appointment is generally not a good practice. A good rule of thumb is always to make an appointment in advance and arrive promptly. If you are late, quickly voice a sincere apology.

5. *Express appreciation at appropriate times.* A simple thank-you can mean a lot. Failure to express appreciation can be a serious human relations blunder. The secretary who works hard to complete a rush job for his or her boss is likely to feel frustrated and angry if this extra effort is ignored. The customer who makes a purchase deserves to receive a sincere thank-you. You want your customers to know that their business is appreciated.

6. *Be aware of personal habits that may be offensive to others.* Sometimes an annoying habit can be a barrier to establishing a positive relationship with someone else. Chewing gum is a habit that bothers many people, particularly if you chew gum vigorously or "crack" it. Biting fingernails, cracking knuckles, scratching your head, and combing your hair in public are additional habits to be avoided.

Letitia Baldrige says that in the field of manners, "Rules are based on kindness and efficiency." She also believes that good manners are those personal qualities that make life at work more livable.[33] A knowledge of good manners permits us to perform our daily work with poise and confidence.

Summary

People tend to form impressions of others quickly at the time they first meet them, and these first impressions tend to be preserved. Leonard and Natalie Zunin describe the four-minute barrier as the average time people spend together before a relationship is either established or denied. In an organizational setting, the time interval is often reduced to seconds. Positive impressions are important because they contribute to repeat business and referrals from customers.

The impression you form of another person during the initial contact is made up of assumptions and facts. When meeting someone for the first time, people tend to rely heavily on assumptions. Many of your assumptions can be traced to early cultural influences. Assumptions are also based on perceptions of surface language. The Zunins describe surface language as a pattern of immediate impressions conveyed by appearance. The clothing and jewelry you wear, your hair style, and the fragrances you use all combine to make a statement about yourself to others.

Image consultants contend that discrimination on the basis of appearance is still a fact of life. The clothing you wear is an important part of the image you communicate to others. Four factors tend to influence your choice of clothing for work: (1) the products or services offered by the employer, (2) the type of person served, (3) the desired image projected by the organization, and (4) the region where you work.

In addition to clothing, research indicates that facial expressions strongly influence people's reactions to each other. The expression on your face can quickly trigger a positive or negative reaction. Similarly, your entrance and carriage, voice, handshake, and manners also contribute to the image you project when meeting others.

Key Terms

primacy effect
four-minute barrier
assumptions
cultural influences
image
surface language
career apparel
unconscious expectations
wardrobe engineering

Review Questions

1. Image has been described as "more than exterior qualities such as dress and grooming." What other factors shape the image we project?
2. Define the term *primacy effect.* How would knowledge of the primacy effect help someone in sales or customer service?
3. Why do people tend to rely more heavily on assumptions than on facts during the initial meeting?
4. Why should career-minded people be concerned about the image they project? What factors contribute to the formation of a person's image?
5. What are some of the major decisions people make about others based on career apparel?
6. What are the four factors that influence your choice of clothing for work?
7. What is meant by the term *unconscious expectations?*
8. Describe the type of speaking voice that increases a person's effectiveness in dealing with others.
9. Letitia Baldrige and Judith Martin have voiced strong support for the study of manners. What reasons do they give for developing an understanding of good manners?
10. Stephen Covey says that changing outward attitudes and behaviors does very little good in the long run unless we base such changes on solid principles that govern human effectiveness. Do you agree or disagree with his views? Explain your answer.

Application Exercises

1. Harvey Mackay, president of Mackay Envelope Corporation, has designed a sixty-six-question customer profile for his sales staff. Salespeople are encouraged to complete the form for each customer they call on. The profile includes such information as birth date, current position, marital status,

professional memberships, and special interests. Mackay takes the position that a salesperson cannot build long-term relationships with customers unless she or he takes a personal interest in them.

a. Do you support the use of a customer profile to build relationships with customers or clients? Explain.

b. What type of organization would benefit most from use of a detailed customer profile? Similar to the one used at Mackay Envelope Corporation?

2. The first step toward improving your voice is to hear yourself as others do. Listen to several recordings of your voice on a dictation machine, tape recorder, or VCR, and then complete the following rating form. Place a checkmark in the appropriate space for each quality.

Quality	*Major Strength*	*Strength*	*Weakness*	*Major Weakness*
Projects confidence	_____	_____	_____	_____
Projects enthusiasm	_____	_____	_____	_____
Speaking rate is not too fast or too slow	_____	_____	_____	_____
Projects optimism	_____	_____	_____	_____
Voice is not too loud or too soft	_____	_____	_____	_____
Projects sincerity	_____	_____	_____	_____

Case 11.1 What You See Is Not Necessarily What You Get

The clothing we wear at work shapes other people's expectations of us. Feelings about people's competence, intelligence, attitudes, trustworthiness, and many other aspects of their personalities are conveyed by the colors, styles, and fit of their attire. Writers for *Communication Briefings,* for example, suggest that women's clothing should fall somewhere between the very feminine, soft and frilly look and the more masculine, dark three-piece suit look to be appropriate in many work settings. And Kathleen Hughes, writing for the *Wall Street Journal,* suggests that women executives should avoid clothes that are too tight and hemlines that are too short if they want to be taken seriously as professionals. Some companies, such as the National Car Rental Company and the Century 21 chain of real estate firms, have begun to require their employees to wear specially designed uniforms, called "career wear," to ensure that the employees will convey the "right" message and instill confidence in their customers.

Just how important is the "right look," and how does what people wear influence our expectations of them? Imagine that you have just checked into a hospital to be operated on the next day. When you get to your room, you are told that the following people will be coming to speak with you within the next several hours:

1. The surgeon who will do the operation
2. A nurse
3. The secretary for the department of surgery
4. A representative of the company that supplies televisions to the hospital rooms
5. A technician who does laboratory tests
6. A hospital business manager
7. The dietitian

You have never met any of these people before and do not know what to expect. The only thing you do know is that they are all women.

About half an hour after your arrival, a woman appears at your door dressed in a straight, red wool skirt, a pink-and-white striped polyester blouse with a bow at the neck, and red medium-high-heel shoes that match the skirt. She is wearing round gold earrings, a gold chain necklace, a gold wedding band, and a white hospital laboratory coat. She is carrying a clipboard.

Questions

1. Of the seven people listed, which of them do you think is standing at your door? Why?
2. If the woman had not been wearing a white hospital laboratory coat, how might your perceptions of her differ? Why?
3. If you find out that she is the surgeon who will be operating on you in the morning, and thought she was someone different initially, how confident do you now feel in her ability as a surgeon? Why?

Case 11.2 Do We Need an Employee Handbook?

Connie Bayer and Rose Lamas met for the first time at a Sales and Marketing Executives (SME) dinner meeting. A strong friendship developed quickly because they had a great deal in common. Connie was a successful real estate broker working for Hilldale Real Estate, a well-established firm serving the St. Louis metropolitan area. Rose was a part-time community college instructor who taught real estate broker courses. Prior to becoming an instructor, she had sold real estate for five years.

After the initial meeting, Connie and Rose met several times at SME-sponsored dinner meetings and occasionally for lunch. At one of these meetings, Connie discussed her plan to start her own real estate business. She explained in detail the type of business she hoped to establish and then said, "Rose, I have been thinking about a partnership. Would you be willing to join me as a full partner?" At first Rose was tempted to say yes. She had also dreamed of owning her own business someday. But she knew that business partnerships often failed. She also knew that a major factor contributing to failure was dissension. She said, "Before I make this decision, I feel we should discuss our basic beliefs regarding business policies and practices."

A few days later, Connie and Rose met to discuss their views on business operations. Here is a portion of that conversation.

CONNIE: I believe that customer relations is a very important key to business success. I feel we should develop a detailed employee handbook that outlines policies and practices in such areas as dress and grooming, use of the telephone, methods of greeting the customer, and service after the sale.

ROSE: I believe that everyone associated with the firm should project a professional image and that good service is the key to business success. But I wonder if a detailed employee handbook is necessary. I feel a handbook is simply a crutch used by managers who do not want to spend time on employee training and development.

CONNIE: I don't think I understand what you mean.

ROSE: When I worked for Hilldale Real Estate, the manager never discussed his expectations in the area of customer service. New employees were given a list of policies and told to read them. I feel customer service requires constant attention. I would want to schedule weekly meetings to improve this area of the business. I would involve the entire staff in making these decisions.

Questions

1. Would you agree or disagree with Rose? Explain your answer.
2. What customer service policies and practices related to the area of positive impressions should be given attention before the new business is opened?

Suggested Readings

Baldrige, Letitia. *Letitia Baldrige's The New Manners for the 90s.* New York: Rawson Associates, 1990.

Baldrige, Letitia. *Letitia Baldrige's Complete Guide to Executive Manners.* New York: Rawson Associates, 1985.

Bixler, Susan. *The Professional Image.* New York: Perigee Books, 1984.

Carnegie, Dale. *How to Win Friends and Influence People.* New York: Pocket Books, 1964.

Collins, Julia M. "Off to Work," *Harvard Business Review,* September-October 1989, pp. 105–109.

Elsea, Janet G. *The Four-Minute Sell.* New York: Simon & Schuster, 1984.
Fenton, Lois, with Edward Olcott. *Dress for Excellence.* New York: Rawson Associates, 1986.
Gray, James. *The Winning Image.* New York: American Management Associations, 1982.
Jackson, Carole, with Kalia Lulow. *Color for Men.* New York: Ballantine Books, 1987.
King, Norman. *The First Five Minutes.* New York: Prentice-Hall, 1987.
Martin, Judith. *Common Courtesy: In Which Miss Manners Solves the Problem That Baffled Mr. Jefferson.* New York: Atheneum, 1986.
Molloy, John T. *New Dress for Success.* New York: Warner Books, 1988.
Thompson, Jacqueline. *Image Impact.* New York: Ace Books, 1981.
Zeldis, Yona. *Coping with Social Situations: A Handbook of Correct Behavior.* New York: Rosen Publishing, 1987.
Zunin, Leonard, and Natalie Zunin. *Contact—The First Four Minutes.* New York: Ballantine Books, 1972.

Vocabulary List

The vocabulary list in this section contains information about the meanings and pronunciations of the words that are underscored in blue in Chapter 18, "Mark Your Books." Your instructor may request you to learn the meanings of the words in this vocabulary list.

Information in Entries

The following entry for the word *pit* illustrates the five types of information that are provided for words listed in this section.

> **pit** (pit) *v.* To set in competition; to set against, match [to *pit* the two best teams in a championship play-off]

1. The *spelling* is printed in boldface: **pit.**
2. The *pronunciation* is enclosed in parentheses: (pit).
3. The *part of speech* is printed in italics: *v.*
4. *The definition* begins with a capital letter: To set in competition; to set against, match.
5. An *example* of the way the word is used is enclosed in brackets following the definition: [to *pit* the two best teams in a championship play-off]

The meaning of each word in the vocabulary list corresponds to the ways the word is used in this book. For instance, the word *pit* has many meanings, including "the hard stone in a fruit [a cherry *pit*]" and "an area where animals are kept [a bear *pit*]." However, the entry above indicates that in this book, *pit* is used as a verb that means "to set in competition."

Parts of Speech

The following abbreviations are used for the traditional parts of speech:

noun (*n.*)
noun plural (*n.pl.*)
verb (*v.*)
adjective (*adj.*)
adverb (*adv.*)

The words in the vocabulary list do not include a conjunction (*conj.*), interjection (*interj.*), or preposition (*prep.*).

Pronunciation Spelling

Interpret pronunciation spellings using the pronunciation key at the bottom of some of the pages in this section. For instance, by using the key you can determine that *chaos* (kā'os') is pronounced using the following sounds:

k
ā as in **pay**
o as in **pot**
s

Vowels

Vowel sounds present the major problem in interpreting pronunciation spellings because the five vowels, *a, e, i, o,* and *u,* are used to represent a variety of sounds.

pat (pat)	**pet** (pet)	**pit** (pit)	**pot** (pot)	**cut** (cut)
pay (pā)	**be** (bē)	**pie** (pī)	**toe** (tō)	**cute** (kyo͞ot)
care (câr)		**pier** (pîr)	**paw** (pô)	**firm** (fûrm)
arm (ärm)			**took** (to͝ok)	
			boot (bo͞ot)	

In addition, pronunciation spellings include the two-vowel combinations found in the term *b**oy** sc**ou**t* (boi skout) and the de-emphasized sound in words such as ***a**go, ag**e**nt, san**i**ty, c**o**mply, and foc**u**s,* which is represented by a symbol called the schwa: ***a**go* (ə'gō). The schwa, which looks like the letter *e* printed upside down (ə), has the vowel sound heard in *of* when the phrase "bag *of* candy" is said quickly (bag əv kan'dē).

Consonants

Consonant letters are used to represent consonant sounds in pronunciation spellings. For example:

half (haf)	phone (fōn)
ghost (gōst)	wrap (rap)
gem (jem)	his (hiz)
knit (nit)	rhyme (rīm)
debt (det)	sign (sīn)

The letters *c, q,* and *x* are not used in pronunciation spellings. The letter *c* is usually pronounced *k* as in *can* (kan) or *s* as in *cent* (sent); the letter *q* is usually pronounced *kw,* as in *quit* (kwit); and the letter *x* is usually pronounced *ks,* as in *tax* (taks).

Accent Marks

Pronunciation spellings usually include accent marks to indicate the relative force with which syllables are spoken. Compare the placement of the primary accent marks (′) in the pronunciations for the verb and noun forms of the word *extract:*

> **extract** (ek-strakt′) *v.* To pull out [to *extract* a tooth]
> **extract** (ek′-strakt) *n.* A passage selected from a book [to read a short *extract* from a long book]

The second syllable of *extract* is stressed when the word is used as a verb [*extract′* a tooth], whereas the first part of the word is stressed when the word is used as a noun [to read a short *ex′-tract* from a long book].

The secondary accent mark (′) is used to indicate stress that is weaker than primary stress but stronger than the stress of unaccented syllables. Primary and secondary accent marks in the following words indicate which syllables receive primary and secondary stress.

rec′ og nize′
in′ dis pen′ sa ble

Say *recognize* and *indispensable* aloud, giving primary and secondary stress to the syllables with the primary and secondary accent marks.

- ☐ **adhere** (ad-hîr′) *v.* To follow closely; to keep to, stand by [to *adhere* to the rules of a game]
- ☐ **adolescence** (ad′l-es′əns) *n.* The time in a person's life that begins with the development of secondary sex characteristics and ends with maturity [to be in high school during *adolescence*]
- ☐ **affiliate** (ə-fil′ē-āt) *v.* To associate, connect, ally [to *affiliate* oneself with worthwhile organizations]
- ☐ **affluence** (af′lo͞o-əns) *n.* Great wealth or riches [the *affluence* of movie stars]
- ☐ **affluent** (af′lo͞o-ənt) *adj.* Financially well off; wealthy, rich [an *affluent* family living in a $500,000 house]
- ☐ **allocate** (al′ō-kāt′) *v.* To set aside for a specific purpose; to designate, earmark, assign [to *allocate* money for rent and groceries]
- ☐ **amass** (ə-mas′) *v.* To gather together or pile up; collect, accumulate [to *amass* a fortune by buying and selling real estate]
- ☐ **amicably** (am′i-kə-blē) *adv.* Showing good will; friendly [respected for dealing *amicably* with others]
- ☐ **ampersand** (am′pər-sand′) *n.* The symbol (&) that represents the word *and*
- ☐ **aptly** (apt′lē) *adv.* Suitably, fittingly, appropriately, properly [to answer questions *aptly* during an employment interview]
- ☐ **assumption** (ə-sump′shən) *n.* Something accepted as true without proof; belief, supposition, theory, hypothesis [the *assumption* that evil deeds will be punished]
- ☐ **autonomy** (ô-ton′ə-mē) *n.* Independence or self-government; the state of functioning independently [unmarried people who value their *autonomy*]

- ☐ **bizarre** (bi-zär′) *adj.* Very odd; strange, weird, outlandish [to wear a *bizarre* costume to a Halloween party]
- ☐ **botch** (boch) *v.* To ruin by poor performance or lack of skill; bungle, spoil [to *botch* a chance for a good grade by not studying]

- ☐ **chair** (châr) *v.* To act as chairperson [to *chair* a meeting]
- ☐ **chaos** (kā′os′) *n.* Extreme confusion, disorder, turmoil, disorganization [*chaos* in a city created by fires following an earthquake]
- ☐ **cognitive** (kog′ni-tiv) *adj.* Involving mental processes [the *cognitive* act of remembering]
- ☐ **concept** (kon′sept′) *n.* An idea, thought, notion [the *concepts* of right and wrong]
- ☐ **context** (kon′tekst) *n.* The entire background or environment of a particular event; frame-

work, surroundings [the inappropriateness of hysterical laughter in the *context* of a funeral]

☐ **convey** (kən-vā') *v.* To communicate in words; to make known, relate, reveal [to *convey* a message by writing a letter]

☐ **crucial** (kro͞o'shəl) *adj.* Of great importance; critical, decisive, essential, urgent [the *crucial* decision to wage a war]

☐ **diction** (dik'shən) *n.* Choice of words; wording [to write papers for college credit using good *diction*]

☐ **diction** (dik'shən) *n.* Choice of words; wording [to write papers for college credit using good *diction*]

☐ **die is cast** (dī' iz kast) An idiom that means "The decision has been made and cannot be changed"

☐ **dilemma** (di-lem'ə) *n.* A situation in which one must select between unpleasant choices [the *dilemma* of whether to remain in a burning building or jump from a high window]

☐ **disclosure** (dis-klō'zhər) *n.* The act of revealing or disclosing; revelation, communication, making known [the *disclosure* of one's affection for another]

☐ **distinctive** (dis-tingk'tiv) *adj.* Having characteristics that are different from those of others; unique, different, special, extraordinary [a *distinctive* way of speaking]

☐ **divert** (di-vûrt') *v.* To turn aside from a course or direction; sidetrack [for police to *divert* traffic around the scene of an accident]

☐ **divisible** (di-viz'ə-bəl) *adj.* Can be divided [A quarter is *divisible* into smaller coins, but a penny is not.]

☐ **elicit** (i-lis'it) *v.* To draw out or bring forth [to *elicit* an answer to a question]

☐ **enhance** (en-hans') *v.* To improve or make more attractive; to heighten, intensify, elevate [to wear clothing that *enhances* one's appearance]

☐ **esteem** (i-stēm') *n.* Favorable opinion or regard; respect [a professor held in high *esteem* by students]

☐ **ethics** (eth'iks) *n.pl.* A code of morals and standards of conduct [the *ethics* of the medical profession]

☐ **facilitate** (fə-sil'ə-tāt') *v.* To make easy or less difficult; to ease, help [a well-written textbook that *facilitates* learning]

☐ **factor** (fak'tər) *n.* A circumstance or condition that brings about a result; reason, influence [a *factor* to consider when selecting a mate]

☐ **feedback** (fēd'bak') *n.* The return of information about an event or activity [to receive *feedback* from an employer about how well one is doing a job]

☐ **futuristic** (fyo͞o'chə-ris'tik) *adj.* Having to do with the future; ahead of its time [a *futuristic* house made entirely of plastic]

☐ **generic** (jə-ner'ik) *adj.* Having the name of a product but not a trademark; common, nonexclusive, unspecified [*generic* aspirin as opposed to Bayer aspirin]

☐ **hierarchy** (hī'ə-rär'kē) *n.* A group of people or things arranged in order, such as order of rank or class [a *hierarchy* of animal life with apes near the top and sponges near the bottom]

☐ **impending** (im-pen'ding) *adj.* About to happen; approaching, immediate, coming [dark clouds warning of an *impending* storm]

☐ **incompetent** (in-kom'pə-tənt) *adj.* Lacking the ability or knowledge necessary for a task; unskillful, incapable, unqualified [an open-and-shut case that was lost by an *incompetent* lawyer]

☐ **inconsistency** (in'kən-sis'tən-sē) *n.* The state of not being consistent, regular, or predictable [The *inconsistency* of his employment made it impossible for him to support his family.]

☐ **indifferent** (in-dif'ər-ənt) *adj.* Having no particular interest or concern; unconcerned [rebellious teenagers who are *indifferent* to what their parents tell them]

☐ **initiate** (i-nish'ē-āt') *v.* To introduce, begin, start [to *initiate* a conversation by saying "hello"]

☐ **intimate** (in'tə-mit) *adj.* To be close, familiar, personal [an *intimate* relationship between husband and wife]

☐ **invalidate** (in-val'i-dāt') *v.* To make no longer in effect; cancel, void, repeal [to *invalidate* a driver's license because of drunken driving]

☐ **limbo** (lim'bō) *n.* A place or condition of neglect or confinement [to be in *limbo* during a ten-hour airplane flight]

☐ **malicious** (mə-lish'əs) *adj.* Deliberately harm-

ə **a**go/a p**a**t/ā p**ay**/â c**are**/ä **ar**m/e p**e**t/ē b**e**/i p**i**t/ī p**ie**/î p**ier**/o p**o**t/ō t**oe**/ô p**aw**/o͝o t**oo**k/o͞o b**oo**t/ oi b**oy**/ou sc**ou**t/u c**u**t/yo͞o c**u**te/û f**ir**m

ful; hateful, spiteful [a *malicious* attack with a hammer]

☐ **marketer** (mär'ki-tər) *n.* An organization or person that sells products to a market [The Gap is a *marketer* of casual clothing.]

☐ **marketing** (mär'ki-ting) *n.* The act of moving products from manufacturers to buyers [the *marketing* of frozen pizza in grocery stores]

☐ **medium** (mē'dē-əm) *n.* A means of communication to the general public that carries advertising [Newspapers are an effective *medium* for grocery advertisements.]

☐ **motivate** (mō'tə-vāt') *v.* To provide a reason to be moved to action; to stimulate, activate, arouse [to *motivate* a student to learn]

☐ **mutual** (myo͞o'cho͞o-əl) *adj.* Shared by two or more people [a marriage for the *mutual* benefit of husband and wife]

☐ **norm** (nôrm) *n.* A standard for behavior that is considered to be appropriate; yardstick, criterion [*norms* that govern the courteous treatment of others]

☐ **outrage** (out'rāj') *n.* A highly offensive or violent act; insult, evil, wrong [The killing of innocent civilians during a war is an *outrage* against humanity.]

☐ **overt** (ō-vûrt') *adj.* Out in the open; apparent, obvious, noticeable, observable [A smile is an *overt* sign of friendliness.]

☐ **perceive** (pər-sēv') *v.* To acquire knowledge by using the senses of sight, hearing, touch, taste, or smell; to sense, observe, detect [by counting, to *perceive* how much money is in your wallet]

☐ **physiological** (fiz'ē-ə-loj'i-kəl) *adj.* Having to do with the functioning of a living organism or its parts [the *physiological* act of breathing]

☐ **prestigious** (pre-stij'əs) *adj.* Having influence or the power to impress; respected, reputable [a *prestigious* address on Fifth Avenue in New York City]

☐ **prevalent** (prev'ə-lənt) *adj.* Common, frequent, widespread, usual [Tipping is *prevalent* in restaurants.]

☐ **profit sharing** (prof'it shar'ing) *n.* A procedure by which employees receive a portion of the profits of a business [to build employee morale with a *profit-sharing* plan]

☐ **profound** (prə-found') *adj.* Thoughtful, deep, wise, intense [the *profound* writings of a great philosopher]

☐ **proponent** (prə-pō'nənt) *n.* A person who argues in support of something; supporter, advocate, booster [a *proponent* of free health care for all]

☐ **rancor** (rang'kər) *n.* Long-lasting and deep-seated resentment; bitterness, ill will, hostility, hatred [the *rancor* that comes from being treated unjustly]

☐ **reassess** (rē'ə-ses') *v.* Evaluate, consider, or look over again [to *reassess* one's primary goals]

☐ **recipient** (ri-sip'ē-ənt) *n.* A person who receives something; receiver [to be the *recipient* of an A in an English course]

☐ **recurrent** (ri-kûr'ənt) *adj.* Appearing or occurring repeatedly; frequent, periodic, regular [a *recurrent* dream about flying]

☐ **reflexive** (ri-flek'siv) *adj.* Automatic, spontaneous, instinctive [the *reflexive* closing of eyes during a sandstorm]

☐ **renovation** (ren'ə-vā'shən) *n.* The state of having been remodeled, repaired, or cleaned up; renewal [the *renovation* of a house that was damaged by fire]

☐ **retailer** (rē'tāl-ər) *n.* A company that sells products in small quantities to customers [the *retailers* who have stores at a local mall]

☐ **segmentation** (seg'men-ta'shən) *n.* A dividing into segments, or parts [the *segmentation* of those in favor, those opposed, and those who don't care one way or the other]

☐ **serial** (sir'ē-əl) *adj.* Arranged in order or in a series [the *serial* number on a movie ticket]

☐ **shoestring** (sho͞o'string') *n.* A small amount of money [to take a vacation on a *shoestring*]

☐ **sputum** (spyo͞o'təm) *n.* Saliva, mucus, phlegm, or other matter coughed up and spit from the mouth [*sputum* on baby's bib]

☐ **strained** (strānd) *adj.* Not relaxed or natural; tense, forced [lack of communication leading to *strained* relations between friends]

☐ **technology** (tek-nol'ə-jē) *n.* The application of science to the solution of practical problems [the use of computer *technology* in planning highways]

☐ **theoretical** (thē'ə-ret'i-kəl) *adj.* Based on theory; unproven, hypothetical [a *theoretical* framework for understanding the workings of the human brain]

☐ **timeliness** (tīm'lē-nis) *n.* The condition of happening at the right time [the *timeliness* of a Christmas card that arrives on December 22]

☐ **timely** (tīm'lē) *adj.* Happening at the right time; well-timed, opportune [a *timely* birth occurring nine months after the beginning of a pregnancy]

☐ **transitory** (tran'si-tôr'ē) *adj.* Not permanent; temporary, fleeting, short-lived [a *transitory* headache that ended when I ate lunch]

☐ **trite** (trīt) *adj.* Lacking originality because of

overuse; worn out, overdone, commonplace ["Quick as a wink" is a *trite,* overworked expression.]

☐ **typify** (tip'ə-fī) *v.* To possess the essential characteristics of something; represent, embody, epitomize [McDonald's *typifies* fast food restaurants.]

☐ **uncommunicative** (un'kə-myōō'ni-ka'tiv) *adj.* Withholding information, opinions, or feelings; silent, quiet, withdrawn [Some people are *uncommunicative* about the problems that disturb them most.]

☐ **valence** (vā'ləns) *n.* The positive and negative reaction that a person has toward an object or event [the *valence* associated with relaxing by watching a violent movie]

☐ **visceral** (vis'ər-əl) *adj.* Pertaining to the internal organs of the body [the *visceral* reaction of an upset stomach]

☐ **volatility** (vol'ə-til'i-tē) *n.* The characteristic of shifting quickly, widely, or unpredictably; variability, instability [the *volatility* of an active volcano]

☐ **wholesaler** (hōl'sāl'ər) *n.* A company that sells large quantities of products that are to be resold to consumers [a *wholesaler* of magazines sold in neighborhood stores]

Glossary

Words in italics within these definitions are also defined in this glossary.

Adjunct. A person hired to teach part-time or for a specified period, such as one *term* or one school year.

Adviser. A teacher assigned to help students select the courses in which they register.

Almanac. An annual publication that contains a variety of information, including facts and statistics about famous people, history, countries, and sports.

Analyze. To separate something into its parts for the purpose of *studying* the parts and understanding how they are related.

Appendix. A part of a book that contains supplementary materials or information; usually located in the back of a book, immediately following the last chapter.

Assistant professor. A teacher who ranks below an *associate professor.*

Associate degree. A *degree* that is usually offered by two-year colleges, often the A.A. (Associate of Arts), A.S. (Associate of Science), or A.A.S. (Associate of Applied Science).

Associate professor. A teacher who ranks below a *professor* but above an *assistant professor.*

Atlas. A book of maps.

Auditory learners. People who prefer to learn by listening and discussing. Compare with *kinesthetic learners* and *visual learners.*

Automatic processing. The effortless *storage* of information in *memory.*

Bachelor's degree. A *degree* offered by four-year colleges and universities, usually the B.A. (Bachelor of Arts) or the B.S. (Bachelor of Science).

Bar graph. A drawing in which parallel bars are used to compare differences in amounts, such as differences in the amounts of fat in various foods.

Bibliography. A list of books, articles, and other sources of information that are referred to by a writer. Same as *references* and *notes.*

Bluebook. A booklet, not necessarily blue, that contains lined paper on which to write answers to *essay questions.*

Bulletin. A booklet published by a college or university that includes information about *curriculums,* courses, and other important facts; a *catalog.*

Bursar. The title of a person at a college or university who is responsible for money transactions; a treasurer or *cashier.*

Call number. Numbers and letters printed on books to indicate their location in a library.

Card catalog. A file in a library that lists books alphabetically by authors' names, by titles, and by subjects.

Cartoon. A drawing depicting a humorous situation, often accompanied by a caption.

Cashier. Same as *bursar.*

Catalog. Same as *bulletin.*

Chancellor. Sometimes the same as *president,* and sometimes the title for special assistant to a president.

Circle graph. A drawing in the shape of a circle that is used to show the sizes of the parts that make up the whole. A circle graph can be used to show what parts of a family's income are used for rent, food, clothing, and other expenses.

Classification chart. A format for recording *notes* about information that explains how two or more people, places, or things are alike or different in two or more ways.

Copyright page. The page of a book that states the year the book was copyrighted or published; follows the *title page.*

Counselors. People who provide students with guidance in achieving their educational and occupational *goals* and in resolving their personal problems.

Credit. A unit given for completion of any study that applies toward a *degree.*

Current goal. A *goal* that helps in accomplishing an *intermediate goal.*

Curriculum. The courses required to earn a particular *degree.*

Dean. A member of the administration of a college or university who is in charge of specified areas of the school's activities, such as a dean of students, a dean of faculty, a dean of instruction, or a dean of a *school* or *division* within a college or a university.

Decay theory. The theory that if we do not use information that is stored in *memory,* we will not be able to *retrieve* it because it fades from disuse.

Degree. A rank given to students who have successfully completed specified courses of study, such as the *bachelor's degree.*

Department. An organizational unit that offers

courses in a specific subject or a specific group of subjects. For instance, a foreign language department may offer courses in Spanish, French, German, and other languages.

Diagram. A drawing that explains something by outlining its parts and showing the relationships between them. For example, a diagram may show the parts and relationships between the parts of the human eye.

Direction word. A word in an *essay question* that informs test takers about the type of answer they are to give. The direction word "diagram" usually indicates that students are to draw a picture and label its parts.

Distractor. A choice for a *multiple-choice question* that is not the correct answer.

Division. *Departments* are sometimes organized under larger groups called divisions. For example, the social sciences division may include a psychology department, a sociology department, an anthropology department, and other departments.

Doctor. Title for a person who has earned the highest *degree* awarded by a college or a university.

Doctoral degree. The highest *degree* offered by colleges and universities, such as the Ph.D. (Doctor of Philosophy) or Ed.D. (Doctor of Education).

Double negative. A phrase that contains two negatives, often the word "not" and a negative prefix, such as "un-" ("not unkind").

Elaborative rehearsal. Same as *rehearsal.*

Encoding. The process by which information enters *memory.*

Essay questions. Test items that require students to give written answers that are usually one paragraph or more in length.

Exercise. In a *textbook,* a *problem* or series of problems.

Extreme modifiers. Words such as "always" and "never" that tend to be in false statements. For instance, "**All** children love candy" contains an extreme modifier, and it is false.

Fill-in questions. Statements that have deleted portions that test takers must supply: "There are __ letters in the English alphabet."

Glossary. A list of words and their definitions; usually located in the back of a book, just in front of the *index.*

Goal. A purpose or objective that is worked toward or strived for.

GPA values. Values given to *letter grades* so that *grade point averages* may be computed. The following values are used at many colleges: A, 4.00; B, 3.00; C, 2.00; D, 1.00; and F, 0.00.

Grade point average (GPA). A number that usually ranges from 0.00 to 4.00 and that indicates a student's average course grade.

Heading. In a *textbook,* a word or words at the beginning of a division within a chapter.

Highlight. To mark important words or sentences in a book using a pen that contains watercolor ink. This is done so that important statements will stand out clearly and not be overlooked while *studying.*

Hour. A unit, usually less or more than sixty minutes, that designates time students spend in classrooms, laboratories, or conferences.

Incomplete grade (INC). A grade given at many colleges and universities when students are doing passing work but have not completed all course requirements. Usually an INC grade is changed to an F or to some other grade if incomplete work is not completed within a specified time.

Index. An alphabetically arranged listing of subjects and the page numbers on which they are discussed in a book; usually located at the very end of a book.

Information-processing model. A theory of *memory* that compares the ways that computers and people process and store information.

Insert. Material set off in a *textbook,* may be enclosed within lines or printed on a shaded background of light blue, yellow, gray, or some other color.

Interference theory. The theory that we sometimes cannot *retrieve* information in *memory* because other memories stored there interfere.

Intermediate goal. A *goal* that helps in accomplishing a *primary goal.*

Intersession. A short session of study offered between two *terms,* such as a four-week session offered in January between a fall term and a spring term.

Introduction. The part of a book that gives the author's explanation of why the book was written. It often includes a summary of the purposes, philosophy, or contents of a book; usually located right after the *table of contents.* This information may also be located in a *preface.*

Kinesthesia. The sensory experience that comes from moving muscles, tendons, and joints.

Kinesthetic learners. People who prefer to learn by being physically involved, such as by doing something or by handling and manipulating things. Compare with *auditory learners* and *visual learners.*

Learning goals. A list of statements or questions at the beginning of a *textbook* chapter that summarizes information in a chapter.

Learning strategy. A set of procedures for accomplishing a learning task, such as the procedures that are used to learn information for tests.

Learning style. The set of procedures that a particular person actually uses to accomplish a learning task.

Letter grade. A grade such as A−, B+, or C that designates the quality of work students do. Letter grades have the following meanings at many schools: A, excellent; B, good; C, satisfactory; D, passing; and F, failing.

Line graph. A drawing in which lines are used to show increasing or decreasing amounts. A line graph can be used to show increases or decreases in the numbers of students enrolled at a college over a period of time.

Long-term memory. The stage of *memory* that holds a vast amount of information for as long as a lifetime.

Map. A *diagram* or other drawing that shows how a topic and details are related.

Master's degree. A degree that ranks higher than a *bachelor's degree* but lower than a *doctoral degree,* usually the M.A. (Master of Arts) or M.S. (Master of Science).

Matching questions. Test items that present two lists and require test takers to associate words or statements in one list with words or statements in the other list.

Memory. The total of what one remembers; same as *long-term memory.*

Midterm. The middle of a *term* or an examination given at this time.

Mnemonic acronym. A *retrieval cue* that is a word made from the initial letters of words to be retrieved.

Mnemonic device. A device used to aid *memory.* "Use *i* before *e* except after *c*" is a mnemonic rhyme for remembering a spelling principle.

Mnemonic sentence. A sentence in which the first letters of words in the sentence are the same as the first letters of words to be recalled.

Multiple-choice questions. Test items written in a format that requires test takers to select a correct answer from among four or five possible answers that are listed.

Name index. An *index* of the authors and other people referred to in a book.

Negative. A word (such as "not") or a prefix (such as "un-") that indicates an opposite.

Notes. Same as *bibliography* and *references.* Also, handwritten summaries of information stated in classes or printed in course *textbooks.*

Number grade. A grade such as 91, 85, or 68 that designates the quality of work students do. Many schools agree on the following correspondences between number grades and *letter grades:* A, 90–100; B, 80–89; C, 70–79; D, 60–69; F, 0–59.

Ombudsman. A special assistant to a *president.*

On-line catalog. A file containing information about books in a library that is accessed by typing authors, titles, or subjects into a computer terminal.

Open-book test. A test during which students may refer to books, and sometimes to notes, as they answer questions.

Orientation. A period of time or a series of events planned to help students adjust satisfactorily to college or university life.

Outline. A summary of information that lists important points in a well-organized manner. In the traditional outline format, details are labeled with Roman numerals, capital letters, and Arabic numerals.

Periodicals. Newspapers, magazines, and other publications that are published at regular intervals, such as daily, weekly, monthly, and bimonthly.

Preface. Same as *introduction.*

Prerequisite. A requirement that must be completed before a student may take a course. For example, the prerequisite for an intermediate algebra course might be a course in elementary algebra.

President. At a college or university, the chief administrative officer, who has ultimate responsibility for all aspects of the functioning of the school.

Primary goal. A *goal* that a person hopes to achieve in the future, such as the goal of graduating from college.

Problem. In a *textbook,* a question to answer, a proposition to solve, or other activity to do.

Professor. The highest rank for college and university teachers, also sometimes called full professor to distinguish it from *associate professor* and *assistant professor.* Also a correct form of address for any person who holds any of the three professorial ranks and an honorary or courtesy title at some colleges.

Qualifier. An adjective that modifies a noun, or an adverb that modifies a verb. In the phrase "young women talking quietly," the adjective "young" is a qualifier of the noun "women," and the adverb "quietly" is a qualifier of the verb "talking."

Quarter system. A system that divides a school year into three parts, usually a fall, a winter, and a spring *term* of about ten weeks each.

Reading. The process used to understand information that is presented in writing. Contrast with *studying.*

Recitation. The act of repeating information silently or aloud to learn it and to be able to recall it.

References. Same as *bibliography* and *notes.*

Registrar. The title of a person at a college or university who is responsible for registering students in courses and for maintaining their academic records on *transcripts.*

Registration. A period of time during which students register for the courses they will take.

Rehearsal. The act of *analyzing* information and relating it to information that is already stored in *memory.*

Retrieval. The act of recalling or recollecting information stored in *memory.*

Retrieval cues. Words or images that help in recalling information stored in *memory.*

Retrieval failure theory. The theory that information in *memory* sometimes cannot be recalled because proper *retrieval cues* are not available.

Review. The repeated *recitation* and *rehearsal* of information to ensure that it can be *retrieved* quickly when it is needed.

Review questions. Questions at the end of a textbook chapter that students may answer to determine whether they have understood or learned information in the chapter.

School. A *division* within a college or university, such as a school of medicine.

Semantic code. A representation of information by its general meaning.

Semester system. A system that divides a school year into two parts, usually a fall and a spring *term* of fifteen to sixteen weeks.

Sensory memory. The stage of memory that briefly registers all information received by the senses of sight, hearing, taste, touch, and smell.

Short-term memory. A stage of *memory* that holds up to nine pieces of information for about twenty seconds.

Skill. An ability acquired as a result of training and practice. *Reading* and writing are skills.

Stem. The part of a *multiple-choice question* that comes before the first answer.

Storage. The act of holding information in *memory.*

Stress. Mental or physical strain that is experienced in response to psychologically or physically demanding events.

Stressors. Events or situations that induce *stress.*

Studying. The strategies used to remember and recall information. Contrast with *reading.*

Subject index. An *index* of the subjects discussed in a book.

Summer session. A period in the summer during which students may take courses for academic *credit* but that is usually not considered a *semester, quarter,* or *trimester* for the purposes of a school's business.

Survey of a book. The examination of the major features of a book, such as the *table of contents, introduction, appendix,* and *glossary.*

Survey of a chapter. The quick examination of introductory paragraphs, headings, pictures, tables, and other features of a chapter to learn what major topics it discusses.

Syllabus. A summary or *outline* distributed by an instructor that states the main topics to be discussed in a course.

Table of contents. A list that shows the page numbers on which chapter headings and subheadings of a book appear; usually located in the front of a book, right after the *title page.*

Take-home test. A test for which students are given questions to answer at home or to study at home before answering them in class.

Tenure. A status in which faculty members, having fulfilled certain requirements, hold their positions permanently.

Term. A period of study that usually ends with the administration of final examinations.

Terminology. Words or phrases that are used with specific meanings when a subject is discussed. The important terminology used in a *textbook* is usually defined in a *glossary.*

Test anxiety. Uneasiness or apprehension students experience because they must take a test.

Textbook. A book that summarizes information about course subject matter. This book is a textbook.

Thesaurus. A book of synonyms.

Title page. The page of a book that gives information about the title, author, and publisher; usually the second or third printed page of a book.

Transcript. The official record of courses taken, grades received, and *grade point averages.* Transcripts are maintained by a *registrar.*

Trimester system. Same as *quarter system.*

True-false questions. Test items that are statements that test takers must decide are either true or false.

Tutor. A person who gives individual instruction to students.

Underline. To draw lines under important words or sentences in a book so they stand out clearly and will not be overlooked while *studying.*

Vice chancellor. Sometimes the same as *dean.*

Vice president. Sometimes the same as *dean.*

Visual code. A mental image of information or an event.

Visualization. An image that can be pictured in the mind and used to recall information. If you picture in your mind the room in which you sleep, you can use the image to recall the information about the room.

Visual learners. People who prefer to learn by *reading* and watching demonstrations. Compare with *auditory learners* and *kinesthetic learners.*

Withdrawal grade (W). A grade given at many colleges and universities so that students may drop courses when they have good reasons for doing so. Usually W grades do not lower *grade point averages* when they are requested within specified time limits or when students are doing passing work at the time of withdrawal.

CREDITS (Continued from Copyright Page)

Page 160: "The Cornell System" from Walter Pauk, *How to Study in College,* 3rd ed. Copyright © 1984 by Houghton Mifflin Company. Used by permission.

Page 176: Definition of *colloquial* adapted and reprinted by permission from *The American Heritage Dictionary of The English Language.* Copyright © 1981 by Houghton Mifflin Company.

Page 176: "The Family" from Ian Robertson, *Sociology,* 3rd ed., p. 128. Copyright © 1987 by Worth Publishers, Inc. Used by permission.

Pages 177 and 178: "The Characteristics of Money" and "The Purposes of Money" from Robert Kreitner et al., *Business,* 2nd ed. Copyright © 1990 by Houghton Mifflin Company. Used with permission.

Pages 179 and 180: "Professions" and "Private Space" from Ian Robertson *Sociology,* 3rd ed. Copyright © 1987 by Worth Publishers, Inc. Used by permission.

Pages 181–183: "How to Improve Your Memory" reprinted by permission from pages 238–239 of *Introduction to Psychology* by Dennis Coon; Copyright © 1983 by West Publishing Company. All rights reserved.

Page 183: "Adjusting to Death" from Robert S. Feldman, *Understanding Psychology.* Copyright © 1987 by McGraw-Hill, Inc. Reproduced with permission of McGraw-Hill.

Pages 184–185: "Listening" from Barry L. Reece and Rhonda Brandt, *Effective Human Relations in Organizations,* 3rd ed. Copyright © 1987 by Houghton Mifflin Company. Used with permission.

Pages 186–189: "Maslow's Hierarchy of Needs" from Reece, Barry L. and Rhonda Brandt, *Effective Human Relations in Business,* 4th ed. Copyright © 1990 by Houghton Mifflin Company. Used with permission.

Pages 191–192: "Emotions" from Douglas A. Bernstein et al., *Psychology,* 2nd ed. Copyright © 1991 by Houghton Mifflin Company. Used with permission.

Pages 195–198: "Television" from Defleur, Melvin, L., and Everette E. Dennis, *Understanding Mass Communication,* 4th ed. Copyright © 1991 by Houghton Mifflin Company. Used with permission.

Pages 198–200: "Conversation" from Rudolph F. Verderber, *Communicate!* 6th ed. Copyright © 1990 by Wadsworth Publishing Company. Reprinted by permission.

Page 280: "Comparison of a Short and a Long Answer to a Question" from Perrin, Robert, *The Beacon Handbook,* 2nd ed. Copyright © 1990 by Houghton Mifflin Company. Used with permission.

Pages 286–309: Chapter 11 from Reece, Barry L., and Rhonda Brandt, *Effective Human Relations in Business,* 5th ed. Copyright © 1993 by Houghton Mifflin Company. Used with permission.

Page 296: "Shopping has become such a nuisance . . ." cartoon. 1988 Mike Twohy; Management Solutions.

SOURCES NOT REQUIRING PERMISSION

Page 68: "Electronic Data Base" from Scott Ober, *Contemporary Business Communication* (Boston: Houghton Mifflin, 1992).

Page 175: "Legalization of Marijuana" from Barbara J. Combs et al., *An Invitation to Health,* 2nd ed. (Benjamin/Cummings Publishing, 1983).

Page 179: "When to Visit a Physician" from Paul M. Insel and Walton T. Roth, *Core Concepts in Health,* 6th ed. (Mountain View, California: Mayfield Publishing Company, 1991).

Index

Assignments

Course Name	Monday *Date:*	Tuesday *Date:*	Wednesday *Date:*	Thursday *Date:*	Friday *Date:*

Assignments

Course Name	Monday *Date:*	Tuesday *Date:*	Wednesday *Date:*	Thursday *Date:*	Friday *Date:*

Assignments

Course Name	Monday *Date:*	Tuesday *Date:*	Wednesday *Date:*	Thursday *Date:*	Friday *Date:*

Assignments

Course Name	Monday *Date:*	Tuesday *Date:*	Wednesday *Date:*	Thursday *Date:*	Friday *Date:*

Assignments

Course Name	Monday *Date:*	Tuesday *Date:*	Wednesday *Date:*	Thursday *Date:*	Friday *Date:*

Assignments

Course Name	Monday *Date:*	Tuesday *Date:*	Wednesday *Date:*	Thursday *Date:*	Friday *Date:*

Study Schedule

	MON	TUE	WED	THU	FRI	SAT	SUN
7—8							
8—9							
9—10							
10—11							
11—12							
12—1							
1—2							
2—3							
3—4							
4—5							
5—6							
6—7							
7—8							
8—9							
9—10							
10—11							
11—12							

Study Schedule

	MON	TUE	WED	THU	FRI	SAT	SUN
7—8							
8—9							
9—10							
10—11							
11—12							
12—1							
1—2							
2—3							
3—4							
4—5							
5—6							
6—7							
7—8							
8—9							
9—10							
10—11							
11—12							

Study Schedule

	MON	TUE	WED	THU	FRI	SAT	SUN
7—8							
8—9							
9—10							
10—11							
11—12							
12—1							
1—2							
2—3							
3—4							
4—5							
5—6							
6—7							
7—8							
8—9							
9—10							
10—11							
11—12							

Study Schedule

	MON	TUE	WED	THU	FRI	SAT	SUN
7—8							
8—9							
9—10							
10—11							
11—12							
12—1							
1—2							
2—3							
3—4							
4—5							
5—6							
6—7							
7—8							
8—9							
9—10							
10—11							
11—12							

Study Schedule

	MON	TUE	WED	THU	FRI	SAT	SUN
7—8							
8—9							
9—10							
10—11							
11—12							
12—1							
1—2							
2—3							
3—4							
4—5							
5—6							
6—7							
7—8							
8—9							
9—10							
10—11							
11—12							

Study Schedule

	MON	TUE	WED	THU	FRI	SAT	SUN
7—8							
8—9							
9—10							
10—11							
11—12							
12—1							
1—2							
2—3							
3—4							
4—5							
5—6							
6—7							
7—8							
8—9							
9—10							
10—11							
11—12							